A LIFE DOWNUNDER

David Burchell was just sixteen when he lost a leg in a train accident, and here he tells of his initial despair, his convalescence and rehabilitation. He was accepted for the Air Force in World War II, and after the war worked on cattle and sheep stations in the Australian outback. Returning to the city, he took up high diving and for fifteen years performed with the South Australian Diving Troupe. He then worked in a remote area for the Shell Company, and he describes life in an outback town. In 1960, he founded the Adelaide Skin Diving Centre and became involved in many exciting stunts and projects. His most important dive was when he discovered the wreck of the cruiser HMAS *Perth* which was lost along with the American cruiser USS *Houston* during World War II in the Battle of the Sunda Strait. In diving circles it is considered as one of the most outstanding single-handed achievements in the history of the sport. The *Perth*'s bell, the object of his search, is now in the Australian War Museum in Canberra. Burchell tells his interesting story with humour.

DAVID BURCHELL

A LIFE DOWNUNDER

An Autobiography

Complete and Unabridged

CHARNWOOD
Leicester

First published in Australia in 1988
under the title of 'My World' by
David Burchell

First Charnwood Edition
published 1999

British Library CIP Data

Burchell, David
    A life downunder.—Large print ed.—
Charnwood library series
1. Burchell, David
2. Large type books
3. Australia—Biography
I. Title
994'.04'092

ISBN 0–7089–9120–3

Published by
F. A. Thorpe (Publishing) Ltd.
Anstey, Leicestershire

Set by Words & Graphics Ltd.
Anstey, Leicestershire
Printed and bound in Great Britain by
T. J. International Ltd., Padstow, Cornwall

This book is printed on acid-free paper

Dedicated to my daughters' children
Sam, Tom, Billy and Sarah
Tom, Jess, David and Steven
Harry, George and Max
And to Sam Eustice (Godson)

Foreword

My first recollection of the author was during my young student days at St Peter's College Adelaide, when I learnt of the untimely accident which was to rob him of the many opportunities to participate in the recognised sporting activities of our school, and social life at that time.

It was whilst still at St Peter's I accompanied school groups to the Adelaide City Baths for training, and various swimming carnivals, that I next remember him well. We would watch in awe as this one-legged young man, a member of the South Australian Diving Troupe, would entertain us and show his exceptional skills from the top platform of the diving tower.

Sport, bred in the Corinthian spirit, as well as being a great character developer, has always brought to those who participate, a spirit of competitiveness and camaraderie, particularly when the people involved have a common interest. In both Dave Burchell's and my own case, that common interest was the sea. Whilst my participation was always with what happened on the surface, Dave took to exploring the virtually unknown world beneath.

Not only did this bring him his own satisfaction, and allow him to climb his own 'Everests', but he shared it with many others whom he taught along the way.

His sense of national pride, resolve, and plain old fashioned 'guts' is clearly illustrated in his endeavours to find HMAS *Perth*, sunk by the Japanese during World War II, in the Sunda Strait in Indonesia. This particular chapter in his life is well documented in this autobiography and allows the reader a closer look at the character of the man.

Dave Burchell, the adventurer, is only part of the total man. Dedicated to his family, successful in business, respected sports administrator and in particular ever ready to assist, not only the disabled, but anyone seeking advice, for wherever he can help, he will willingly give of his time.

So whether as an adventurer, family man, businessman, sportsman, or just a good mate, this monopode is one of that rare breed of person of which there are too few in this world, let alone South Australia. Like all people that know him well, I'm sure I'm a better person for the experience and the world would be a happier place if there were more David G. Burchells.

Sir James G. Hardy
Adelaide
9 November 1988

1

We had just turned 16, Don McLeay and I, when that train accident so dramatically altered our lives.

It was during the Christmas holidays and we were on our way home from a cycling trip, but as we were running late for the start of the school term, we decided to catch the train at Keith in order to be back in time.

It was a hot day in February 1941 and Mac and I sat side by side out on the access platform of the carriage to greater enjoy the feeling after four weeks pedalling bikes, of glorious effortless speed as the train swept along. But unbeknown to us between Tailem Bend on the river and Murray Bridge some 20 kilometres further on, there was a gangers' siding built close to the track. It was a solid structure with the wide steps made from inch thick jarrah planks and as the train roared through the siding the top step caught our dangling legs, slamming into them with tremendous force.

My legs hit first and the blunt leading edge of the step ripped into me with such a whack that it tore my right foot off just above the ankle and smashed my left leg before throwing me violently sideways into Mac. Then, cannoning off him, I was hurled through the air to finally thump, far behind, in an unconscious spreadeagled heap at the bottom of the railway embankment.

Mac was also swept off, but fortunately when we hit he was holding the handrail of the carriage and somehow managed to hang on.

Then, even though he was dragged the full length of the rough timber siding, with a superhuman effort he hauled himself back onto the carriage.

Mac's first thought was that I'd gone under the

1

wheels and immediately he tried to scramble to his feet to get inside and stop the train. But there was something wrong with his legs and looking down he saw they were at odd angles and he realised they were both broken.

Dragging himself across the carriage platform to the door leading inside, he banged on it with his clenched fist until after what seemed an eternity someone came.

'Stop the train — stop the train', he gasped when the door finally opened. 'It's my friend — he's fallen off . . . '

★   ★   ★

At first, in the operating theatre of the Murray Bridge Hospital, I had very little conscious feeling. There was no pain or curiosity, no fear or awareness of surroundings or of what had happened. Just the ghostly white shapes that alternately appeared and then, wraithlike, swirled away. I do vaguely remember the lights, those bright lights and the heady smell of ether as I mindlessly drifted until the anaesthetic took its roaring, head spinning effect and I slipped away. Then there was nothing.

★   ★   ★

My mother was having a rare night out at the pictures in Adelaide when the hand printed notice appeared on the theatre screen. Mum's heart skipped a beat and a cold tingling feeling swept through her — for the message read . . . **'Mrs Burchell, Please come to the Manager's Office'**.

The war was on, my brother Murray was in the AIF and like all mothers at that time the dreaded anticipation of just such a call was always at hand.

In the office, the embarrassed manager silently

handed her the phone. ' Is that you Patty?' asked the distressed voice on the line — it was my adopted Aunty Kit with whom we lived. 'It's David!' she said. 'He's had a terrible accident. They've just rung from the hospital at Murray Bridge — he's lost a leg — we must go up there at once.' What Aunty Kit didn't say, but knew she would have to tell Mum during their long drive to Murray Bridge, was that the Matron had told her they must hurry — I was in a bad way — and that I may not last the night.

★ ★ ★

For the next week, through one crisis after another, I struggled in a nightmarish world filled with hallucinations, pain and terror. The lucid moments, with their flashes of conscious reason, were oddly the worst. Once in a terrifying nightmare, in which a looming dark shape kept coming and coming, trying to envelop me, I desperately shrank back, yelling and punching at it trying in vain to escape.

Suddenly my mind cleared and the shape changed its form and I realised that this terrifying thing was in reality my dear mother and that I was punching her in the face as she tried to reach me and hold me down.

I must have hurt her, for I was a strong boy and I remember she was crying, but somehow I knew in my despair and confusion that the reason for her tears was not because of my blows. I'll never forget how utterly appalled I was when I realised what I had done.

Another occasion was the day it was decided to set my broken left leg, which had a nasty triple compound fracture and was badly swollen. It was towards the end of that first week and up till then the doctor, who had apparently expected me to die, couldn't see much point in setting it.

However, as I was still hanging on he had the

unenviable task of making a decision — the problem being that as I was too far gone to take any more anaesthetic, he knew that the leg would have to be set whilst I was conscious. The shock and pain of this would, he felt, more than finish me off.

But then if the leg wasn't set and somehow I did live, he also knew that gangrene would set in and he'd have to amputate. This he also felt would more than finish me off.

It was a classic example of the old joke — 'Which do you want first — the good news or the bad?' But I don't think the doctor quite put it that way when he discussed it with my mother.

When they came for me on the morning of the leg setting I was still wild eyed and panting from the terrors of my latest hallucination.

It is strange how you remember these things, but I vividly recall that in the nightmare I woke to find my head was on back to front and that as hard as I tried to tell people, no one would listen. Desperately I'd turned from one to another with the awful news, but I couldn't reach them and I was swamped with a heart-pounding panic at the unnerving feeling of being utterly alone.

Up in the operating theatre, the instant the doctor firmly placed his hands on my swollen shin, I snapped out of the world of delirium.

Gasping at the pain of his exploratory touch, I instinctively made to sit up, but was further confused to find that I was held down by some straps across my chest. At the end of the table the Matron, white faced, was holding my foot and with her back to me a theatre sister was holding my bent knee. Between them, with his strong hands, stood the doctor.

Then as the Matron pulled in one direction and the Sister pulled in the other, the broken bones were drawn apart and the doctor did his best to thumb them together into some semblance of order.

It was a dreadful business and I'm sure they didn't like it any more than I did and although initially I tried to control myself it was a pretty feeble effort. For as the agonizing affair kept going on and on I soon lost what little endurance I had and very shortly I began to yodel like a Swiss mountaineer. My cries must have carried for Don McLeay, who was in a bed at the other end of the hospital, told me later that finally he'd buried his head under the pillows in an effort to escape them. Lord only knows the effect it must have had on my mother and Aunty Kit who were also somewhere there listening.

To me, the next week or so passed in a confusing blur. I was still unaware of what had happened — of where I was or that I'd lost a leg and during this period I apparently nearly died all over again. The cumulative effects of the shock of the injuries, the concussion, the loss of blood and a heart attack from a clot all added up to one endless crisis.

But despite the doctor's sombre predictions, a flicker must have kept going and eventually I started to pull out of it. Even then full consciousness only came slowly, through a series of odd, unrelated incidents.

At first these lucid times were short and infrequent, but as my condition improved the quantity of drugs I was being given was decreased and their side effects of nightmares and hallucinations decreased with them.

They were strange days for although I can still clearly recall recognizing and speaking to people, it seems very odd that when consciousness did unexpectedly appear, I had no query or curiosity about the unfamiliar environment in which I found myself.

Early one morning I awoke and was pleased to see my brother Murray sitting beside the bed. He was in uniform as a sergeant in the 2/9th Armoured Regiment AIF and being immersed in a book, at first he didn't notice that I was awake. It didn't occur to me that it was unusual he should be there and I remember lying quietly, just looking at him, as we hadn't seen each other in months for he was attached to a jungle warfare school at Canungra in Queensland.

I'd always idolized my brother as he had everything that made up the true hero. Three years older than me, he was not only a perfect and a bright student but had also been captain of athletics at school.

Murray glanced up from his book and was startled to see me watching him. Quickly leaning forward he took my hand 'G'day boy', he whispered softly, 'How are you feeling?'

I found that I couldn't do much more than smile back at him and glanced down at his hand. It was strong and tanned and I noted without much interest that mine was dead white, nothing more than skin and bone, like a claw. I wanted to tell him how good it was to see him, but felt strangely weak and couldn't summon the effort it required.

Then out of the blue I murmured, 'My legs feel cold'. Poor old Murray did a double take and his eyes darted from mine to the mound made by the cage supporting the bedclothes. 'Your legs feel cold' he stammered, 'er . . . which one' Then his courage deserted him as he had no desire to be the one to tell me what had happened. 'Hang on a minute', he said, 'I'll be right back'.

I must have drifted off again for when next I opened my eyes Matron Trixie Randall was there. She was an exceptional woman, a fine nurse and a legend along the river, with her ties to the Murray going back to her grandfather, Captain Randall, who was a respected river boat skipper back in the 1800s.

Mum told me later that to Matron Randall and her staff at Murray Bridge, as often happens in hospitals, I had become something rather special and during those first critical weeks they had put everything they knew into keeping me going. Even during the times when the

6

situation appeared hopeless, Mum told me they had selflessly nursed me around the clock, never once giving up.

Now that I had turned the corner their professional pride and hopefully affection, was strong and they were proud of me for hanging on and because I represented a victory in an area of contest where victories are rare, they were justifiably proud of themselves.

This feeling of achieving the ultimate accomplishment, that of saving a life through sheer skill and dedication, would be unique to the nursing fraternity. All of whom would have experienced it and would understand what I mean.

However at that time it wouldn't have made what Matron Randall had to say any easier.

'David' she said, 'I have to tell you something and I want you to be a brave boy'. No doubt hating the job, she paused for a moment before continuing, but she didn't beat around the bush. 'You have had a bad accident', she said, taking my limp hand. 'You have been very ill — you are much better now — but we had to amputate your leg'.

In the silence that followed Matron Randall studied me anxiously to see how I'd taken it, as she was concerned at the possible effects of the emotional shock that such news could bring. She needn't have worried, the whole thing went straight over my head and I lay there still waiting for the news for which I'd been told I had to be brave.

As the silence continued, like a pathetic village idiot, I smiled and nodded to indicate that I was ready.

As it turned out I was fortunate in not understanding what the Matron had tried to tell me, as I was spared that single, traumatic revelation most amputees have to face.

For as time passed, already in my subconscious mind the seed of the knowledge that I'd lost a leg had been sown and this gradually grew, along with my returning awareness, until finally I couldn't remember exactly when it was that the realization came.

As our health improved, Mac and I were allowed visitors and the first of these included our Headmaster from school, the Reverend Guy Pentreath and my Form Master, Bob Vollugi. I was rather embarrassed at seeing them as I knew I hadn't been a model student. The last time the Head had spoken to me was one day in his study some months before, when he had invited me to touch my toes so that he could all the better lay six of the best on my backside.

Actually I didn't think the crime for which I was to be caned was all that bad. All I'd done was to assist in playing a few jokes on an Hungarian academic refugee that the Reverend Pentreath, an Englishman and great humanitarian, had helped flee Hitler's Europe to become our English master.

Sufficient to say the Head was not amused.

Mr Vollugi, my form master, was in a different category. His was a more familiar face and although he generally found the need to cane me once a week, I don't think his heart was really in it. Along with his other duties Bob Vollugi was also the school's athletic coach and my brother, being school captain, was his favourite, and while he considered I played around too much in class I think he hoped that one day I might change my ways and become a good student and a champion runner like Murray.

Seeing him so unexpectedly that day at the hospital, with a concerned look on his face and a watermelon as a present under his arm, I knew that I'd played too much on his good nature and high regard for my brother and I felt ashamed.

Now after all these years I realize I needn't have been so embarrassed, for to the Head and Bob Vollugi I was just a normal boy, doing normal smart-arse things.

What I didn't appreciate was that they considered Mac and me as their boys and that their concern at our accident was total.

★ ★ ★

As my mother had responsibilities to her work in Adelaide as well as to me in Murray Bridge, it was decided that as soon as I was strong enough I should be moved to the city.

After about four weeks, propped up with pillows in the back seat of a friend's car, I came down to the Memorial Hospital in North Adelaide where Mum had arranged a bed for me.

I had rather an unpleasant introduction to the Memorial Hospital, where for the first time I really came face to face with the extent of my leg injuries.

At Murray Bridge the primary concern had been for me to survive, with the legs being of secondary importance, but now the position was reversed. The doctors at the Memorial, knowing of the desperate circumstances under which the left leg had been set, wanted to check the breaks to see how they were healing and the plaster cast which had been so painfully applied was removed. I sat up in bed intending to watch, putting on a brave front and while I don't quite know what I'd expected, the first sight of damage done to my once strong quick legs really shocked me. The left, misshapen, wasted and wobbly, with the bones not yet set, was scarred with deep open lacerations, while the right, the ultimate horror, ended in a heavily bandaged stump.

Slowly, so as not to draw attention to myself, I leaned back against the heaped pillows and closed my eyes.

This time my mind was quite clear, unlike the previous occasions and I was horrified by the implication of what it all meant. 'Oh God', I thought, my chest starting to heave with a sickening panic as the significance of the brutal facts swept on through me.

Those hopelessly crippled legs — that obscene stump.

At that moment I knew — that no matter what — or for how long I lived — I would never run again.

I'd been Junior Champion at Pulteney Grammar, our former school, but now I'd never become Captain of Athletics at Saints like Murray, which in my conceit I'd always secretly considered to be a foregone conclusion. There would be no more football, or hopes of joining the Navy and finally most frightening of all — how was I going to cope for the rest of my life with virtually no legs.

In the hope that no one would notice my utter despair, I turned my face away towards the wall as the tears of self-pity started to sting my eyes.

★   ★   ★

The next two years were pretty tough going. When Mac's legs finally mended he went back to school but after only a few weeks he slipped while trying to kick a football and broke his right leg again.

My stay at the Memorial lasted another four months, but when the bones in my leg knitted and the plaster was removed the leg was so fragile it couldn't stand any weight and the only way I could move about was to be pushed around in a wheelchair. However, the great day eventually came and I was allowed to leave hospital and go home.

I was still rather weak, apparently too weak, as after a few days I was back in the Memorial again with pneumonia. Also the bone below the knee on my right leg had become infected with Osteomyelitis, an aftermath of blood poisoning from the early days at Murray Bridge and for the next year I was in and out of

10

hospital in unsuccessful attempts to get rid of it. They were boring frustrating months and I'm sure that convalescence can be as bad a time as any, for it is the time when the patient is not ill enough to be in hospital and yet not well enough to help himself at home.

I was more than fortunate in having my mother and Aunty Kit to help me, for although my friends rallied round and took turns in pushing me about in the wheelchair, it was really Mum and Aunty Kit who bore the brunt. They were wonderful women and although they came from a generation that lived through two World Wars and the Depression, rarely did life get them down.

I was to find that Osteomyelitis is a miserable disease, for each time the latest outbreak was beaten, the Osteo would erupt again in a different spot. These eruptions would take the form of any angry boil-like sore, indicating the continuing inflammation that was still active deep within the diseased bone and I grew to dread the sight of them. Each time this happened it meant another trip to the Memorial for an operation and although this was bad enough the continued outbreaks meant I couldn't be fitted with an artificial foot, as the stump not having a chance to heal, was always too swollen and tender to take any weight. It was certainly a very depressing time. For months my shattered left leg, still skin and bone and misshapen, was too fragile to stand on and the only way I could move around the house was to drag myself about on the floor with my arms.

I became lonely and bored with too much time on my hands, as Mum left early each morning for her work, Aunty Kit had her time pretty well taken up and all my friends were away at the war. However it wasn't all bad. Wednesday was a big day, as there was a matinee at the local picture theatre on Wednesdays and with a bit of wheedling I could always talk Aunty Kit into pushing

11

me in my wheelchair to the theatre. She had plenty of other things to do but she never let me down and we'd set off in high spirits for the Piccadilly theatre where I would join the other smattering of misfits who made up the Wednesday afternoon audience.

Also eventually the leg strengthened enough to bear my weight and with the aid of my crutches, 'Arthur' and 'Martha', I started to move about outside on my own. Then a splintmaker Mum had contacted made me up a peg-leg, using a caliper for support and although it may have looked a bit weird I was delighted, as in no time I mastered its idiosyncrasies and could walk without the aid of crutches. In addition by now, with all the work they were getting, my arms and shoulders had started to build up and to strengthen my good leg I dusted the cobwebs off my pushbike and each morning before the traffic built up would go for a ride.

At the start these sojourns were fairly shortlived, as the strain on the freshly healed breaks made them ache, but slowly the strength in the leg returned and with my friends Arthur and Martha resting across the handle-bars, ready in case of some unforeseen accident, in time I could push my way around the district in complete confidence, exhilarated by the feeling of this newfound independence.

By then my leg had become strong enough for me to carefully hop and while cosmetically it hasn't returned to its former shape, even with all the work it has since done and all the abuse it has taken, the battered thing has never once given me any further trouble.

2

Slowly and tragically the war years dragged on.

My mother was now in charge of the women's section of the war-time Manpower Department, Murray was away in the islands with his regiment and all my friends were in one service or another. Each morning with a sense of dread we would read the casualty lists in the paper, as apart from all the other lads whom we didn't know, four of my friends had already been killed.

When Bryant Sedgely, who lived next door to us and with whom we grew up, was listed as missing-in-action with the Air Force in Sicily, my frustration at not being able to get involved in the war reached a peak.

Bryant, although a year older than me, was my special friend and we had always been together. He was a gentle fellow and as a boy had a beautiful singing voice, but he was never much good with his fists and in our relatively harmless gang fights with the locals, in which Murray was always the officer and Bryant and I the privates, it was my job to protect him. He was like a brother, but now he was gone and I felt his loss deeply.

When the war broke out I was about fourteen and right from the start I made up my mind that if it lasted long enough I would join the navy. With the accident to my legs the situation changed, but Bryant's death haunted me and I grimly decided that at least I had to give it a go.

Sprucing myself up, I put on my peg-leg and took care in choosing which of Murray's two sports coats I'd wear, finally picking the one, although it was too big and hung on me, that made me look broader in the shoulders.

Creeping quietly out the front door, so that Aunty Kit

wouldn't see me, I started on the long tram and bus trip to the Naval Installation at Birkenhead.

It was quite a walk from the bus stop to the installation and I had to stop several times as I stumped along to ease the chafing from the caliper. But as I approached the main gate I was pleased and heartened to see that the sailor on guard was watching me closely. I needn't have been too flattered.

Fortunately, or is it unfortunately, we don't always see ourselves as others see us. I thought I looked great, but the sailor saw a different picture — a skinny kid fresh out of feet on the starboard side, dressed in an oversize set of sails — it was probably the first break all day in the boredom of guard duty. Blissfully unaware of the reason for the sailor's interest and straightening my shoulders and puffing out my chest in an attempt to fill Murray's coat, I picked up my step and strode along in what I imagined to be a naval manner.

I'd planned what I was going to say. The intention being to open with a smile and come right out and tell them — in case they may not have noticed, as I didn't want to trick anyone — that I was a bit light on in the foot department and although I knew I wasn't quite ready yet, soon I'd be getting my artificial leg.

Then I was going to ask if there was still room in the navy, as there had been in the old days, for one-legged sailors. This I felt would make them laugh and put them on my side. They might even sign me up then and there and not wait for the wooden leg.

When I came face to face with the sentry, his size momentarily overawed me as he seemed to have grown a lot taller and I could see that under the smart round rig and gaiters he was built like a prizefighter. In my confusion I lost the initiative, but I don't think it made any difference.

The sailor looked me up and down, especially down to where I was conscious of my empty trouser leg flapping in the sharp breeze.

'Well Long John,' he said brusquely, 'what do you want?' I felt the colour rising to my face and stammered something about wanting to join the navy.

'Christ', he exclaimed disgustedly, 'we've got a waiting list as long as your arm of blokes wanting to join the navy. They wouldn't take anyone who even had the top joint off his little finger.'

Just then an officer called to him from inside the gate and the sailor sprang to attention and marched off.

I stood there on the footpath not knowing quite what to do, but when he opened the gate and without so much as a backward glance disappeared inside and closed it behind him, even I started to get the impression that my interview for the navy was over.

After waiting for about ten minutes, in the forlorn hope that he might come back, I turned away and started the long walk back to the bus. Only this time as I stumped along on the peg-leg, with my face flaming at the thought of the mess I'd made of it, my spirits were so low that I didn't even try to fill out my brother's coat.

I'd heard of Douglas Bader of course and how with both legs missing after an aircraft crash he'd fought back to again become a successful fighter pilot, but after making enquiries I found that I didn't have the necessary academic qualifications to train for a pilot, but might just make it as an airgunner. With this in mind I started an all-out campaign of attack on No. 5 Recruit Centre for the RAAF in Adelaide. Unfortunately for him, the Senior Medical Officer had a kindly streak and instead of sending me on my way he made the mistake of saying he would see what could be done about my being enlisted as an airgunner.

For weeks I plagued him until finally he threw up his hands in surrender and promised to give me a medical examination. The first thing to come out in the medical was that I had osteo and this gave the doctor the out for

15

which he was no doubt seeking.

Not that he didn't appreciate my zeal, but I'm sure he considered it hopelessly misguided and he not only welcomed the osteo as a reason to scrub me, but also as a chance to let me down as lightly as possible.

Telling me that the Air Force couldn't consider anyone with that sort of complaint, he closed my file and didn't proceed any further with the examination.

This didn't dismay me, as I'd really always known I couldn't join any of the services until I had an artificial leg, but now that there was a real chance I could get in, it started me thinking of ways to hasten things along.

I made an appointment with the surgeon who had been treating me and told him about being turned down by the Air Force because of the osteomyelitis and asked if I'd be better off if we got rid of the disease permanently, by amputating the leg again above the knee. At first he wasn't too keen on the idea, as he felt it was a case of the cure being worse than the complaint and went to some lengths to explain the tremendous difference between above and below knee amputations. The below knee being far more desirable as the prosthesis used with this type of amputation is really not much more than an artificial foot and is more easily and efficiently controlled by the amputee than a full leg.

However I was ready for this and pointed out that the bone below my knee was in such a mess from the Osteo, and all the operations, that it would never be able to stand the weight and chafing of an artificial leg anyway.

Finally he agreed to discuss it with my mother, who after a great deal of thought, anguish and no doubt a prayer or two, gave her consent.

The night before my leg was to be amputated for the second time I lay in bed at the Memorial full of misgivings, with a sick feeling spreading under my ribs as my courage and determination started to go.

I had a pretty fair idea of what the operation would

be like and shuddered at the thought of the dreadful stainless steel saw, of which unfortunately I'd once caught a glimpse when previously in the operating theatre.

Panicky questions were coming fast. What if the doctor was correct in his original assessment, with the cure being worse than the complaint. — Once the knee was amputated it was gone forever. — Hadn't I been through enough, without volunteering for this. — Could I really make Aircrew. — What if a cure for Osteomyelitis was developed next week?

I ran my hand down my thigh and rubbed the knee, flexing it several times. The kneecap functioned smoothly, with the big sinews at the sides healthy and strong and it was with a sense of betrayal that I thought of what was going to happen to it. Filled with melancholy I recalled the happier times when this knee had driven my leg down the running track, or pushed my bike, or sent me bounding into the surf and the knowledge that it wouldn't be there tomorrow did little to raise my morale. In the midst of these depressing thoughts I was vaguely conscious of a woman coming into the room and at first in the dim light I thought it was one of the nurses checking on me, but when she sat by my bed I realized it was my mother. She must have gone to some trouble to make the long walk alone at night on the offchance that I'd still be awake, but mothers seem to know instinctively when they are needed most and Mum knew this was one of those times.

I'm sure she read and understood the reason for my white face and troubled look as soon as she saw me. She didn't speak, but her grip on my hand tightened and somehow the strength and understanding my mother always showed flowed into me, reinforcing my flagging spirit until the mounting fears that had sapped my determination appeared as paltry and unworthy.

17

Mum

Slowly my courage returned and fiercely I returned her grip, wanting to let her know that everything was all right and that I was ready. For although not all the tenseness and loss of nerve had left me, I felt grimly committed and wanted to get the thing over and done with.

Suddenly I felt very tired and closed my eyes as the sedative I'd been given must have taken its effect and now with Mum's calming presence beside me, I slept.

I don't remember her leaving.

* * *

To most amputees, the initial introduction to an artificial limb factory is a bit of a shock and my case was no exception.

Filled with joyful anticipation I arrived at the Repatriation Department where the legs are made and waited impatiently for my name to called. After what seemed an interminable time I was finally taken into the workroom where I was startled to see a profusion of arms and legs, in various stages of completion, hanging from pegs around the walls.

I'd never seen an artificial limb before and the sudden appearance of all these naked, life-like looking replicas, dangling in rows as if they were prepared and ready for some unthinkable cannibalistic feast, to me made an unnerving sight.

Also the men working in the factory really fitted the scene as they were tough old characters, short on tact and sympathy, who between them had lost an assortment of limbs during the first war.

Spotting my dismay, one of them approached and it further disconcerted me when I saw that he had a half finished leg, complete with shoe and sock, sticking out from under his arm.

'What's the matter lad,' he asked roughly. 'Did you think you were the first bloke to lose a leg?' Not waiting for a reply he added, 'We don't need a war to keep us in business, all we need are motorbikes on the road. How did you lose yours — bet it was a motorbike.' His name was printed on the breast pocket of his overalls and even though I was still off balance I wanted to let him know how sharp I was at noticing things like that. So hoping it didn't sound too presumptuous, using his Christian name on so short an acquaintance, I replied, 'No Ralf, actually I fell off a train.'

He gave me a sour look and turned to his mate who had wandered up, 'This kid says he came a gutser off a train,' he said disgustedly, 'I owe you two bob.' To pass the time, they had bets on how new customers lost their legs.

I was interested to see that this second chap's name was also Ralf and thought that would be handy as I wasn't too good at remembering names, but when a girl came in from the office with my card and her name was Ralf, I started to get suspicious. 'How come you are all called Ralf?' I whispered to her when the others were out of earshot.

They didn't seem to be a happy crowd, as she also gave me a sour look 'R..A..L..F..' she spelt out loudly for all to hear, emphasizing each letter, 'stands for Repatriation Artificial Limb Factory. What are you trying to be, some sort of smart Alec?'

Waiting for my leg to be finished was a lengthy and frustrating business. The people at R.A.L.F. wouldn't be hurried and the several fittings that were necessary were spaced weeks apart. But eventually the time passed and R.A.L.F. rang to say the leg was ready. That night I was so excited at the prospect of collecting it the following morning that I couldn't sleep.

I had the same unforgettable feeling a boy has on Christmas Eve, when he is almost sure that tomorrow he will be getting his first pushbike, or later in life, his first car and each hour preceding the event seemed like an age.

For at last, after nearly three years, I would stride down the street on two feet — no crutches — no empty trouser flapping round the odd looking peg-leg, which had always caused curious stares from normal pedestrians. Now I'd be one of them — now, I too, would be gloriously anonymous. Soon I could be an Airgunner and when that happened the war was as good as over.

I guess I expected too much too soon. The leg was a disaster and I found I couldn't stride anywhere.

I was so laden down with the unaccustomed weight of it and the mass of straps, belts and buckles that were part of prosthesis technology in those days, that to move at all required the steadying aid of both my crutches. Even then the movement was jerky and uncontrolled, resulting in countless busters.

I was very disappointed and my initial reaction after the first few painful days, by when the chafing from the leg had caused several large raw spots, was to chuck the thing in the corner.

I suppose this was normal enough. I was only young and had waited so long with such high expectations, that when the leg didn't immediately measure up, I was hit with an anticlimax downer. However this state didn't last long and after giving the leg a spell for a couple of days, during which I regularly swabbed the sore spots with metho, to toughen the skin, I started again.

This time the efforts were rewarded, soon one crutch was discarded, then the other, until after a week or so I could walk reasonably well with just a stick.

Very pleased with myself and the progress made, I smugly decided that I was ready to sort out No.5 Recruit Centre, RAAF, as I was now confident that I had them over a barrel.

The catastrophe that dashed my hopes of ever making Air Crew, happened during the eye test at the Medical Examination. I knew the Medical would be demanding and had qualms about some aspects of it, but the last thing I'd expected was trouble with my eyes. However there it was — irrefutable — I failed to pass the eye test. Now, after all these years, I can almost laugh at the irony of it. For out of all the tough and complex tests that comprise an Air Crew Medical, — any of which in my poor physical condition I could have reasonably expected to fail, — I was scrubbed on the one thing I hadn't even considered.

I was devastated and dejectedly returned to my job as a skin-classer, which I'd had for a year or so since doing a wool classing course. My work grew duller and less interesting with each day that passed, until one night a week later, when we were preparing cattle hides for appraisal, the phone rang. It was one of the WAAAF's who had befriended me at the recruit centre. 'There's a ground staff intake next Wednesday, bound for initial training at Shepparton,' she said. 'You can be in it if you like.'

'The ground staff', I thought, mind racing. It wasn't Air Crew, but it was the Air Force. Once I got in and was posted overseas anything could happen. My spirits rose.

'Thanks', I said, 'Put me on the list, in fact thanks very much.' It was so sudden I found it hard to believe and slouched back in the chair a bit dazed, but after a moment or two it sank in and with a whoop I grabbed for the phone to break the news to my mother and Aunty Kit.

★ ★ ★

There was no doubt about it this time, I was in.

I had a brand new number which I couldn't remember and I'd taken the oath of allegiance, been photographed and finally lined up with about twenty-five other chaps, ready to march to the railway station. There we were to take the train to Melbourne, on the first leg of our trip to Shepparton.

As we marched out of the door into King William Street, I caught sight of my mother on the footpath. If it was the last thing she did, she was determined to see me off. I gave her a wink and a grin as we crossed the footpath and tramped off down the middle of the road.

By 1944, the year I enlisted, most people in the street were so accustomed to seeing groups of young men in civilian dress making the trip to the railway station that they hardly gave them a second glance. No bands played and with the exception of a few hearty 'you'll be sorrys' called out from chaps already in the services, we straggled along in stony silence.

But no, we were not entirely ignored. The policeman on point duty at the North Terrace intersection, at the sight of the group bearing down on him, held up the traffic with a fine flurry of hand signals.

His action allowed us to turn the corner with at least some semblance of dignity. Some of us anyway. Before we reached him it was quite obvious that with my slower gait, I was going to be left behind and by the time I made the corner the rest of the mob were about level with the steps of Parliament House.

The policeman watching the squad out of the corner of his eye and satisfied that they had gone a decent distance, was all set to wave the traffic on when he saw me hobbledehoying along about twenty yards behind. He was then faced with making the decision between either arresting me as being some kind of nut, or holding up the rapidly banking traffic until I'd passed.

But the guardian angel that protects our police force must have been on the job that day, for the officer's attention was somehow attracted to the grim-faced woman on the footpath, who keeping pace with me was sending him her own set of hand signals.

To my great relief he let me pass, for my mother, who comes from a long line of Scots would have felled him on the spot if he hadn't.

Mum and I marching side by side eventually made the railway station, where I reported to the worried corporal in charge who had just convinced himself that he had lost one of his flock before even leaving Adelaide.

To thousands of RAAF ground staff personnel, No. 1 Recruit Depot Shepparton represented their first contact with the mysterious ways of the Air Force. It was here that truck drivers and clerks, mechanics and salesmen were drilled, bawled out, marched and inoculated.

At good old No 1 RD they had their teeth pulled, their equipment inspected on short-arm parades, were instructed on how to handle a rifle and to eat the Air Force 'balanced diet'.

23

To some the transition from civilian to service life was not easy, but like thousands before us we survived and eventually the great day came when Flight 1290 passed out and the airmen who comprised it were posted to units and squadrons as Air Board saw fit to send them.

With a few others I was sent to No 1 ES Ascot Vale for further training. Ascot Vale — in peace time the Melbourne showground — was as vast and confusing as a city in itself and here thousands of RAAF and WAAAF personnel were trained as fitters, cooks and clerks. I'd been mustered as a clerk stores assistant and after two months of hi-tech training found that I could fill in a voucher — with the correct number of carbons — with the best of them.

The main speculation at Ascot Vale was where we were to be posted next, as this was the end of our training and the next stop could be anywhere.

I didn't mind so long as it was out of Australia, but occasionally I had the disquieting thought that I'd only get as far as Darwin or somewhere up in North Queensland, but I'd shrug it off thinking, 'They wouldn't do that to me.'

Actually I was tipping New Guinea, as there were some important stores units up there and I reckoned that's where I'd go. But when postings were finally announced, AC1 Burchell D.G., Clerk Stores Assistant, was posted to No 14 Stores Unit which I found to my horror was in Waymouth Street, right in the heart of down-town Adelaide.

I never quite forgave the Air Force for pulling such a lousy trick and for the next eighteen months staged an all-out battle with Air Board in an effort to change the situation. At first I was quite confident that the mistake — as that's all it could be — would soon be rectified and I would be on my way. But after awhile, with my hopes going up and down, I started to get despondent. Even several high-ranking officers whom I made it my business to get to know and who promised to help me, for one reason or another were all unsuccessful and as the months went by I continued to go to war each day on a tram.

The final blow came in the form of a signal from the Air Member of Medical Services to an MO whom I was currently pestering in Adelaide. It read, 'This airman will not — repeat not — be sent overseas under any circumstances. The subject is to be considered closed!'

For the rest of the war it seemed I was stuck with the defence of my home town and attending to the mountain of paperwork, apparently necessary to keep our planes in the air, and to puzzling over how the RAAF motto 'Per Ardua ad Astra' could possibly apply to me.

3

Immediately after the war I teamed up with Ken Langley, a friend from school who had just been discharged from the AIF. We had ideas of applying for land grants under the War Service Rehabilitation Scheme and while we waited to see if we were eligible, we took jobs as station-hands on a property in South Australia's far north.

There was an acute manpower shortage in the bush after the war and the stations were desperate for men, which was the reason Ken and I were offered the jobs, as our only qualification was that we were available. We turned up at the station on the mail truck and the manager, who had been hoping for a couple of experienced ringers, took one look at Ken in his heavy hob-nailed army boots and jungle greens and decided Langley definitely wasn't The Man from Snowy River. But when he saw me his eyes lit up, for here without doubt was the true colt breaker.

I'd been more cunning than Ken, as before we'd left the city I paid a visit to R. M. Williams, The Bushman's Outfitter. Appreciatively the manager eyed me up and down, taking in my high heeled elastic-sided boots, white moleskin pants, plaited 'roo hide belt — with the tricky secret buckle — and red checked shirt. He was a bit startled at my hat — a black Stetson — which was a size too big and made my ears stick out. But the girl at the shop said it made me look like Clancy of the Overflow and as it was the last one they had I really had no option but to take it.

Conscious of this scrutiny I casually leaned against the side of the truck and tried to roll a cigarette from the makings, which was a trick I hadn't quite mastered, and all the tobacco fell out. The manager didn't seem to notice and surreptitiously I screwed up the empty paper in my hand, but when I started taking our gear from the back of the truck and hauled out my crutches, his eyes narrowed. 'Bust your leg off a horse?' he asked and as the thought struck him, he added rather menacingly, 'Hope it's all right now.' 'Well no', I replied, pleased at his apparent interest. 'Actually I've only got one. I use the crutches when I get tired and a bit sore from the old wooden leg, or when I ride a horse.'

The manager made a sort of strangling sound and I was concerned to see that he had suddenly taken on the appearance of a shattered man. However, as he came from a long line of resourceful bushmen who had only survived in their tough environment by making the most of limited opportunities, he quickly regained his poise. Making a snap decision about his two new men he put Ken in charge of a truck, which carried all the camping and shearing plant and made me the camp cook.

I'm sure the only reason I managed to hold the job as cook, was because no one else would take it. Being the 'greasy' as the cook was called, was rated rock bottom on the station's status list, a point made quite clear by the head stockman the first day we were out in the camp.

Lining the men up, he said bluntly, 'The first bastard to complain about the dude's cooking, gets his job.'

The job of being camp cook was terrible and for awhile, especially at first, I had hopes that there would be complaints, but unbelievably in all those months there were none.

I'd always been a keen horseman and originally learned to ride on a cunning little Shetland pony at Ceduna, where Bryant Sedgley and I went for holidays staying with his grandfather and uncles. Like most Shetlands, when they have had enough of you, she

27

would just dump me and go galloping home leaving me to walk.

But this treatment didn't deter me and right up to the day Don McLeay and I had the train accident — when I'd been riding Queenie Langdon's prize chestnut gelding on their property at Kongal — I was never happier than when I was on a horse.

We all have a few talents and one of mine was good balance. Good balance could possibly be thought of as a minor ability, but it has been very helpful to me in my life with one leg. Especially in sports in which I've been able to participate, such as high diving when I had to stand on the leading edge of the tower or do handstands and in horse riding where balance is equally important.

When first I had my leg off below the knee the loss of the foot hardly affected me at all on horseback. For by removing the offside stirrup and learning the knack of mounting by vaulting instead of the accepted manner, I could get up. Then once astride, the grip that was available from my knees was mostly all that was required and I rode that way for two years.

After I had my leg off above the knee and was fixed up with an artificial one, along with looking forward to joining the Air Force I was also looking forward to wearing the leg on horseback and using two stirrups again.

However, this turned out to be as disappointing as not making air crew, for I found that the leg's weight and lack of flexibility made it stiff and awkward and that it was quite unsuitable for riding as it upset my balance.

After a couple of tries, with the leg flying in all directions, I gave it away and went back to riding without it. This was OK so long as I didn't fall off, as sometimes if I had it would have meant a long hop home, especially out in the bush, where if I'd bounded along through the scrub there was the chance of being mistaken for a kangaroo and being shot by some short-sighted hunter.

But this didn't happen and although I rode hundreds of miles mustering sheep on Miller's Creek Station, while Ken drove the truck from one camp to the next with my wooden leg, crutches and cooking pots, I didn't once fall off.

But even if I had parted company with my horse I knew that help wasn't far away. For although the regular station hands gave Ken and me the usual verbal hard time, dealt out to all greenhorn city-slickers, they always kept an eye on me. There was nothing pointed about it and it was never mentioned, but when we were out on the run mustering I noticed that every now and again one of them would appear over a ridge — take a look — and then disappear again.

Station people are like that.

Being the cook didn't preclude me from normal station duties, in fact the only difference I could see between me and the other chaps was that I got up earlier and went to bed later.

When Ken and I first arrived at Miller's Creek they were crutching — the term used when only a sheep's backside is shorn to prevent blowfly strike — and every few days we would move and set up a new camp. Then while the rest of the men finished mustering the paddock and crutched the adult sheep, Ken and I would mark the lambs.

Marking is a term used for notching their ears — for identification — cutting off their tails and de-sexing the rams. It's a bloody business and the method used — a sharp knife and strong teeth — offended Ken's sensitivities so much that he decided to catch the lambs and hold them while I cut and bit.

Consequently by the end of each day I was so covered in gore that it looked like I'd gone three rounds with the current world heavyweight boxing champion.

They were running over 25 000 Merino sheep on the station when we were there, which makes for a hell of a lot of ram lambs, but by the end of it I felt I had a personal interest in all of them. For how could you bite someone's balls off and not feel some intrinsic sense of responsibility towards his ruined future.

Finally Christmas came and our time was up and Ken and I rolled our swags. Then in the same mail truck on which we'd arrived nearly a year before, we headed back down south to Adelaide.

After a couple of week's spell in Adelaide we headed off once again to the bush, this time to the more sophisticated and closely-settled part of South Australia, the South-East.

I had been talking to Max Monfries, a friend of my brother's, about getting experience down there and Max, who was a Shell agent at Naracoorte told me that he knew of a place looking for men and would fix it for us. This was duly done and before long Ken and I were on our way.

Killanoola Station, one of the large original properties in the Naracoorte district, has since been split up into blocks for closer settlement under the War Service Rehabilitation Scheme.

However, when we arrived it was all the one property and whilst only a pocket handkerchief in size compared with Miller's Creek, its rich clover covered paddocks carried as many sheep to the acre as Miller's Creek did per square mile.

The large staff comprising the manager, three jackeroos, a married couple and four station hands, were all kept pretty busy since South-Eastern stock demands far more attention than those in the north.

The main reason for this is the climate. In the north, where it is dry and hot the sheep are only handled a couple of times a year, at shearing and lamb marking.

Occasionally, as happened when we were up there,

crutching after a rain is necessary, for the sheep scour after eating the unaccustomed green feed. But other than this they are left pretty much alone even during lambing.

In the south where it is cold and wet, the problems of combating disease in stock are greatly increased and to keep his sheep healthy the southern stockmen must be constantly on the job inoculating, drenching, dipping and crutching. On top of this during lambing the southerner is out in all weather playing midwife to his valuable ewes.

Ken and I were met at the train in Naracoorte by Rob McEwin, the manager of Killanoola, and while he was driving us out to the station he remarked casually, 'Max Monfries tells me one of you boys has had a lot to do with horses.'

I knew he couldn't possibly mean Langley, who at the very mention of the word horses had lost all interest in the conversation.

I smiled smugly thinking he was just making polite conversation, for I knew the horse had long since ceased to be a beast of burden in the South-East. Casually stretching my legs out so that he could all the better see my by now scuffed R.M. Williams boots and cooking stained no longer white moleskin pants, I admitted modestly that I'd forked a few broncs in my time.

McEwin looked relieved and said, 'Well, I'm certainly glad to hear that. We have a horse stud on Killanoola and at the moment we're having trouble with the stallion. My chaps aren't used to horses and he's got them a bit bluffed, but I'm sure you'll be able to teach him some manners.'

Jerking the suddenly traitorous boots back out of sight, I said, alarmed 'A stallion, now wait a minute, I haven't had anything to do with blood horses.'

'That's all right' laughed McEwin, pleased at what he thought was now my genuine modesty. 'You can't kid

31

me, as soon as I saw the way you were dressed I took you for a horseman. You'll do nicely.'

We had finished lunch when McEwin came in; I was in the middle of an interesting discussion with the male half of the married couple, Doc Bilsborough, who had played league football for Port Adelaide.

'Come with me when you're ready', said McEwin, obviously meaning 'like right now', 'and I'll introduce you to the horse'.

I noticed as I stood up that Doc looked at me hard, as if he wanted to remember what I was like before it happened. He told me later he had already composed the story he would tell — 'Yeah', he was going to say, 'I was there the day it happened, I wouldn't say I knew him well mind you, he'd just turned up actually. He only had one leg, said he'd lost it when a horse he was breaking rolled on him up north somewhere; it was terrible what happened, a proper devil that stallion was.'

When we approached the stables the stallion at the sight of us started whinnying and running around his loose-box in tight circles, eyes rolling. Full of advice Rob McEwin said from behind me, 'There's no real vice in him, just remember the important thing is don't let him see you're afraid,' and pressing a length of rubber hosepipe in my hand he pushed me through the loose-box door. I just had time to appreciate how the Christians in Rome must have felt as they entered the lion's den when the stallion charged.

I'd never hit anyone or anything before in my life and hesitated, preferring to try for evasive action and talking reason into him with a strong authoritative voice like you see people do in the movies.

It was nearly fatal. The stallion's first ear-flattened teeth-bared rush nearly did for me; the snap as his teeth came together just clear of my arm sounded like a rabbit trap going off. My yelp of fright was neither strong nor authoritative and as he came in for the

Me and the Stallion 'Anton Hill'

second time I knew I had to hit quick and hit hard, so discarding the psychological approach I started in to clobber him with the hosepipe for all I was worth. I reckoned that I could argue with my conscience and the RSPCA later.

The rubber hose, about two feet long, was ideal for the purpose. It made a lot of noise as it hit and whilst it undoubtedly stung, didn't inflict any lasting damage. Fortunately for me the stallion wasn't really bad or I wouldn't have stood a chance; in fact, being what he was he probably viewed the fight in the light of rough horseplay. True he was all set to have a go at the start, especially after I'd hit him the first couple of times, but after awhile his rushes grew less determined and his maddened squeals less terrifying.

Finally he stood with heaving flanks and dropped head at the far side of the stall, covered in sweat and shaking all over with spent fury. I was a proper case too and the fight hadn't finished any too soon as far as I was concerned.

Leaning back against the wall, I stood with arms hanging nerveless at my sides for the moment unable to move and thus we regarded each other.

When I considered I could make it I shoved off the wall with my shoulders and staggering through the loose straw on the floor approached him, shaking hand outstretched. The horse flattened his ears and snickered. Hoping it was just pride I kept on going and taking care not to touch the welts on his neck and shoulders that I'd made with the hose, I started in to soothe him.

After that first day the horse and I became firm friends and apart from the time he nearly sexually assaulted me in a moment of passion I had no further trouble with him.

There were twenty broodmares on Killanoola and it was the stallion's and my job to get them in foal. It was a serious business, for me anyway, and many was the hour I spent pouring over my stud book making sure each mare was receiving our proper attention. Actually the time I put in on 'Burchell's Brothel' as the stud was smartly nicknamed, only constituted about fifty percent of my activities, the rest of the time being spent with the other chaps on general sheep work.

Life was certainly different on these South-East properties from what it was up North. The distances around the run were naturally much shorter and I found the Northern bushmen's saying that you 'couldn't change out of second gear between gates' was pretty well correct.

Tiger snakes were a menace and when I was getting feed for my horse at night I often got the uncomfortable feeling that there could be one in the next sheaf of hay. At times when I was out exercising him we would see their sinister shapes with distinctive markings as they lay coiled in the long grass, or half hidden under a bush.

I would always know if Anton Hill, the stallion, sighted one, as snorting with fright he'd leap sideways and if I wasn't careful likely as not he'd dump me right on top of it.

They were good days and at week-ends Alan Reid, a friend of Ken's and mine, would come over.

Reid's visits were always popular; he had a car and this meant we could all get off the chain and go into Naracoorte.

After about six months on Killanoola it became obvious to me that although I was restocking the horse population of the South-East, admittedly with some assistance from the stallion, I wasn't furthering my cause much.

For some time Ken and I had realized we weren't getting anywhere with the Land Settlement boys and it appeared we were wasting our time pursuing the chance of getting our own blocks.

Ken however wasn't fully convinced and decided to try a bit longer. But I, either lacking his tenacity or thinking I knew the Land Settlement Board better than he did, decided to 'scratch 'er out', as the old bushmen say when they have had enough.

Waiting until the shearing was finished, I bade my horse a sad farewell and returned once more to Adelaide.

A swallow dive off 'the roof' at the old Olympic Pool

Diving from the Adelaide City Bridge at an aquatic carnival

4

After returning home, being loath to cut my ties with the land entirely, I applied for a job with one of Adelaide's stock and station firms. Here, at least, I felt I could still mix with stockmen and share their problems.

Working in the city however had its compensations. The regular hours and free week-ends allowed me to take up again the sport of high diving, which had been interrupted by my sojourns into the bush.

My career, if it could be called that, as a high diver actually spread over about a fifteen years and started when I was a kid still at school. But it reached a peak in the late forties when I returned to Adelaide after working on Killanoola.

The first time I'd dived off the top tower at the Olympic Pool was about five years earlier when I was sixteen, a month or two before I lost my leg. I can still remember the occasion quite clearly. It was a hot Saturday in early summer and Buck Ashby and I had sat up on the 'roof' as they call it in the trade, for the best part of the morning trying to pluck up courage to dive off.

Every now and again we would worm our way out to the edge of the platform and peer from its dizzy height at the pool far below.

Although I tried to kid Ashby into diving he wasn't to be conned and eventually almost in desperation I stood up and half fell and half dived.

My dive, roughly resembling the flight of a bag of wheat was memorable in only one respect. It was the only time, in what subsequently must have been thousands of dives, that I landed so flat that I didn't even get my back wet. Jimmy Hall, the pool attendant, duly recovered my body from the water and Buck, who watched my performance in thoughtful silence made a snap decision about his diving future.

Crawling on his hands and knees so that no one would see him, he made his way across the platform and sneaked surreptitiously down the stairs.

However this time, four years later, with the encouragement of Tom Herraman — known in the diving circles as the tallest pygmy in the world — and Don Brown, both of whom were State Champions at various times, I decided to take the game on more seriously.

I couldn't compete in open competition, as some of the compulsory round of dives necessitated running take-offs. But by concentrating on the stationary dives and those requiring handstands, I built up a sufficient repertoire to qualify as a member of the State Diving Troupe. The Troupe, which comprised ten top class springboard and tower divers, was much in demand at the local night swimming carnivals and over the years as its reputation grew, was invited to put on exhibitions at aquatic events all over the State.

This involvement did a lot for me, both physically and mentally, as highboard diving is a tough, disciplined sport and while it built me up physically at the same time it did a lot for my confidence. For I found that to make myself hop out to the edge of the tower with a gusty wind blowing and balance on one leg, or hold a handstand, until I was ready to drop away to the pool far below was mostly a confidence thing — a state of mind — a skill that had to be worked at and developed just as much as those required to control the dive on the way down.

It was a great feeling of accomplishment to be part of a complex pattern of eight divers, all going off the tower at once, knowing I could handle my part in the split second timing and teamwork that was necessary with everyone twisting and turning in the glare of the spotlights.

There were the bad nights, when the rain howled in and the crowds stayed home, or for no apparent reason dives became gutsers. But they were good days to me and it was a real morale booster to be part of it all.

Also at this time, through an association with Reg Lindsay a fellow member of our swimming club who could sing, play a guitar and yodel in a manner that rivalled Hank Williams, I briefly entered the world of show business.

As I'd always been able to yodel, Reg and I teamed up as a duo and performed during the half-time intervals at swimming carnivals. We were so successful that Reg started getting ambitious and entered us for an audition for Australia's Amateur Hour, the BIG thing in radio show business in the late 1940s.

Australia's Amateur Hour
We both sang the same song

39

We survived three auditions and to my surprise and Mum's horror, as she considered yodelling quite barbaric, old Reggie and I got on the show.

The half a dozen other acts, all of which seemed more classy than ours, included a small boy dressed in a blue velvet suit who played the violin, a choir comprising twenty girls and a plump woman who had a real go at 'They call me Mimi' from 'La Boheme'. Although Reg claimed that none of these acts would worry us and that we'd kill them, as the great night approached I became more and more apprehensive for I knew we had a big problem . . . Reg was a very nervous performer.

Even at a swimming carnival, where we had a captive sympathetic audience, Reg could get so nervous that at the last minute he'd start singing something entirely different to the song we'd chosen. This was all very well down at the swimming pool, where the crowd would just laugh as I tried to catch up, but it would be a different story if it happened while on air to most of Australia's radio audience.

I could imagine us up there on the stage and while I started off with 'The Love Sick Blues', Reg — glazed of eye and out of control — could quite easily launch into 'The Freight Train Yodel',

However, on the night of the concert, before a packed house in the Adelaide Town Hall, Reg and I sang our number.

Fortunately we both sang the same song and it really went quite well. We didn't win, as after the votes were counted, including the extra ones that Mum and Aunty Kit phoned in at the last minute, we were pipped at the post by the kid with the violin.

Soon afterwards Reg went to Sydney where he overcame his nervousness and built up such a successful career as a Country and Western singer, that today he is one of the most popular performers in both Australia and America. A far cry from singing in a dressing gown at the old Olympic Pool, but I guess we all have to start somewhere.

Probably one of the greatest characters to grace the Olympic Pool was Don Brown.

A born comedian, Don was just as adept at fooling with the clowns in the Diving Tripe as winning State titles with the Diving Troupe and he had several classic clown dives that were show-stoppers.

One I remember was a running Molberg or Full-gainer off the top tower. Dressed in neck-to-knee striped bathers he would continue to run right through the reverse somersault and would still be running when he hit the water.

In another he would sit reading a comic while balanced on the end of a plank which was protruding from the edge of the tower. One of the other clowns, in full view of the crowd below, would creep up behind him and start sawing through the plank. The mental anguish waiting for the board to break would have the spectators in turmoil, but Don wouldn't move a muscle, even when it did eventually snap and would plummet down still sitting and still reading.

He possessed that touch of genius and finesse that stamps a top performer and could, by just stepping off the tower seemingly doing nothing, still make the crowd roar.

His witch dive when he rode a broom down and his Colonel Light dive depicting Adelaide's first surveyor — copied from the statue on the hill — were all gems and although he won the State high-board title from Tom Herraman in serious competition, there is no doubt that it is as a clown diver Don Brown will be best remembered.

One of the funniest things that happened during my time with the diving troupe, was the day they shot Ern Beatty out of a cannon from the Glenelg jetty.

The stunt was the highlight of an aquatic carnival

Ern 'Cannonball' Beatty and I doing a duo from the top tower

organized to aid local charities and Ern, billed as the 'Human Cannonball', was the star performer.

The cannon itself, an impressive looking affair made of tin, was mounted on a platform above the jetty with its nine-foot red barrel pointing rakishly skyward.

The organizers had one small problem. The impetus to shoot Ern on his spectacular journey was provided by a heavy coil spring wound down by a ratchet type jack and sometimes the jack without warning would slip, allowing the cannon equally without warning to fire.

Now this information was withheld from Ern, as his friends considered it to be of minor importance and anyway he had enough on his mind. The day of the carnival was ideal, cloudless and hot and by the time Ern jumped up onto the platform beside the cannon a large crowd had gathered.

Ernie, always the ham, had gone to some trouble to look his part. Dressed from neck to ankle in white underwear, with a flowing purple cloak and a crash helmet, he stood accepting the plaudits of the crowd with all the aplomb of a man about to be shot into space. His anxious friends, who were more concerned about the temperamental firing mechanism than Ern's moment of glory, wanted to get on with it and without further ado proceeded to stuff him down the cannon's barrel. But the old 'Human Cannonball', unwilling to relinquish the limelight and being unaware of the need for any rush, managed to prolong his time by hanging by his armpits in the cannon's mouth. From this somewhat uncomfortable position he continued to acknowledge the cheers from the festive crowd below. It was at this moment the cannon fired.

In the initial conception of the stunt it had been planned that Ern would slide down, deep inside the barrel and stand with his feet on the round platform covering the spring with his arms above his head. When the cannon was fired he was to fly out in a graceful swallow dive. However . . .

The unexpected firing so caught Ernie unawares that for the first part of his flight he seemed paralysed. His arms hung limp at his sides, his thin legs encased in their white underpants trailed behind and the confident smile to his fans still remained on his lips. It was as if his body had moved too fast for his mind and it wasn't until he reached the apex of his arc of flight and his mind caught up that he came to life.

With a wild yell of surprise and terror Ern galvanized into action with his arms and legs flailing started in on the first of his unscheduled somersaults.

The onlookers could never agree how many somersaults Ern did that day. Ern himself was willing to swear that he saw the mob on the jetty go past six times,

43

but as he had severely bruised heels at the time his testimony wasn't counted.

★ ★ ★

During the winter months of this period I devoted my spare time to following that sport peculiar to our country, Australian Rules Football. A fast moving open game with heavy body clashes it is a real crowd-puller and is just about a religion in the States in which it is played.

Every Tuesday and Thursday night after I knocked off work I'd track out to the Prospect Oval and watch my team practice.

Ian McKay the captain, who also worked at Elders the stock firm where I was employed, often came with me on my Harley Davidson motor bike outfit and while the boys practised under the critical eye of the coach, Ken Farmer, I'd stand around and watch.

Sometimes on these occasions and when I was watching athletics I'd really rue my one legged condition, although normally I never thought much about it. Naturally it had its drawbacks at times but mostly these could be overcome. But football, the game I'd most like to have played, was beyond me and to add to my frustration my team, North Adelaide, who were never noted for their consistency kept me and the hundreds of other supporters in a constant state of anxiety.

Ian McKay, sensing all this and seeing a way in which he could ease it, did some lobbying around the club. Consequently I was elected to the position of thirty-fourth Vice-President and became a junior member of that august group of senior supporters. Being a VP didn't mean that you could pick the team each week or give pep talks at half time, but I was happy. I was really a part of the club, a sort of official and became so carried away with my status that for a while I became a title dropper. Making sure of course when casually mentioning it during conversation, to say that I was 'a' vice-president, never the 'thirty-fourth'.

5

With the diving and swimming in summer, football in the winter and riding a friend's polo ponies in between, my spare time was pretty well accounted for.

But busier days were ahead and when I applied to join the Shell Company as a country representative, I couldn't possibly foresee the many different paths down which this innocent-sounding job would take me.

Six of us including my old mate Ken Langley, who had finally given up any thoughts of going on the land, successfully finished the four weeks' induction school into the ways of the oil industry. We were waiting somewhat impatiently in the staff manager's office to learn to which country area we had been assigned. In a way it all reminded me of waiting for a posting in the Air Force. Some areas naturally enough were considered a lot more attractive than others and there was plenty of conjecture going on about where each of us might go.

I remember the West Coast came up as an area to be avoided. Due to its great distance from Adelaide and shocking roads, it was generally considered as the back of beyond by South Australian company representatives.

One chap who was a bit of a humourist but in reality dreaded the thought of being sent anywhere west of Whyalla, was carrying on properly.

'You could die over there', he wailed, 'and Head Office wouldn't know about it for months.'

The rest of the fellows laughed, but they were anxious just the same. I didn't really care, I'd been to Port Lincoln and Ceduna on holidays when still at school and had driven over the inland section a couple of times on trips to Perth . . . the West Coast had

46

always seemed all right to me.

The conversation ceased as the staff manager, clutching a sheaf of files, came briskly through the door.

'Sit down gentlemen', he said sitting down himself behind his desk. 'I suppose you are all anxious to know where you are going.'

Opening the first file he studied it briefly and looking across at Norm Duncan said, 'You, Mr Duncan, will be the company's representative at Kadina'. Norm let out a sigh of relief. Kadina was a nice little town in a good area, handy to Adelaide. His wife should be happy enough with that.

One by one the staff manager went through his files sending chaps, some with families and some without, to new jobs and new lives all over the State.

Ken landed Balaklava in the lower north and the humorist an area on the river in the Upper Murray. Finally he looked at me and with a smile said, 'And you Mr Burchell, are going to Tumby Bay on the West Coast.'

'Tumby Bay sir?' I queried frowning slightly, 'never heard of it', at the same time realizing that the sudden flash of irritation I felt proved I must have cared where they sent me after all.

'Oh, it's about four hundred miles by road from by here', the staff manager replied easily choosing to ignore my abruptness, 'good beach, excellent swimming I understand, you should enjoy it'.

'Hell', I thought, getting a bit savage, 'I've done as well as anyone in the school, why me?'

But business doesn't make many mistakes and although I couldn't see it at the time the Company was doing me no disfavour. Two days later, with all my worldly goods packed in the back of my new Holden car I reluctantly set off for the West Coast and Tumby Bay.

I think I liked the place as soon as I saw it. The town right on the sea with only the wide sweep of the beach separating the houses from the water looked a bit dry and dusty, but as it was late summer this was only to be expected.

I drove slowly around and when I'd had a good look searched through my briefcase for the piece of paper with the Shell agent's name and address. 'Jack Jameson', it read, 'Tumby Bay'.

'They could have put his full address on it', I thought, 'but I guess I'll find him'. I was to find him all right, just as I was also to find many other people in this quiet pleasant looking town, a town which on this warm Sunday afternoon was half asleep and completely indifferent to the fact that its population had just risen by one head.

The territory with which I had been entrusted by the Company covered the bottom of the Eyre Peninsula, from Port Neill on Spencer's Gulf to Mount Hope on the Great Australian Bight and in it Shell had ten agents in ten different towns. My job was to look after the Company's interests generally by working in close contact with the agents and calling on their customers at least twice a year, ironing out their complaints and problems.

The topography of the area was such that I spent about half my time operating from Cummins, a town situated in the centre of the lower Eyre Peninsula, for its pub offered the only accommodation for miles. It was here that I commenced a brief career as a football coach. Every night after we'd finished opening gates, Jim Cronin, a lad employed by the Cummins Agent, and I would retire to a paddock on the edge of town and play football. Or more correctly, he would play and I'd yell at him, full of advice on where he was going wrong.

In due course our activities were noticed by Ron Wedd, the captain of the Cummins Reds, the team for which Jim played. He must have been impressed by the noise I made yelling at Jim, since one night he stopped and asked if I would consider coaching the Cummins Red team.

Although never one to underestimate my capabilities, I hesitated. 'What do I know about coaching a football team?' I thought. 'These jokers take the game pretty seriously, if I muck it up they'll probably run me out of town on a rail.'

But the temptation was enormous. What an undreamed of opportunity, coach of a football team. They even wore North Adelaide colours.

'Perhaps', I reasoned, 'I can base my coaching on Ken Farmer's techniques'. I'd watched him coaching for years, something must have rubbed off. As the thoughts raced through my head I stared down at the football I was spinning end over end in my hands as if, like a crystal ball, it could give me an answer.

It was unheard of, in a way even preposterous, a one-legged coach who had never played a game. I could well be the laughing stock of the district. But perhaps with the aid of the Great Footballer in the Sky, Ken Farmer and a lot of luck I could do it. Grinning at Ron and fervently hoping we'd still be friends at the end of the football season I said, 'She'll be right, when do we start?'

It didn't take much to reorganize my work so that I'd be handy on practice nights, although some of the Cummins farmers received more than their scheduled two calls and for the next three months we battled and worried over the team.

But it was worth it. In the Grand Final of the Great Flinders League that year Cummins Red beat Kapinnie by three goals, taking out their first premiership for five years.

During the long hot summer which followed, the aquatic attractions of Tumby Bay beckoned and Peter Langford, one of the schoolteachers who boarded with

49

me at the guest house, and I banded together with two local lads in purchasing an ancient fishing boat. We reckoned on doing a bit of cruising and taking the local belles for trips around the bay. With the aid of Jack Jameson, who seemed to be able to repair anything, we went over her and after a repaint and patch or two renamed her *Zarefa*.

Our initial ideas of cruising around with three or four girls on board never really eventuated for the boat became an immediate favourite with every kid in Tumby Bay, so much so that even the shareholders were never certain there'd be enough room left for them.

I didn't mind really. I found it was handy as an incentive in my learn-to-swim classes. Only swimmers were allowed on board and generally the sight of the *Zarefa* with up to twenty kids as passengers cruising around the jetties was enough to make the most lethargic learn-to-swim pupils dramatically renew their efforts.

It would seem Australian country towns have a great capacity to use their imported population to the full. Oil companies, banks, stock and station agents and the Education Department with their schoolteachers provide a never-ending flow of young males into the country areas. These are readily absorbed into the local football and cricket clubs, or if the town is larger, also into service clubs, such as Apex.

In my case, since I wasn't much use as a footballer, the town found me other work to do. Almost before I knew it my Saturday mornings were taken up with the kid's gymnasium class, which somehow I found I was also running.

Our equipment which was pretty meagre, had been resurrected from a heap of old gear that had been lying in a shed behind the supper room for years. It comprised three medicine balls that the smaller girls found hard to lift and the larger boys found ideal for breaking windows, two tumbling mats and a tired vaulting horse.

With this fairly unsuitable collection of equipment I did my best to teach them the rudiments of body control and balance.

The children who turned up each week may not have been the best gymnasts in the world but they certainly would have gone close to being the noisiest. At times the racket in the old supper room was deafening. Like most kids though they'd rise to the occasion when needed and their item at the annual concert was not only a highlight of the evening to the audience, but always to me as well.

The annual concert was real entertainment. Johnny Hendriksen the local barber would always do his conjuring tricks. They were the same every year until one night someone sabotaged his carefully prepared props and his whole act fell apart along with the audience.

Other acts that always seemed to stand the test of time were the male ballet, comprising the entire football team complete with boots and Ivy Greenslade's rendition of 'My Hero'. It must have been the only song she knew and everyone hoped that this year she'd make the top note, but she never did.

I was foolish enough to sing a song one year. It was the hit number, 'Worried Mind' which was fairly appropriate, for as the time came closer for me to sing I was getting pretty nervous, so I decided to join the boys of the ballet behind the hall who were bolstering their courage by giving a bottle of Four Crown Port a nudge.

Normally I didn't drink but when Peter Langford said urgingly, 'Come on, Burch, a few swigs of this and you'll sound like Perry Como', I decided that for the sake of the audience I'd better join in.

It was a lie of course, as any representative of AA would have been glad to inform me. Perhaps I overdid it. Anyway I didn't sound like Perry Como at all, all the port did was make me forget the words. Even then I didn't think I was too bad, at least I finished the song.

But I hadn't reckoned on the Tumby Bay critics who are pretty severe on their performers. As my last Four Crown-soaked note lost itself in the rafters of the old Institute, Audrey Williams, the mother of one of my gym kids called out bitterly from the back of the hall, 'There's no doubt about you Burchell . . . as a singer, you're a bloody good swimmer'.

The gales of laughter that immediately followed from the rest of the audience told me that perhaps she was right and from then on I restricted my singing to bouts in the bathroom at the guest house.

As the months went by several other spare time jobs came my way.

One was the Married Women's Gymnasium Class which sprang from a humble enough beginning, with half a dozen young matrons wanting to take off weight and ended up a full-scale operation involving nearly thirty females of all shapes and sizes.

Every Thursday night in neat rows they covered the main dance floor pounding away at their exercises, based on preseasonal swimming training that I'd picked up in my swimming days, although I told the girls they were doing high frequency low resistance calisthenics which sounded more impressive. At Christmas each year we would have a dinner at the pub, just me and thirty women. Life on the West Coast was tough all right.

The news of my dazzling success as a football coach in Cummins drifted over the Yallunda Hills to Tumby Bay and I was asked to coach the Tumby team. I should have rested on my laurels, for while at Cummins we won the premiership, the first for five years, at Tumby the team under my expert guidance lost their first premiership for five years.

True it was only by a point and if it hadn't been for Alan Aldenhoven playing for the opposing team . . . but, ah well, that's the way she goes.

Generally on Sundays along with most of the other Anglicans I attended morning service at St Margaret's Church and the Reverend Blaxell, no doubt in an effort to ensure my more regular attendance, suggested that I read the lessons for him. As he said it would help him with the service I agreed and it became my regular job each Sunday.

One day after the service as we were tidying up, he asked me if I'd ever considered becoming a Lay Reader. The question coming out of the blue as it did, caught me without an immediate reply. Whilst I admired and respected the parson it had never crossed my mind to become involved in the work of the church.

Like many younger members of my faith I had always taken my religious responsibilities fairly lightly.

My infrequent trips to church were inspired more by the desire to please my mother and perhaps to conform to the accepted social pattern in which I lived, rather than in answer to any call or need I felt within myself.

To my discredit my first reaction to the parson's question was one of embarrassment at what the boys would say, 'They ribbed me enough when I started reading the Lessons', I thought; 'what will they say to this?'

Alwyn Blaxell, seemingly unaware of my embarrassment continued quietly. 'It's just that in the event that I am sick', he said, 'you could carry on.'

A disturbing mental picture of Alwyn, lying for months in hospital whilst I 'carried on', flashed through my mind. I could see my weekly sales report to the Shell Company, 'Sorry, no fuel sales again this week, but I baptised three children and buried poor old Mrs Thompson'.

The sales manager would be most impressed,

53

especially as he was not only a martinet, but also a staunch Roman Catholic.

As kindly as I could, for I certainly didn't want to hurt his feelings, I told Alwyn I couldn't do it. He accepted my reply in silence and after hesitating a moment or two under the guise of stacking some hymn books I slipped guiltily out the vestry door.

Three weeks later dressed in the Lay Reader's badge of office, a cassock and surplice, I was up at the altar lighting candles. In the pocket of my coat hanging from a hook in the vestry, was my licence, Number 229, signed by Richard, Bishop of Willochra.

Alwyn had won, in fact according to him as he handed me my licence, the issue had never been in doubt.

From then on I assisted him generally with the services each week and the contact with him was both interesting and rewarding.

When the day came and he told me he had been made a Canon and had been offered the much larger parish at Port Lincoln, I wasn't dismayed. The thought of looking after St Margaret's until a new man arrived didn't seem to present any problems at all. As it turned out I quite enjoyed it, even though Sunday became my busiest day of the week. But I did find that it was one thing to just read the Lessons and quite another to conduct the entire service. But at least we had all the hymns I liked, such as 'Onward Christian Soldiers' and during the next six months that elapsed before the new minister arrived, if anything the congregation of St Margaret's increased in number.

I was never quite sure if this was due to the stirring sermons I read from 'Sermons for Lay Readers' that Alwyn gave me when he left, or the fact that I could only make the service last three-quarters of an hour.

★　★　★

One day Leo Carr, the Shell Agent in Cummins and I were out canvassing the district for fuel orders. It was a blistering hot day and in an attempt to beat the heat and be more comfortable I'd left my leg under the bed in the Cummins pub, preferring to wear shorts and use my crutches.

We were approaching a gate on the side of the road which led to a farm house and I started slowing down, intending to turn in.

'Not much point in calling there' Leo said, 'this chap's a Mobil customer.' 'Ah, well it might be our day' I replied and in we went.

After the usual pleasantries the farmer suddenly asked 'Well, I suppose you're here for business?' 'Er — yes — of course' I replied 'how can we help you?'

'Let me see' he said thoughtfully, 'I guess I'll need thirty drums of diesel for the harvest and say ten drums of motor spirit. What's your lighting kerosene like?' 'First rate' I said brightly 'and we've coloured it blue so that kids don't think it's lemonade.' 'That's a good idea' he said, 'I'll have a couple of drums of kero.'

I glanced across at Leo, he raised his eyebrows and shrugged as if to say 'Well, you just never know.' We tidied up the order which was a beauty, arranged for the delivery and after thanking the farmer, continued on our way.

I was pretty impressed by my ability in nailing an order from an opposition customer and for the next half hour subjected old Leo to a lecture on the sales techniques I'd used. Obviously they were successful and I thought they could help him in the future. But apparently he'd been working too hard and must have been tired, as I noticed him stifle a yawn and close his eyes after the first couple of minutes.

The next day Leo ran into the same chap in the street in Cummins.

'Isn't it terrible about that young Shell rep.' the farmer said.

'Why!' exclaimed Leo, startled, 'what's happened to him?'

'What's happened to him?' echoed the man, shocked at Leo's apparently heartless attitude. 'I saw him in the town only a couple of weeks ago and he was all right. Then yesterday when you both turned up at the farm, he'd lost a leg. I don't know what the Mobil agent will say but I just had to give him an order.'

* * *

The two most significant things that happened to me at Tumby Bay, not necessarily in their order of importance, were learning spearfishing and getting married.

The spearfishing started when Dave Jones, a farmer friend of mine from out west of Cummins, returned from an overseas trip bearing a speargun and mask as a present for me. I could hardly wait to try them out and excitedly took them back to Tumby.

It was unfortunate that it happened to be mid-winter, but before the icy water drove me out I'd seen enough to realize that here indeed was a sport.

I'd heard about Cousteau and his new dimension, but in 1951 skin diving was virtually unknown in South Australia and anyone expressing an interest in it was regarded with grave suspicion.

For weeks afterwards as I'd come empty handed and shivering out of the water the locals would give me the works.

'Didn't get too many today Dave', they'd say and the line fishermen would call out, 'Don't spear 'em all Dave, leave some for us'. They would then dissolve into laughter at my optimism, imagining that I could catch fish underwater.

After a while I was inclined to agree with them. At first I blamed the speargun that Dave Jones had given me, as it was a fool of a thing with a friction trigger release, a system that was never successful, and was just about as dangerous to the user as the fish. But finally I had to accept the fact that it wasn't the gun's fault entirely, and that my lack of technique was probably the main reason why I returned each time empty handed.

However the day my new Lyle Davis speargun arrived from Queensland my luck changed. I was working along the outside of the Tumby Bay reef when I saw the sight every spearo remembers for the rest of his days. His first really decent sized fish.

The fish was lying half asleep on the clean white sand and short weed that comprised the sea-bed and as I lined him up, I thought, 'I'm sorry, old chap, but at least you'll make spearfishing history in Tumby Bay'.

We subsequently shot hundreds of fish up and down the coast and it became a regular thing on weekends to visit different spots and do a bit of spearing. It was on one of these occasions that we encountered our first shark.

About a dozen of us were fishing in a small bay, known locally as Hamilton's Beach. It was a favourite spot and one we often visited for there were generally plenty of fish on the reef which ran between the heads of the bay.

On this day there didn't seem to be many about and as it was pretty cold we soon drifted in twos and threes back to the shore. One of the crowd a bit keener than the rest stayed behind on the reef in an effort to bag a particularly good fish he'd been stalking. Nobody took any notice of him; we were far more interested in getting warm around the fire and it wasn't until his cry of 'Shark!' came to us that we realised in fact that he was still out there.

We jumped up anxiously scanning the bay, noticing

My first fish

An afternoon's catch at Tumby Bay
with Peter Dabovich

that the lad was safe enough for the time — he was perched on the only bit of rock on the reef that was still above water — but there, halfway between him and the shore was the dreaded triangular fin.

Calling to the boy to stay where he was, which I guess was a bit unnecessary, I hurried across to where I'd left my gear. There was only one thing to do and that was to swim out and get him. With the tide coming in, the rock would soon be covered and there was no time to get a boat.

As I picked up my speargun I suddenly felt a damn sight colder than when I'd come out of the water a few minutes before. Sharks were very much an unknown quantity in those days and the thought of swimming the hundred yards out to the reef and then back again with one for a companion was fairly unattractive.

As I sat down at the edge of the water to put on my gear Gerry O'Brien one of the truckies from the Highways Camp squatted down beside me.

'What are you going to do?' he asked in his Irish brogue.

'Go out and get him', I replied, amazed at how casual it sounded. 'He's my responsibility; I talked you boys into this.'

Gerry, the original wild Irishman was cut to the quick that I'd even considered going without him.

'Your responsibility be buggered', he exploded. 'It's Jasus you think y'are is it?' and sprinting back to the fire to get his mask and flippers, called back over his shoulder, 'Don't you leave that beach without me'.

In spite of the sobering thought of what I knew I was about to do, I couldn't help smiling to myself. Somehow, I wasn't feeling so cold any more and when Elmer Lloyd in a quieter voice but in his own way just as determined said, 'It's my brother out there Dave, I'm coming too', I was almost warm again.

I guess we were about halfway out to the reef when I

59

first heard the screams from the women on the beach. Raising my head above the water I looked in the direction they were pointing and there, about thirty yards away, coming straight at us was the shark.

Dropping my head back underwater, I indicated to the others that he was coming and we lined up three abreast with spearguns at the ready. We had decided beforehand not to fire unless as a last resort. We had no idea what effect the spears would have on the shark's tough hide; they could well only annoy him.

As he circled us, despite the natural terror he instilled it was difficult not to admire him. Sharks are a coldly efficient bit of mechanism; I understand they are one of the few creatures that have remained physically unchanged since the beginning of time, their original physical concept being nigh perfect.

The effortless way this chap glided round us made me realize how slow and cumbersome we humans are even with the aid of modern equipment.

On the way out to the reef he made several passes, but at no stage did he come any closer than ten feet. We collected Elmer's brother off his rock and then headed back to the shore which seemed a mile away. The shark only appeared twice on the way back and at his last pass I had difficulty in stopping Gerry from taking a shot. I reckoned we were doing fine without antagonizing the thing by bouncing spears off his nose and eventually we made the shore without any trouble.

Subsequent experience with sharks has taught us that we had little to fear. This had been a Bronze Whaler, a fish eater and most unlikely to attack a man.

The one we encountered that day was quite large, ranging from ten to twenty feet in length, depending on who out of the four of us was telling the story.

Learning spearfishing, compared to getting married, was a piece of cake. I'd always had an eye for girls, but apart from my wife there has only been one other whom

I could have married. However that's another story and as any married man will appreciate I've already placed myself on thin ice by even mentioning it.

I forget when I first noticed Ona Davies, but it wasn't very difficult to notice her since she was the belle of the district.

Her father owned a property about fifteen miles back in the Ungarra Hills and soon after I started pressing my suit I was invited out to the farm for Sunday dinner.

Sunday dinner in the country is a pretty big deal, often involving relatives and friends as well as the host's family. Such was the case that first day Ona asked me out there.

Her relatives include the Schramms and Roedigers and as everyone knows these families comprise about half the population of the eastern Eyre Peninsula. The men are mostly tall with heavy black eyebrows and hawk-like noses and like most descendants of the pioneering families they are self-reliant and good farmers.

The accepted leader of the Schramms was Uncle Jim who for years chaired the Tumby Bay District Council and the fact that he still had a sense of humour was probably as much to his credit as was the OBE he was awarded for the effort.

Uncle Jim, backbone of the RSL and Grand Lodge office-bearer, could be a hard man. He referred to agents, company representatives and in fact anyone who didn't grovel in the dirt raising sheep or grain for a living as 'bloody parasites' and consequently my appearance at his cousin's table for Sunday dinner was little short of an insult.

His great mate and counterpart Uncle Wilf, chief of the Roediger clan, wasn't much different and with one or two other uncles we sat down at the table.

Their attitude towards me pained me somewhat, for secretly I admired and respected these men. They had

61

all been good sportsmen in their day and their civic-minded approach to district matters combined with their qualities of natural leadership quite impressed me. But as far as they were concerned I wasn't even there. About the only people who recognized my presence were Ona, her mother and young Paul Schramm, a lad of five or six who thought I was the ants pants. It was Paul who caused my downfall.

'Show Dad how you can do a handstand David', he implored from his place at the small table where the kids were sitting. Earlier I had been showing him how to do a handstand on a fence post and he'd been greatly impressed. But I shook my head; sitting at a loaded dinner table was hardly the time or place.

But then again I thought, perhaps it wasn't a bad idea at that. There was no chance of a mishap, as handstands had always been a speciality of mine and in my high diving days I had several tricky presses I used to do off the tower.

It would certainly make these characters sit up and take notice, especially if I did one on the end of the table, so giving Paul a wink I shifted a couple of plates to make room for my hands. Ona's mother, getting a bit anxious said, 'Do you think you ought to David? Dinner is ready now'.

Giving her a confident smile I replied, 'She'll be right, won't take a minute' and from a sitting position at the table I pressed into a handstand.

I don't know how it happened, perhaps I broke my concentration listening for the murmurs of approval that never came, but almost immediately I lost my balance. When you lose your balance in a handstand the alternatives are simple enough, you either fall over on your back or start walking.

In that agonizing split second when I knew I was gone the former seemed unthinkable, so I started walking.

Ona and me on the beach at Tumby Bay

The first thing my left hand hit and knocked over was a large jug of salad dressing. As my right hand came through it landed smack in the middle of a bowl of beetroot in aspic and this dreadful stuff sliding from beneath me threw me further off balance and I completely lost control.

I waded down that table like some upside-down freak out of a nightmare leaving behind a trail of destruction defying description, and I didn't stop until I landed flat on my back, draped across the lap of Uncle Colin. As I lay there staring up his ample left nostril my mortification was very nearly overwhelming.

This unfortunate beginning seemed to set a pattern and our courtship followed a rough path. Ona's father, Jack Davies, only tolerated me around the place to please his daughter. I did have an ally in her mother though, who liked me and considered I was a reasonable, albeit slightly crazy, catch. Also as it was a dry year I had to put off asking Jack if I could marry his daughter until it rained, since he was worried about his stock.

When I did ask him he was far from thrilled at the thought of the proposed union and asked Ona in front of me if she was sure she knew what she was doing.

We were married the following April at the Methodist Church in Tumby. It was a good show. The reception went on all night, ending up at the farm where it took Ona's mother two hours to cook breakfast of bacon and eggs for the mob.

6

I don't know why I left the Shell Company. I can hardly blame it on Port Pirie, the area to which Ona and I were sent after Tumby Bay. Perhaps after eight years I felt I needed a change. Anyway leave I did, lured by the offer of a sales manager's job with a new firm in the city. I think I realized I'd made a mistake the first week I started, it was an awful job and I hated every minute of it. However I stuck it out for twelve months then, at my step-father's suggestion, decided to go into business on my own.

He offered to help me in obtaining agencies from interstate, but I wasn't sure and it was with a very heavy heart that I bade my wife and four kids goodbye as we left for Melbourne to find a manufacturer who wanted an agent in Adelaide.

Aristoc Industries at Glen Waverley were our big hope. They manufacture steel furniture of all types and we felt if we could crack their agency all would be well.

I still don't know how we did it, but the result was that we returned home with the Aristoc franchise and also one for Airdive Equipment, a crowd at Prahran I'd heard about who made SCUBA.[1]

I don't know which was the harder to get off the ground, the furniture or the diving. Practically no one in Adelaide had heard of either, Aristoc being virtually unknown and the number of scuba in South Australia could have been counted on one foot.

---

[1] The word Aqualung is actually a trade name, the correct term if referring generally to a compressed air lung is Scuba, the initials of Self Contained Underwater Breathing Apparatus.

However I hired a small shop in an Adelaide back street and with great pride and some trepidation hung up my shingle. The window on one side of the door read Adelaide Skin Diving Centre and on the other Featherston Interiors.

It seems a long time ago that Don McLeay and I assembled the first three scubas on the floor of our sitting room.

The scubas or lungs arrived from Airdrive Equipment in pieces and at one stage, we thought we would end up with four instead of three before we straightened it all out.

There was one each for McLeay and me. The third was for John Scammell, an old mate of ours who protested loudly that he didn't need a scuba. I overruled him as I badly needed the extra discount allowed for three units on the one order.

Mac and I a few months before, had joined the Underwater Explorers' Club, a struggling little group with half a dozen members who were giving free lessons in the Henley Baths.

We'll never forget our first time down. My instructor was a cop appropriately named 'Snook' Godliman, an original member of the Police Aqualung Squad and by the time he had led me on a circuit of the murky pool I was a complete convert.

At the same time Mac was being instructed by Felice Wittwer, the only girl in the club and judging by his enthusiastic comments every time he surfaced I could tell she was doing a good job.

We went diving at every opportunity after that and by the time the three scubas arrived from Airdive we were starting to get the hang of it.

Realizing we owed him some consideration, we gave John Scammell a ten minute schooling with his new lung and promptly dragged him underwater with us.

From then on at weekends, they both helped me run

With Don McLeay on the Port Noarlunga jetty

training schools. We started off at Port Noarlunga Reef, a spot about twenty miles from Adelaide and then used various suburban swimming pools for a year or so. I found swimming pools were not the best for scuba training. For one thing we never seemed to be able to obtain exclusive use of them when we wanted it and for the other they are generally not deep enough.

One day I saw an article in the *American Skin Diver* magazine describing a training tank at the Marina Diving Centre in Vancouver and I realised that this was what we needed in Adelaide: a tank. The next day I rang Don Mitchell, an engineer friend of mine and told him what I had in mind.

Drawing up the plans, to an engineer like Don

Members of the SA Police Underwater Recovery Squad during a training session in the tank

Mitchell who was used to designing complicated bridges, was a breeze; but building the tank and installing it was a different proposition.

The steel shell, twenty-two feet high and eight feet in diameter proved difficult to handle. We had to juggle its unwieldy bulk one hundred feet up a narrow lane at the end of which was a right angle turn into a small back yard but with the aid of the Electricity Trust, a crane and most of the divers in Adelaide pushing, we got her in.

This was only the start of our troubles, but a month later with great ceremony we had the official opening. The fact that the water was a muddy brown was unfortunate — the filters hadn't caught up — but since Adelaide people are used to muddy water it was hardly noticed.

I've lost track of the number of people who have learned to dive in the tank, but it would run into thousands. For not only have many sport divers taken their first tentative drags on a demand valve in it, but so also have trainee divers from the Police, Marine and Harbors Board, Engineering and Water Supply, half a dozen other government departments and hundreds of Boy Scouts and school kids.

Over the years I spent, or so it seemed, about half my time underwater. A lot of it could be described as hack work, even mundane perhaps, training other people, but to me it was always interesting. Even the long hours at night in the tank after having finished with the furniture for the day, have had their moments.

But because diving and mixing with other divers had become part of our business, opportunities for the less mundane always seemed to be presenting themselves.

These came in many forms and we became quite expert at recognizing them . . . a chance remark, a casual meeting or an article in a magazine. Such things have sent us off on trails to sunken ships, to diving in subterranean caves and nearly to the limit of compressed-air breathing two-hundred and seventy feet down on the edge of the Continental Shelf itself.

There have been dives for the hell of it in flooded gold mines and dives in the muddy Murray River recovering speed boats and outboard motors. We stood by in full diving gear whilst Donald Campbell made his bid for the world water speed record on Lake Bonney and at times, even created a record or two of our own.

At other times days have been spent in library archives, searching the yellowed pages of ancient newspapers for clues to the exact locations of old wrecks.

In all we have spent many hours diving and many more talking about it and I'd like to think we have in

I gear up Mac Laurie's son, Jock, before taking him for his first dive

our way contributed our sixpenny-worth, or perhaps I should say, now that Australia has gone to decimals, put in our five cents.

* * *

The chap didn't really mean to get in my way, but he was making a pretty good fist of it.

I was filling scuba cylinders out in our compressor room and as everyone who has done this job knows, it's something you have to keep your mind on and it doesn't help to have someone standing all over you.

He wasn't a diver and not having seen cylinders filled before was barraging me with irritating questions.

As the gauge crept round past the 2000 psi mark he started to get alarmed and yelling in my ear over the noise of the compressor, asked what would happen if one of the copper pipes burst.

Feeling a bit mean but seeing my chance I called back

70

over my shoulder eyes still on the gauge.

'How do you think I lost my leg?'

I finished opening the next cylinder and glanced back to see how he'd taken it. He'd gone; the compressor room was empty.

7

Not only did we convince ourselves that scuba was the best medium for underwater breathing, but over the years we have done a sizeable job influencing many others as well.

Until the advent of the scuba, all diving was done by conventional divers using heavy canvas suits, lead-weighted boots and bronze helmets, generally known as hard-hat gear.

Nowadays however, the modern lighter equipment of the scuba and hookah[1] divers has all but taken over and with the exception of a few die-hards and operators who can't afford the conversion, the hard-hat era is finished.

This state of affairs, accepted now by commercial contractors and navies throughout the world, was resisted fairly strongly at the outset. There were probably as many reasons for this as there were men diving, but apart from the financial angle which was considerable, high on the list would have been prejudice.

This prejudice and resentment was built up by many conventional divers against the swarms of sportsmen and even worse, women, who were invading their hitherto private domain.

Consequently, when it was suggested to a hard-hat diver of many years standing that his equipment was old

---

[1] When a diver breathes air through a demand valve similarly as in scuba, but instead of having a cylinder on his back, his air is supplied by means of a long hose connected at the surface to either a low pressure compressor, or a large cylinder of compressed air.

fashioned and his methods were clumsy, it was a case of look out!

Further if it was hinted that to be in the swim he should get with it, throw off his long woollen underwear and climb into a wet suit, it could well mean spearguns for two and coffee for one.

Our first major victory in this regard was with the Royal Netherlands Harbours Works, a Dutch firm who had won a contract to carry out the marine work at Port Stanvac Oil Refinery.

Netherlands, who had been engaged in contract diving for some eighty years, had been honoured with the title Royal by the Dutch Government for their services to the industry. They had always used conventional gear and when I called on them and suggested they try applying skin diving techniques to their work, they nearly drop-kicked me out the door.

'We know all about skin divers', Bill Romeyn the head diver told me bluntly, 'we had one in the Persian Gulf on the last job; he was no good. He knocked up too quick'.

Determined not to give up easily I pressed on. 'There were good divers and bad divers' I admitted, 'also good gear and bad. You are reasonable men; why not come up to town and try it for yourselves?' I raced on a bit desperately as I could see Bill's attention was fast leaving me.

'Yeah, we'll do that one day', said Romeyn.

It was obviously the brush-off and I thought I'd lost my cause. But with one one last try I said, 'Well, can you make a definite time? I'd like to put you in our diving tank and I want to make sure I'm there when you come'.

Bill showed his first flicker of interest. 'Diving tank', he queried, 'you have a diving tank.'

Seeing my opportunity I immediately launched into a harangue on the tank and its virtues. In the end, to shut me up, he made an appointment for Wednesday of the next week.

* * *

Bill's head broke the surface.

'Well, what do you think', I asked, confident of his answer since he had been fooling around on the bottom of the tank for nearly half an hour.

'She is good', Bill replied delightedly, 'it would be ideal for inspections and light work, but I don't know about heavy jobs'.

'Well that's a start anyway', I said, taking the lung off him, 'it's more than you would have admitted a week ago.'

Bill laughed and said, 'If you think this is good for hard work, perhaps you know some divers who want to work for us at Stanvac. I'll need two or three soon.'

I thought Brian O'Grady could be interested and perhaps Frank Alexander. Also Bruce Berry was looking for something to do during the winter months.

'Yes', I said to Bill, 'I reckon I know a few boys who could be starters. Let's know when you want them'.

Subsequently these chaps, along with a few others did practically all the diving at Stanvac and nurturing the seeds I'd sown finally convinced Bill that Scuba and hookah were the answer.

So complete was their influence that long before the job was finished Netherlands packed all their hard-hat gear away and used skin diving equipment only.

When the Stanvac contract was finished and Bill was about to leave and go off half-way around the world to his next assignment he said to me, 'Well Dave, our company has been diving hard-hat for over eighty years and yet we had to come to a little out-of-the-way place like Adelaide to completely change our methods. I don't mind telling you', he went on, 'We would never have finished the job on time if it hadn't been for Scuba.'

Since then we have converted many government and semi-government departments to Scuba. There was the Engineering and Water Supply where we trained Brian Cotten to dive deep into reservoirs and crawl up water filled pipes. The Marine and Harbors Board, when more than a dozen of their conventional divers were converted to hookah in schools at Adelaide and Port Lincoln.

Of the others, including private contractors, the most interesting possibly would be Geosurveys.

I'd met Reg Sprigg, the managing director of Geosurveys, a couple of times at Don McLeay's. Highly rated as a geologist, he applies the dedication no doubt learned early in his career in isolated lonely field work, to everything he does.

Reg's lieutenant and number one trouble shooter was Darby von Sanden, a mountain of a man whose official title of Operations Manager covered the difficult and demanding task of keeping seismic crews happy in dreadful out of the way places, helicopters in the air, fuel and supplies pouring into camps all over Australia and information pouring out.

My first contact with Geosurveys was when von Sanden rang and invited me to join Peter Warman, of the Police Underwater Recovery Squad, in the training of ten of his geologists to Scuba.

I agreed to assist and off and on I've been worried by Geosurveys and the Von ever since.

Peter Warman I'd known for a long time. A tough, efficient policeman, Peter had been in charge of the Police Underwater Squad for several years. Along with his colleague, Colin Williams, he has led the squad in and out of some of the roughest dives, underwater ones that is, imaginable.

When Peter and I arranged a meeting to draw up a training program for the Geosurvey's geologists, I was all set to go a bit easy on them. None of them were very fit and both Reg and Darby, who were also to be trained, were not exactly lads anymore.

But Peter wouldn't hear of it. 'Be buggered', he said, 'if they want to learn to dive they'll get the full treatment, right from the start'.

I laughed and already started to feel sorry for our pupils, for I knew only too well what Peter's ideas on the full treatment would mean.

Warman, a disciplinarian, liked everything done on the double. During the training of the police candidates for his squad, the only time he would allow the poor characters to wear flippers was when they were running from one place to another. Also it was woe betide anyone who made the mistake of jumping in with his weight belt under his Scuba harness, or after coming out, forgetting to turn off his air.

His methods were more severe than mine, but with a little give and take between us we drew up a comprehensive program. This covering a three week period, including both the practical and theoretical aspects of diving.

The theory side involved lectures on diving physiology, psychology and physics. The practical ranged from snorkel training in a private pool, half-mile swims without gear in the open sea, mask clearing and initial free ascents in the tank, to more serious techniques required for deeper dives and staging against bends. Also we threw in as many sudden and unheralded acts as Peter and I could dream up, in an effort to gauge each pupil's reaction to the unexpected.

The first week saw four of them flunk out, but the balance including Reg and Darby saw it through.

Towards the end it was with a certain amount of pride that we watched the six geologists sitting on the bottom of the tank without masks, calmly breathing in turn off the one Scuba. It wasn't a bad effort considering none of them were active swimmers and had all more or less been pushed into it.

All the sea dives during the course were done from Geosurvey's sixty-foot research vessel Saori, a name derived from the initials of South Australian Oceanographic Research Institute. Each time we went aboard my eyes were drawn irresistibly to the large yellow and black diving chamber securely lashed to the gantry on her stern.

The chamber, designed by Darby to take gravity meter readings on the sea-bed, was as yet untested and I was bursting for the chance to be first man down. As it turned out, I needn't have worried. When starters were called I had no rivals for the honour, for Peter wouldn't have a bar of it and the others were not experienced enough. The interesting part as far as I was concerned was not so much going down in the chamber but escaping from it when it was on the sea-bed.

The theory involving the escape from submarines and the like is nothing new and in other parts of the world submariners have been using the principle to save their lives for years.

But this represented the first opportunity we'd had in South Australia to have a go and I didn't want to let the chance slip by.

It didn't take much to convince Reg and Darby that it was unwise to send a man down in the chamber if in the event of an emergency he couldn't crash out of it and the test was placed on the list of official activities.

On the last day of the course we tested the chamber. After the grind of the previous three weeks this last day, which was a sort of passing out parade, was like a holiday. Also we had some visitors on board, including most of Geosurvey's directors and the entire Police Diving Squad.

Consequently it was with a festive air that Saori ploughed her way out past the breakwaters at Outer

Harbor, to the preselected spot where the tests were to be made.

The second step was to do the simulated escape and then if all went well run the Geosurvey's personnel through in turn. By the time we reached the test area I was already in my wet suit and within a few minutes of dropping anchor was ready to go.

Darby, who was in charge of the winches, gave me the nod and ducking under the gantry I climbed up the iron ladder welded to the outside of the distinctively painted steel hull.

The chamber itself, a massive thing standing ten feet high was cylindrical in shape and constructed from half-inch steel plate. Its all-up weight of over four-and-a-half thousand pounds was raised and lowered by two nine-thousand pound breaking-strain nylon ropes, powered by compressed air winches.

At the top was the round entry hatch, the opening and closing mechanism which was operated by two hand wheels allowing the hatch to be operated from either side.

The inside, whilst not being exactly spacious had ample room for the gravity meter operator, usually a geologist, to work his complicated equipment. A telephone kept him in contact with the ship above.

At eye level were three equally spaced two-inch thick glass portholes. Through these the geologist could make visual observations of the sea-bed, or if there were divers down, keep contact with them whilst they were collecting their sand and rock samples.

All things considered the chamber was a beauty and a credit to von Sanden whose ideas she represented.

As part of the test program included flooding the chamber, all the expensive equipment had been removed from the inside and when I lowered myself down through the hatch it seemed larger than I remembered it.

The extra equipment I had with me didn't take up much room. Apart from a depth gauge, weight belt and mask, the only bulky item was a Scuba, to be kept ready in the unlikely event of the hatch jamming and preventing me from getting out of the chamber after it was flooded.

The weight belt was necessary for a wet suit can have up to a ten-pounds buoyancy factor and the diver in a wet suit without weights floats uncontrollably like a cork.

Once inside I closed the hatch and gave Darby the thumbs up through one of the portholes to lower away. It's a strange sensation for a diver to be underwater in a dry capsule. The view through the portholes is the same but somehow you are not part of it and as I watched the free moving Scuba divers escorting mc down, I understood how a man in a prison cell must feel when looking out of barred windows, he observes the birds flying freely past.

On the way down I checked the hatch cover for possible leaks. All was well and as the depth of water was only forty-five feet, in a minute or two I could see the sea floor coming up. With a slight jar the chamber hit sending up a cloud of sand and mud which temporarily obliterated my vision.

The disturbed sediment was soon cleared away by the current and after I'd received the all clear from the chaps outside I started to flood the chamber by turning on the two seacocks located near the floor. The twin jets of water came through the valves with surprising force and in no time at all the floor was awash. Placing the Scuba in a handy position in case I needed it in a hurry, I spun the control wheel of the hatch cover to the open position.

All I had to do now was wait until the internal air pressure which was being compressed by the inrushing water, reached the ambient or surrounding water

79

pressure of the sea outside. Until these pressures were equal it would be impossible to open the hatch.

As the water level inside crept higher and higher, I witnessed the odd sight of the depth gauge on my wrist registering the pressure increase, for although the water level was only to my waist the gauge was reading twenty feet.

To pass the time during the slow process of flooding, I wrote rude messages on my slate to the boys outside. But after a few exchanges of greetings the first trickle of water started leaking through the hatch over my head, indicating the pressures were nearly equal and the time had come to get out.

By now the water level was nearly up to my chin and suppressing a mild wave of claustrophobia at the thought of the hatch being jammed, I took a couple of deep breaths and standing on the ledge that usually housed the gravity meter instruments pushed against the hatch as hard as I could. The result was like standing under a waterfall.

The heavy spring-loaded hatch after a slow start suddenly flew open and as the air inside, compressed to about two-and-a-half atmospheres, was released and took off for the surface forty-five feet of water pressure poured in.

Waiting a second or two until the boil-over had subsided, I swam out the open hatch and free ascended to the surface.

It was agreed by all concerned that the escape had been most successful and after some discussion on the technique involved I took each of the Geosurvey's chaps down in turn. It was fairly crowded as this time we intended to use Scuba and by the time two people and two lungs were jammed in there wasn't much room. However, they all went well and at the conclusion of the test it was decided that a mask and Scuba be kept in the chamber as standard equipment

'I'm OK'
Escaping from the chamber during tests

and this proved to be just as well.

For although at the time of the practice run everyone considered the knowledge gained would never be used, within three weeks due to a series of unfortunate incidents the chamber was lost out in the Gulf in a hundred feet of water.

Jonas Radus, the geologist on board at the time, remembering his escape drill calmly crashed out through the hatch and using the emergency Scuba swam back to the surface lugging his gravity meter with him. The chamber none the worse for the experience was recovered two days later.

Since then Geosurveys, using this technique, have completed hundreds of dives and gravity meter surveys searching for oil and minerals in Australia and New Zealand. These gravity meter readings which determine the changing in mass in sediments, provide critical information to the geologist and physicist.

After an area has been subjected to a gravity meter survey and is found to have possibilities and more accurate information is required, the more sophisticated and costly techniques of seismic are employed. If the combined information received from the two surveys presents the picture that the geologist wants, the area finally becomes a potential drilling target.

An interesting point is that a major problem confronting people operating underwater surveys is the limited time they can use their divers in a day.

The basic reason for this is that bogey of compressed air breathing, diver's bends. The bends, a form of paralysis brought on by the absorption of nitrogen into the fatty tissues of the body, particularly in the brain and spinal cord, is directly influenced by three contributing factors: depth, duration of the dive and the degree of exertion of the diver.

Contrary to popular belief amongst non-divers, depth alone doesn't produce bends. For instance a diver can carry out a dive of few minute's duration, known as a bounce dive, to depths of two hundred feet and come straight back to the surface without ill effect, or conversely he can stay down in shallow water of up to thirty feet for hours and also come straight up without trouble.

The problem of bends only arises when the two factors, depth and time at depth are combined, the position being accelerated if the diver is required to perform heavy manual work, for the harder he works the more nitrogen he will absorb.

There are several sets of tables governing permissible times at various depths and whilst these vary according to the individual ideas and principles employed by the people who made them, the end result is the same. The deeper the dive, the less time the diver can stay down without staging.

Staging is the term applied to the decompression stops the diver must make if he overstays his maximum allowable time. If this occurs it is then necessary to make a controlled ascent, staging or stopping at lesser levels thus allowing the excess nitrogen absorbed to be removed from the system.

Unfortunately staging represents time and time is not the ally of underwater survey. In our Gulfs where the depth of water ranges from eighty feet to one-hundred-and-forty feet, a diver can possibly carry out half-a-dozen four or five minute bounce dives a day without trouble before his time is up. After this if he continues to dive, his accumulated time under forces him to stage.

On oil survey work a station is set up and a gravity meter reading taken every three miles and in Geosurvey's case this is done in the chamber. At every alternate station divers go down and collect the all-important sand and rock samples from the ocean floor, at the same time obtaining a detailed report on the incidence of marine growth and fish life.

Generally as the work starts at dawn and finishes after dark the normal complement of divers soon use up their time and the contractor is forced to face several unattractive alternatives.

He either continues to use his divers, consequently slowing the whole operation down to a crawl with time-wasting staging, or he can break the rules and send divers down on their own instead of pairs, thus doubling his diving time. As a last resort he can invite his friends along for free sea voyages, on the condition they bring their own wet suits.

The people included in this latter group have had a pretty rough time and frequently have been shanghaied and forced to breathe copious quantities of compressed air in furthering the interests of underwater surveys.

But there have been few complaints from those

impressed and in every case the diving accomplished has been most interesting and rewarding.

When possible to save the divers' time away from their usual employment, Saori sailed on ahead, loaded to the gunwales with gear and the divers flew out later in the aircraft to the nearest convenient landfall to pick her up, contact being established en route by ship-to-aircraft radio.

These oil surveys have taken us from the Continental Shelf out from Robe near the Victorian border in the South-East, to the shallow tidal mud flats at the head of the Gulf in the North.

There have been days when we have looked up from the sea floor and viewed the ship riding at anchor one hundred and forty feet above, almost as clearly as if there was no water at all.

At other times with the visibility reduced to a few feet, the tide rip could be so strong that if a diver lost his grip on the heavily weighted shot line he would be swept a quarter-of-a-mile away by the time he surfaced.

When approaching the Continental Shelf, the mariner doesn't need the aid of the echo sounder to tell him when he has arrived. The dolphins soon let him know. There are hundreds of them leaping and flashing, row upon row, right on the exact line where the sea floor shears away from a mere six-hundred feet of depth to twelve-thousand feet a few miles further on.

Out there a hundred miles from land where the water is far too deep for diving, we have watched fascinated at the story being told by the echo sounders, with the graphs recording the underwater mountain ranges and wonder as divers are apt to do, if perhaps one day . . .

But we know it is a forlorn hope and are filled with the sadness and the frustrations of all pioneers who can visualize the potentials and possibilities of their chosen field, yet know that these goals will not be attained in their lifetimes.

The surety of the knowledge that it will be done is some consolation. It is certain that future generations of divers pushing down further and further will overcome the present problems and in time will explore and work the precipitous chasms and valleys of the Shelf. It will be they, these as yet unborn divers who will carry out the farming of the countless tons of fish that show in the huge schools on the echo sounder charts and who will also in time lead to the recovery of the vast mineral deposits that lie waiting for the use and ultimate benefit of man.

Saori, driven tirelessly by her crew in the quest for more and more knowledge, has sailed over the awesome depths of Jeffrey Deep, one of the biggest and least known deeps of the world, where the sounder nearly runs off the graph in an effort to record the twenty-thousand feet.

Further inshore, in lesser depths but still too deep for diving we have gathered around on the deck as the diver-type bottom sampler is hoisted back on board.

Shaped like a bomb and weighing eight hundred pounds, it drops with the speed of a rocket, driving the eleven foot sample catcher up to the hilt in the sea-bed thousands of feet below. The compacted clay and sand samples thus brought up provide the geologist with further vital information and although it is a hit and miss effort with chance and luck playing a big part, at four-thousand feet what else can you do? Nothing . . . yet.

★ ★ ★

'Forty-four fathoms', said Arno, eyes on the sounder graph. 'Will that do you?' Arno, the skipper of Saori, was pretty blasé by now about people stepping over the side of his ship whilst at sea. They always seemed to

85

come back up again and he'd long since ceased to worry about it.

I made a quick mental calculation. Forty-four fathoms equals two hundred and sixty-four feet — plus eight for the ship's draught — just over two hundred and seventy feet. 'That'll do fine, Arno', I said, 'how about coming down with us?' His reply, flavoured by fifty years as a skipper of a coastal ketch, was unprintable.

As Arno cut his engines I hopped across the deck to my diving gear, lying checked and ready by the gap in the rail. Reg and Darby were already shrugging their lungs on and after thoroughly checking them both out I slipped into mine and in a minute or two we were ready to go.

The ship's position was approximately fifty miles off Beachport in South Australia's South-East and we were about to make our first dive in excess of two hundred and fifty feet. The event was one that I'd long awaited, since the opportunity for deep dives is limited in our shallow coastal waters.

Three days before Colin Semmler, Geosurvey's pilot had flown Reg, Darby and me down to Robe where Saori was waiting and after a day or two out on the really deep stuff we had come back inshore to do some diving. We had done one bounce dive to two hundred and five feet the day before, but this one to two hundred and seventy was what we'd been waiting for.

My job was to ride shotgun on the other two and whilst I was not worried about Darby, for he keeps his mind on the job, I was a bit concerned about Reg.

The old Sprigg, like most truly dedicated professionals, gets so completely carried away and lost in his geological fossicking that I'm sure he forgets where he is. It makes no difference if he is underwater or in the middle of the Simpson Desert, his environment means nothing to him.

To add to my problems Reg was an air sucker and without any trouble at all when we dived to two hundred and five feet he all but flattened his 80 c.f. cylinder, whilst Darby and I came up with ours still two-thirds full.

It was obvious we had a problem with Reg and his air, in diving to two hundred and seventy feet. To overcome the possible air shortage we secured three spare Scubas to the shot line one hundred and fifty feet down and to overcome Reg's personal idiosyncrasies I gave him a pep talk on his responsiblity to himself and to others. I don't think he appreciated it much, as he told me quite briefly and concisely when I'd finished, to get stuffed.

The three of us sitting side by side on the deck at the gap in the rail, legs hanging over the side, were ready to go. The shot line was on the bottom and we had two hookah hoses down ten feet in case emergency decompression was necessary.

Our plan was for Reg to go first, then Darby and then me. We were to keep visual contact with each other and physical contact at all times with the shot line. We were to go down quickly, stay two minutes on the bottom and come straight up.

We were using SeaBee lungs, with the usual tactile-type pressure gauges on the high pressure line. From these gauges we would be able to tell if it was necessary to change over to one of the spare lungs tied to the shot line on the way back up.

I gave Reg the nod and placing his hands over his face to protect his mask he slipped feet first over the side. Next went Darby and allowing a few seconds for them to get clear I followed.

There was quite a sea running and as weights are not worn when doing deep dives — due to the extreme pressure the wet suit loses its buoyancy factor — it is necessary for the diver to pull himself quickly down the shot line to keep clear of the plunging ship. Immediately I hit the water I spun around and taking hold of the white nylon rope started pulling hand over hand as fast as I could. But due to the extreme depth and the influence of the tide, the rope which up on deck had appeared taut was in effect slack and with Reg and Darby hauling themselves down thus tightening it, all I was getting at the top was free line.

The force with which Saori's hull hit almost stunned me and I thought it must have dislodged the regulator off the cylinder valve behind my head.

'Blast!' I thought with great feeling as desperately I hauled on the slack line. 'I'll have to go back up and check for possible damage to the regulator.' Just as the ship was poised to deliver her next crushing blow I started to get some purchase on the rope, and managed to move down a few feet. Here I stopped and whilst my head cleared, quickly felt behind me as best I could in an effort to check the regulator. It seemed OK and whilst I knew I should go back up it would mean missing the dive and leaving Reg and Darby on their own.

'Not bloody likely', I thought, 'they'd never let me live it down', so flipping over I pulled myself down the line for all I was worth.

The water was a beautiful royal blue and the white shot line seemed to stretch on into infinity. At about eighty feet my suit started to lose its buoyancy and at one hundred and fifty feet, where the spare lungs were tied, I was all but neutral.

At two hundred feet, although getting darker, the visibility was still good and soon after I could make out the shadows of the sea floor. At two hundred and twenty feet I could see the tiny figures of Reg and Darby on the bottom.

Deep diving is really quite an experience and as the sea-bed comes into view and starts to take shape below, the diver gets the same impression an astronaut must feel when looking down at the earth spread out beneath him. A feeling of unreality, no doubt brought on by nitrogen narcosis or 'rapture of the depths' adds to the sensation. Although 'rapture' never affects me in open sea dives like it does if we are diving in fresh water, such as in the confined shafts and rock fissures of the volcanic system at Mt Gambier, this I think subscribes to the theory that narcosis is partly psychological, for diving in confined spaces has never appealed to me like diving in the sea.

As I reached the bottom at two hundred and seventy mark it was time for Reg and Darby to start their ascent and giving me the 'I'm OK!' sign which I returned they shoved off.

Holding the shot line in one hand I gazed around at the unusual scene. 'So this is what it's like', I thought, 'it looks like a garden, with the coral and white sand'.

A particularly good specimen of Bryazoa or lace coral caught my eye. It was as big as a cabbage and taking out my knife from its sheath on my leg I carefully cut it away from its rock base. It would make a good trophy.

I noted the rare sight of the indicator needle on my depth gauge hard round at its maximum reading of two hundred and fifty feet and checking my watch I was surprised to see that already nearly half my time was gone.

At this stage I was unaware as to what extent Reg and Darby's powers of observation had been affected by narcosis and as the three of us were desperately keen not to waste the dive I reckoned it was time I stopped gazing and started looking.

Settling down I made a concentrated effort to memorize pertinent details, such as the amount of rock and marine growth per square yard, types of coral and fish life.

Using the shot line as an axis I did a complete three

hundred and sixty degree sweep, mentally noting points as I went. A small school of fish of a type I hadn't seen before kept pace and regarded me silently with goggle-eyed curiosity. I gave them a wave and had difficulty in determining if I'd done it for fun or if it was the narcosis getting the better of me.

Finishing the sweep I tried hard not to forget what I'd seen and a glance at my watch told me it was time to leave. Carefully cradling the lump of fragile Bryazoa in one hand I pulled myself up the rope with the other and slowly made for the surface, leaving the small school of fish to their silent lonely domain.

Five minutes later back on the deck of Saori, the three of us compared notes and impressions with almost boyish enthusiasm.

I was pleased with Reg, he'd done a perfect dive coming up the moment Darby signalled him. He even had a few pounds of air left in his cylinder.

I checked the pressure in the 80 c.f. cylinder I'd used; the gauge showed eight hundred pounds. Not bad considering it included the dive to two hundred and five feet the day before.

I needn't have worried that Reg's powers of observation would be affected by the depth. His trained geologist's eye had missed nothing and any information Darby and I had to throw in only served to corroborate the mental picture he already had.

Reg, excited by the geological importance of the dive, was pouring over the samples we had brought up. Lumps of rock, quite meaningless to me had him really jumping.

He badly wanted my Bryazoa but I told him he was definitely out of luck and carefully carried it off and hid it. Previous experience having taught me that Sprigg is not to be trusted when it comes to pinching other people's samples.

I was really pleased with the dive. We had bounced to

90

two hundred and seventy feet without decompression and while I was sure it could be done, it was good to have actually done it. Darby was also pleased . . . to be back on deck again.

★ ★ ★

As I came in the back door Ona looked up from peeling potatoes in the kitchen. 'Ah, you're back,' she said, smiling brightly, 'have a nice dive?'

'Yep', I replied, 'did a deep one yesterday off Beachport'.

'Oh', she said interested, 'what was it like?'

'Just like a garden', I sighed, the memory of it all still fresh in my mind 'just like a beautiful garden'.

Ona, acting like any wife whose husband completely lacks horticultural interests, couldn't let the opportunity go by.

'Is that so, just like a garden', she said and then added as dry as you like, 'I wouldn't have thought you could recognize one'.

8

An interesting point and one that will surprise many South Australians and also one that indicates the vast number of ships that are at the bottom of the seas, is that between the years 1837 and 1961 there have been nearly four hundred officially recorded shipwrecks in our waters alone.

If a relative isolated backwater like South Australia can have four hundred shipwrecks in only one hundred and twenty years, what must the sea beds of the great shipping lanes of the world be like. As spanning the maritime centuries and combining both the result of natural disasters and wars, there would have to be tens of thousands of ships.

Some of ours were small ships, the list showing dozens of cutters, brigs and whalers, but the majority were large barques and steamers. A few were recovered and recommissioned, most were a total loss, with names such as *Marion, Jessie Darling, Songvaar* and *Corio* becoming part of our history.

There was the ill-fated *Star of Greece*, wrecked at Port Willunga in 1888, from which some of the local divers recovered a cannon. Also the *Admella* which went on the rocks at Cape Banks in 1859, taking with her to their deaths over seventy passengers and crew and yet by a strange twist of fate several racehorses, on their way from Adelaide to Melbourne, survived by swimming ashore, one even winning a race soon afterwards.

At one time or another every Scuba diver in Adelaide has been on the local wrecks *John Robb* and *Norma* and to a lesser extent the *Clan Ranald*, lying upside down in eighty feet of water off Troubridge Hill, but we are always looking for new ones.

One trip involved a safari to Stun Sail Boom River on the isolated southern coast of Kangaroo Island.

It was here on that wild desolate coast, under the expert guidance of two local islanders Don Dixon and Doug Seton, that we searched for and found the stark remains of the once proud and beautiful four-masted French barque, *Montebello*. Hounded by a gale one black night in 1906, she'd driven straight in onto the rocks and in minutes of striking was a total loss.

Another time on Kangaroo Island we dived on the steam powered merchantman *Portland Maru* in the turbulent waters off Cape Torrens. At the base of the seven hundred foot cliff lay the rusting remains of the Japanese freighter and as we swam through her engine room clouds of startled sweep flowed around us, no doubt excitedly discussing this intrusion from the alien outside world.

It was John Rathbone who first thought of looking up the histories of our wrecks in the old newspapers, held by the Public Library Archives and he and I have spent many hours poring over these fascinating eye-witness reports, describing the shipwrecks and tragedies of years long since gone.

One particular wreck that always intrigued Rathbone and me was the *Loch Vennachar* and once in an effort to find her, along with Ross Curnow, we risked our very lives for two days, trailing two-hundred yards behind the cray boat *Canowie* on an improvised sled made out of a piece of driftwood.

To say that we risked our lives, although a bit dramatic, is virtually true. This is real shark country, the home of the White Pointer and on previous trips down there I'd seen several, one measuring seventeen feet which was caught less than a mile from where I was looking for a lost propeller.

I guess none of us will forget those lonely turns on

the sled. For if ever a diver resembled a seal — the Great Whites natural food — it would have to be while gliding along in total silence, clad in a black wet suit, at the end of a two-hundred yard rope. To make it worse we could only stare straight ahead. What might be following behind and possibly closing in fast, we could only imagine. I for one, did a great deal of imagining.

The crew of the *Canowie* wrote us off as lunatics, but so great was our desire to find the *Vennachar* that the three of us took turns on the sled until we'd used up all the air in the ten Scubas we'd laboriously carted over the sandhills.

But skimming the sea bed about eighty feet down we really saw the wonders of nature, as the underwater scenery off this cruel broken coast is awesome in its wild beauty.

Thick green-yellow kelp, growing in clumps up to ten feet from the ocean floor is everywhere and the bottom, a riot of huge tumbled rocks interspersed with valleys and large dark caves, presents an ever changing panorama.

Blue Groper, four and five feet long, unused to moving out of anyone's way shifted reluctantly at our approach and once, by leaning over the side of the short plank we were using for a sled, I actually touched one with my hand as I went by.

However while we enjoyed the scenery well enough we found no trace of the ship and it was not until a full decade later that the *Vennachar* was found — fifty yards North from where we started our search going in a Southerly direction.

That area finally claimed John Rathbone, for he was drowned a few months later while attempting to cross from the mainland to the island in an open boat. His death sat heavily on those of us that knew him, for he was not only a competent, courageous diver and pioneer, but he was also a good husband and father and a good mate.

Some of the names of ships listed as wrecks stir the imagination to the full and as I read a brief account of the sinking of the schooner *Experiment* off the Althorpes in 1881, I couldn't help but conjecture on just whose dreams had gone down with her. Obviously the *Experiment* as such was not a success.

Other names such as *Emma, Agnes* and *Ethel*, while no doubt meaning something to their owners, appear plain and unexciting and one tends to skip over them in the search for the more imaginative. There are many of these and again we had no trouble painting mental pictures of tall graceful ships bearing the names *Apollo, Resource, Summer Cloud, Tigress* and *Triumph* and even though their loss must have been tragic at the time, being something of a dreamer, to me it would almost seem preferable to have them die proudly fighting their last battle in their natural environment, than to be torn apart and broken up by the impersonal hands of the shipwreckers.

★ ★ ★

It was a small brass lantern, so heavily encrusted with calcified marine growth that it was difficult to recognize. With great care I pried it loose from the upturned lamp locker, where it had lain for over half a century and swam back up to the surface. Later metallurgy boys at the Adelaide University helped me clean it by using a solution of sulphuric acid and water and when finally we were able to take it apart we found that the fuel container still held some sludgy kerosene and four inches of cotton wick. The wick was washed in warm soapy water and dried in an oven. The sludge I badgered the Shell Company into centrifuging and after the impurities were thrown off we had a dessert spoon full of kerosene.

This and the wick were put back in the container and after fifty years lying seventy feet under water the lamp, in its original condition, was relit.

* * *

As Phil Houston and I walked up the steps to the hotel foyer, I noticed that the Fijian porters seemed to be grinning more than usual, but wrote it off to their natural good humour. We had just returned to the Sky Lodge Hotel at Nandi, Fiji's international airport, after three weeks knocking around some of the four hundred islands that make up the Fiji group.

For the first two weeks we'd had for company a Sydney TV unit, who were making a series of films featuring Ron Taylor and Ben Cropp.

But for the last week after the filming was finished and the unit had gone back to Australia, Stan Brown the captain of the inter-island schooner *Mororo* which had been our home, made us an offer that was too good to refuse.

He suggested that Phil and I might like to spend a week with some Fijian friends of his on the remote island of Mbulia, in the Kandavu Group, fifty miles South of Suva. Stan assured us that the Mbulia islanders were mostly friendly and that the majority of them had given up cannibalism and also that the diving in the Astrolabe Lagoon, in which the Group was located, rivalled the Great Barrier Reef.

We readily accepted and had a tremendous time living and diving with the Fijians, but now it was all over and incredible as it seemed, within a few hours we would ourselves be back home in Australia.

As we dumped our mixed assortment of diving gear and trophies on the hotel foyer floor I grinned happily back at the friendly sea of faces, noticing as I did so that a couple of chaps were glancing upwards above my head. Following their lead I looked up and there firmly tied to the hotel's swinging sign-board was my faithful wooden leg Mercury.

Three weeks before, along with several other items not wanted on voyage, I'd left Mercury in the tender hands of the Irish-American manager of the Sky Lodge, Paddy Doyle and apparently he'd been having a whale of a time with it ever since.

During the day he displayed it as a tourist attraction

With Phil Houston and friends
Mbulia Island, Fiji

in the foyer. At night I was told he would completely shatter the nerves of the tired Qantas and Pan- Am crews, as they quietly eased their tensions at the bar, by bursting through the door with the long suffering Mercury — complete with shoe and sock — sticking out from under his arms.

Attracting their attention with a wild rebel yell he would then call out dramatically, 'Quick you guys, come outside, there's been an accident'.

9

Unfortunately the waters in South Australia are notoriously bad for sharks, as in addition to our share of Bronze Whalers, Hammerheads and Tiger sharks, we are one of the world's headquarters for that terror of the seas, the White Pointer or Great White.

Our reputation is such that it has lured big game fishermen, including the legendary Zane Grey, to our shores in efforts to bag their world record catches.

It was to Dangerous Reef out from Port Lincoln on the West Coast, that Ron Taylor suggested the American film producer Peter Gimbal try for his now historic underwater shots of Great Whites, when shooting the film epic 'Blue Water — White Death'.

Consequently that first question asked of a diver by a non-diver, 'What about the sharks?', is not easy to answer if you wish to still appear as being of sound mind.

I've found that no matter what I say the questioner is left unconvinced, still believing that to be a diver you have to harbour some sort of bizarre death wish, with diving in waters where there is a chance of a shark attack being on par with riding through a lion park on a pushbike.

How you handle the problem, and it is a problem, is a personal thing. Some beginners never do, especially if they see a shark on their first dive. Often when this happens diving gear is advertised for sale under the caption, 'Bargain — used only once'.

Then there are the divers who have been in the game for years and have never seen a shark, but who at their first fright have never gone back in again.

An example of this was Charlie Oliver, one of the

original spearfishermen in the Port Lincoln district. Charlie was a strong swimmer and completely without fear in the water. So much so that most of his spearfishing exploits, when he would swim alone out to far off reefs and islands, were considered as foolhardy.

I'd always thought of Charlie as being quite special and when he called on me some years later, I was really pleased to see him. After awhile I asked, 'How's the spearfishing going?'

'Given it away mate' he replied, 'I lost my nerve'.

'YOU lost your nerve', I said unbelievingly, 'Why, what the hell happened?'.

'Well', he answered, 'I put in a season as a deck hand on a shark fishing boat with some mates of mine from Lincoln and one day we snagged this bloody big Pointer. He'd got himself tangled up in the lines and we had to pull him along side to cut them off. He'd pretty well had it, but the skipper said, 'Hey Charlie, take the twelve gauge and get up in the bow. If he starts to give us any trouble give him both barrels'.'

'Well they winched the big bastard up until his head was about two feet away from where I was squatting by the rail.

'I'd never seen one before and it was a strange feeling to be so close and staring straight into his cruel black eyes. This didn't worry me any and I was just thinking about giving him one — when it happened.

'He must have been in his death throes, although he wasn't thrashing around or anything, but he started to work his jaw and this bloody great mouth came open right in front of me. The lips peeled back and there were these teeth, they were triangular, with the edges all serrated like sharp steak knives and behind them this tunnel-like gullet.

'I crouched there like I was hypnotized and couldn't tear my eyes away from that opening and closing mouth that could gulp a man down in one bite.

100

'I went cold and started to shake as I thought of all the times these big sods must have been cruising around near me and right then and there I made a decision.

' 'Charlie old boy' I said to myself, 'that's it. You've just given up spearfishing', and I haven't been back in since.'

While I had to laugh at Charlie's description of the reason for his retirement, I couldn't help but agree with his decision. The chances were he wouldn't have lasted much longer the way he'd been going.

Although no one fully understands the behavioural patterns of sharks or is able to explain why sometimes they attack and sometimes they don't, or why at certain seasons they are meant to be in certain areas and yet they are not — or vice versa, we have learnt that large spearfishing competitions, when twenty to thirty spearos are all in a restricted area at once, can be a dangerous game.

However it should be clearly understood that Scuba diving and spearfishing are two totally different sports and that there is a big difference in the risk of shark attack between the two. For where Scuba divers don't spear fish and spearos do, it logically follows that the radar-like impulses of pain and fear that a speared fish emits, which attract sharks from extraordinary distances, must put the spearfisherman in greater danger. For to the cruising shark these impulses are like the sound of a cook in a mustering camp ringing the dinner gong.

In the early 1960s spearfishing was a competitive sport on an International scale and we had State, National and World Championships, with Australians of the ability of Taylor, Cropp, Rodger and Fox all in world class.

But within the three-year period — 1961 to 63 — when a spearfisherman was attacked each year by sharks, the big competitions in South Australia finished.

The first attack occurred in March 1961 when Brian Rodger was mauled by a White Pointer during a spearfishing competition at Aldinga, south of Adelaide.

Savaging his leg and arm it then unaccountably backed off and left him struggling in a cloud of his own blood.

Rodger, a fine physical specimen and very fit, used his spear gun rubber to wrap a makeshift tourniquet round his thigh, twisting it tight with his diving knife. Then not knowing from one second to the next if the shark would attack again, he started the long swim back to shore.

Finally, so weakened by loss of blood he was all but passing out, but just offshore in answer to his now feeble calls for help a boat picked him up.

After reaching the beach quick-thinking friends rushed him to the hospital, where the doctors replaced four litres of lost blood and put over two-hundred stitches in his leg and arm.

The next year, again in a competition, sixteen-year-old Jeff Corner was all but bitten in halves by a White Pointer at Carrickalinga, a few miles south of Aldinga.

At that time spearfishermen were working from surf skis and Alan Phillips and Murray Bampton, who were diving near by from their skis, in a fine show of courage carried him to shore. Tragically, by the time they reached the beach, Jeff Corner was dead.

We thought we'd learnt something from these attacks and the next year it was decided that pick-up boats would cruise the area when big competitions were in progress. The idea being that speared fish be taken out of the water as soon as possible, thus minimizing the attraction for sharks.

Rodney Fox had just handed up his catch to a boat and after reloading his speargun was ready for his next dive when a huge Pointer, coming from nowhere, hit him with such force that it tore the snorkel from his mouth and the mask from his face.

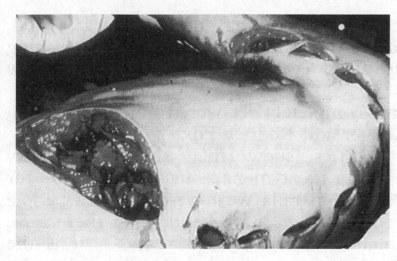

Rodney Fox

Surging through the water with Fox clamped in its jaws, the monster nearly drowned him, but after taking him to the bottom twice it suddenly let go.

Shockingly mauled, with his punctured lungs exposed through crushed ribs and left forearm stripped to the bone, Rodney was hauled into the pick-up boat.

Again, as in the case of Brian Rodger, his friends acted quickly and within the hour he was on the operating table at the Royal Adelaide Hospital.

I was home that Sunday afternoon when Peter Warman from the police rang and told me of the attack. I immediately rang Brian Cornish, who was an Honorary Orthopaedic Surgeon at the Royal Adelaide and he got me straight into the Casualty Department.

Sometime later I was grimly standing by a barouche in the recovery room on it was what was left of Rodney Fox.

They had worked on him for hours, but even in my inexperienced eye the effort had apparently been in vain, as for the last ten minutes there hadn't been the slightest sign of life. Sick with the horror of it all I was about to turn away when suddenly his eyes opened and he looked straight at me.

'G' day Dave', he said with a grin, 'sorry I can't sit up and entertain you'

It is interesting to note that the next year, 1964, South Australia won the Australian Spear Fishing Championship Team event, which was held in New South Wales.

In our team, completely recovered and undeterred, were Brian Rodger and Rodney Fox.

Although statistics show that sharks, relatively speaking, are not a great menace to swimmers — for instance in South Australia we have had more people killed in car accidents on a weekend, than there have been shark fatalities in twenty-five years — it is the appalling thought of actually being eaten alive by another living thing that is so horrific.

In this regard our last two fatalities have been especially bad. In 1985 a young mother of three children was attacked while snorkelling near Tumby Bay and in September 1987 a Scuba diver was taken while collecting scallops off one of our popular beaches. In both instances the victims were completely devoured. The attack on the Scuba diver sent an especially cold chill through the diving fraternity as it was the first time in Australia that a person using Scuba had been taken by a shark. Up till then we had thought that somehow we were immune or perhaps hoped we were immune would be more correct, as I don't know of a Scuba diver who hasn't the thought of sharks somewhere in the back of his mind.

During the thirty or so years that I've been diving I've seen a few sharks — not many — but apparently the ones you see are not the ones to worry about. For in every case I know where divers have been hit, they were unaware of the shark's presence until the moment it attacked. Why sometimes sharks don't attack when they are in a position to do so is a mystery.

I had an instance of this once at the Barges, a popular local dive about three miles out from Port Stanvac. It was during an official UEC outing and we had just finished taking twenty-four trainee divers down the ninety feet to explore the three steel hulks that had been abandoned on the sea bed.

Ours was the last boat to leave and as I was pulling the anchor and idly watching for it to come into view through the clear water, a huge White Pointer slowly cruised up from the depths. He followed the anchor right up to the surface and for a moment, as I hauled the pick in over the side, I thought the shark was going to keep on coming and join us in the boat.

But after coldly staring at me for a second or two with black fathomless eyes, he rolled over and effortlessly glided along the side of our fifteen-foot runabout.

'Bloody Hell', I breathed, just having time to register that the shark was longer than the boat, then over my shoulder said quietly, 'Hey Ernie — take a look at this'.

Ernie Foody, my friend, business colleague and at times unwilling companion on many exploits, was not a diver and had no intention of becoming one. He's worked with me in my various business projects for over fifteen years, is a cabinet maker by trade, can fix anything and is a great fan of Ona's — whom he quite incorrectly feels has a hard life.

He is very aware of my shortcomings and limitations and is convinced — probably quite correctly — that if it hadn't been for Ona and himself I would have sunk without a trace years ago.

This day Ernie had been sitting for hours hunched up in the stern of the boat, miserably green with seasickness.

He didn't move at my call and just urged me in no uncertain terms to finish getting the anchor in so that we could return to Terra Firma, which he vowed he'd never leave again. Then suddenly without warning the great black back of the Pointer slid past three feet off his left elbow.

105

'What't that?' he shrieked, spinning around and going a shade greener.

In spite of the seriousness of the situation I had to laugh. 'That's a White Pointer', I said conversationally and in an effort to cheer him up added, 'Now I don't want you going over the side and attacking him with a knife'.

But it didn't seem to cheer him at all. 'Oh God', he whispered, raising his eyes longingly towards the far distant shore, 'Let's get the hell away from here'.

By this time the shark had moved off to about twenty yards and was gliding round us in a wide circle, his sinister dorsal fin cutting the surface. Then after a couple of minutes he just eased down beneath the sea and disappeared as silently as he came.

Thinking about the shark on the way back to shore, I couldn't help wondering why it hadn't made its appearance sooner. It must have been lurking in the vicinity all the time we were diving and as we had taken the trainees down in separate small groups, we had been underwater for a considerable time. Also after the dive people were swimming around on the surface visiting friends on other boats and generally skylarking about within the perimeter of the half-dozen anchored craft.

I went cold at the thought of what could have happened.

It could well have got me first.

I always claimed — with great modesty — that I was the only person in the club who had the knack of finding the Barges with visual bearings. Consequently when I said we were on them it was my job to go down first and make sure we had at least one anchor securely hooked. I couldn't help shuddering at the knowledge that I must have been alone down there with this monster.

Then why the shark didn't attack over the next two hours, when there was a veritable smorgasbord of soft, plump little bodies from which to choose — nobody knows.

That it wasn't hungry is unlikely — sharks are known to have insatiable appetites.

It may have been sick, although it looked and moved as if in perfect health.

That it was frightened by our numbers is laughable — the Great White is frightened of nothing.

The only conclusion I could make as I steered the boat back to shore, with a subdued Ernie bouncing around uncomfortably in the back, was that as far as sharks are concerned — we still have a lot to learn.

10

It was cold and wet in the old mine and the muffled voices of the fellows up ahead floated eerily back along the horizontal shaft.

There were fifteen of us in all. Miners with heavy boots and powerful battery operated lamps on their helmets, skin divers in wet suits, reporters and harassed television cameramen. The latter, rapidly ruining their clothes in the effort to protect their expensive equipment, were moaning the loudest.

The event that had led up to this slipping and sliding around was the discovery of a 100-year-old mine by a friend of mine, Ian Clarke, on his property at Ashton in the Adelaide Hills.

With the aid of a torch Ian had cautiously followed the mine about 120 yards in to where it ended at a water-filled winze or vertical shaft. By the time he'd reached the winze he was pretty excited, which I suppose was understandable. It's not every day that you find a gold mine in your backyard and he was burning with curiosity as to the extent of the workings in the flooded section under his feet.

Assuming from the size of the drive that these workings could be quite extensive, the next day he rang and asked if it would be possible to dive down the winze and see what led off it in the way of other drives. Already he had ideas of pumping the mine dry and making his fortune.

I'm not mad about mines with their confined dark tunnels, but Ian assured me that the drive was like walking down Rundle Mall and his description of the flooded winze made it sound like the Olympic Pool, so I decided to have a look for him.

I asked Bruce Berry to come along as a stand-by diver. Nothing worries Bruce and he is a handy chap to have around in an emergency.

During the week prior to the dive some of the boys from the UEC said they wanted to come along and watch. This suited Bruce and me well enough as it meant we could off-load all the heavy gear, lungs, weight belts, ropes, batteries, et cetera, onto the spectators.

Our friends the Press, attracted by prospects of obtaining good copy with stories of skin divers and flooded gold mines also wanted to come. This was all right by us too. 'She'll be right', I told them, 'it's like Rundle Mall down there'.

Of course I should never have believed Ian Clarke in the first place. After the first ten yards I was all set to turn around and crawl right out again. Only one thing stopped me; there wasn't room to turn around.

I'm sure anyone with even slight claustrophobic tendencies would have felt uneasy. Imagine a narrow black tunnel, seven chaps in front and seven behind, all lugging heavy equipment. No room to even sit up, knowing there was ninety feet of earth and rock on top and faced with the depressing knowledge that there was over 100 yards to go.

Just as I was really getting a yen for the great outdoors the drive opened up and whilst it didn't get any wider than about three feet at least you could stand up.

The increased size of the drive must have had a heartening effect for by the time we reached the winze my claustrophobia had left me. This was just a well, for in the light of the torches and television sun guns the black flooded shaft looked far from inviting. In fact Bruce and I both agreed that it was the most unattractive patch of water we had ever considered diving in.

We had chosen the equipment we intended to use with care and had settled on 72 c.f. standard lungs, incorporating tactile-type high pressure indicators.

These are plunger type pressure gauges that retract as the air pressure in the cylinder decreases. They are ideal for diving in dirty water, since the diver can always tell the air pressure left in the cylinder by touch rather than by sight.

We were wearing full length wet suits and double our normal sea weights. The reason for the extra weights was that we wanted to be negatively buoyant so as not to bump the ceilings of the flooded drives and invite cave-ins. We'd left our flippers off, for with the extra weights we intended to crawl more than swim.

Our underwater lights comprised a sealed-beam spotlight hooked by a cable to a twelve-volt battery and two torches. The calibrated shot line, which was to serve as a signal rope as well, showed the water in the winze to be just under fifty feet deep. Our plan was simple enough. I was to go down first and if a drive off the winze was found, signal Bruce to come down. He, controlling the shot line would then wait outside the drive entrance whilst I followed it in.

With the thermometer reading the water temperature at forty degrees Fahrenheit, I eased gently in so as not to dislodge any mud. I needn't have troubled, the water was filthy and after going down about ten feet I let the spotlight go.

The light being buoyant shot to the surface like some live thing that was only too glad to get back to the relative comfort of the drive above. For a moment I was sorry I'd let it go, for whilst it was useless for seeing anything at least it turned the inky black into a comforting deep orange.

However dirty water was nothing new and almost immediately I forgot about the light in my concentration on the job ahead. Lowering myself cautiously down the shot line I felt the hard still perfectly square outline of the shaft with my free hand. Mentally I complimented the unknown miner who must have spent years digging with pick and shovel making the shafts. They were a work of art and I couldn't help but wonder what drove him on. The lure of great riches? Or perhaps just an experienced expert miner plying his trade, content to earn his living as he best knew how.

Finally my probing foot touched the loose shale and rock at the bottom of the shaft and I thought, 'If there are going to be any drives this is where we'll find them'. Feeling carefully over each wall in turn, it was something of a shock to find that the fourth wall wasn't there. Instead there was a large gaping hole into which, quite unwillingly I slid foot first.

I lay in the drive not moving; this was by far the most likely spot for a cave in and we had decided before the dive to treat any such area with extreme caution.

Very gently I started feeling around me. The drive was about three feet wide, but not as high as the one on the upper level. The ceiling seemed sound enough and slowly I groped my way back out through the entrance to the winze.

Giving the shot line two tugs which was the signal for Bruce to come down, I propped myself into a corner and waited. I remember thinking that it is a pity you can't smoke under water as I could have done with a fag. Before long I could hear Bruce coming and the next thing he was standing on my head.

We eventually sorted things out with Bruce beside me I took his hand and traced around the opening of the drive for him. He tapped me on the shoulder to indicate he understood the position and I went back into the drive foot first. Lying on my stomach I pushed myself backwards further and further along the shaft, feeling the sides and ceiling as I went. I suppose I was about twenty feet in when I felt rather than heard, the roof cave in between me and the winze.

At times we all have our moment of truth and I had one right then. Suppressing an almost uncontrollable desire to panic I wormed my way back to the entrance. 'Was it blocked?' was my first thought. No, not quite, there was a gap at the top. Stretching my arm through I could feel Bruce's legs as he stood out in the winze.

I lay there in that coffin-like hole for a minute or two forcing my rapid breathing rate, a sure sign of panic, back to somewhere near normal.

All divers are taught in their initial training that the greatest danger to the diver is himself. Uncontrolled panic has no place anywhere, especially under water and more accidents are caused by it than any other factor. I had pounded this point at hundreds of trainee divers and I remember thinking as I lay there, 'Ok. Here's your big chance old feller'.

By the time I was back to breathing on a five-second cycle I'd worked out a plan. I dared not try to force myself through the opening with my lung on, in case I dislodged the regulator from its O-ring fitting on the cylinder valve behind my head. If this happened I would have immediately been without air to the demand valve or mouthpiece and my five-second breathing cycle would have been reduced to something like five years, the time I reckoned it would take to dig me out.

Therefore I had no option but to reverse back down the drive again to where I could move more freely, take the cylinder off, then keeping the demand valve in my mouth return to the entrance and push the cylinder through and wriggle out after it.

Crawling a few yards backwards down the drive I quietly and carefully struggled out of the harness and then pushing the cylinder in front of me headed back to the entrance.

It was simple enough to slide it through the opening and as I couldn't think of any other way to attract

Back in 'Rundle Mall'
Bruce Berry and I surface from the
50 foot deep winze

Bruce's attention I belted him on the shins with it. He complained rather bitterly afterwards that I needn't have been so rough, but he was pleased to feel it just the same.

Crouching down he felt the cylinder and instantly realized what I'd done. Running his hand carefully along the low pressure hose to me at the other end he gave me a reassuring pat on the head and as I started to worm through he drew the cylinder gently out into the winze. I followed in hot pursuit.

Things were a bit confused for awhile. It is difficult for divers to communicate with each other at the best of times, but in the dark it's just about impossible. After a couple of false starts we finally got the message through to the boys up top to haul away and Bruce and I, dancing cheek to cheek like two puppets on a string controlled by an incompetent novice, rose jerkily to the surface.

Relativity is a strange thing. As we surfaced and looked around at what before the dive had seemed to be a dark confined area but now looked spacious and brightly lit, it crossed my mind that Ian Clarke was right after all. The upper drive was just like Rundle Mall.

★   ★   ★

'How about putting on a Scuba exhibition at the State Swimming Championships Saturday night?' Tom Herraman asked. 'You can do what like so long as it doesn't take more than five minutes'. 'OK son' I replied, at the same time thinking 'This will be a good chance to try out my stunt'.

For some time I'd been working on an idea for just such an exhibition. Occasionally we were asked to put on Scuba acts at swimming carnivals and nothing is more boring than a skin diver jumping in a pool and once in just blowing bubbles. My idea was to place a

114

We were all pleased to get out into the open again

lung, mask, weight belt and flipper on the bottom at the deep end of the pool, then after climbing up to the top platform of the tower, dive in, put the gear on under water and swim off. It was all very dramatic and as a stunt ought to be a beauty.

The day before the Championships I slipped down to the pool with a set of diving gear and had a trial run. Actually putting gear on under water is a simple operation and one that every diver is taught in his initial training. The gimmick was diving off the tower. The trial went off without a hitch and pretty pleased with myself I turned up the next night all set to please the large crowd.

Modestly I listened to the build up that I'd written out for the announcer being read over the loudspeakers. 'For the first time in Australia, ladies and gentlemen', the voice boomed, 'Dave Burchell will attempt the amazing feat . . . '

On cue, making a great show of measuring distances I deposited the diving gear on the bottom of the pool and amid the expectant hush from the spectators started climbing up the tower.

I was about half-way up when the thought came to me that the turn deserved a better dive than the plain header I'd done in the practice run. 'How about a handstand somersault', I thought smiling down at a good looking girl in the second row of the stand. 'You could do a press from the sitting position and really slay 'em'.

The fact that I hadn't done one for twelve months didn't matter. Hell no, not to the great Burchell; I'd done a million of them ... one thing about an old trouper, he never forgets his act.

The handstand went well and conscious of the effect I was making I held it straight as an arrow, poised ready to fall away into the somersault. I was just overbalancing when I thought about breathing. I needed plenty of air to last out until I found the lung. Should I take one now, or watch the water until the last split second and take one on the way down? 'Quick, make up your mind', I thought, but it was too late. I was on my way.

For the next few seconds I was busy controlling the dive and forgot about my eyes which, remaining open like a light switch I'd forgotten to turn off, stared straight ahead as I speared in. Hitting the water from ten metres with the eyes open temporarily renders your vision to being on a par with Mr Magoo without his glasses.

I tried to find the lung on the bottom. Hell how I tried. The first thing I grabbed in my visual fuzz was a water inlet grating. Then I swam blindly into the wall at the end of the pool cracking my head and finally I ended up frantically trying to extract a non existent demand valve from an under water light.

My mortification was so complete that I considered staying down without the lung and the pain in my eyes from their chlorine impregnated douche was nothing compared to the verbal lashing I was handing myself.

Finally I had to come up and holding on to the side of the pool tried to sort out the sea of blurred faces looking at me. Out of the haze came Tom Herraman's voice.

'That was a classical exhibition', he remarked bitterly. 'How about doing it again later when the proper clowns are on; you should feel more at home then'.

11

In 1963 the Underwater Skindivers' and Fishermen's Association of Australia voted our State as the venue for the annual Spearfishing Championships and the local controlling body chose Penneshaw on Kangaroo Island for the site.

Naturally it was desirable to obtain as much publicity for the Championships as possible, in order to ensure a successful roll-up of interstate competitors and it was felt a publicity stunt of some kind was called for.

With this in mind I sought out Mac Lawrie, a friend of mine who operates a slipway and commercial diving business at Port Adelaide. Mac, for the dour Scot that he is, had a very inventive mind when it came to risking my neck and on several occasions had dreamt up stunts for me to do to promote skin diving.

Sometimes his ideas which at the least are hair-raising were not altogether practical and I'd have to back off, but on this occasion, I was prepared to take the chance.

As I headed off down the Port Road towards Mac's slipway from which he operated his small fleet of diving and work boats, my thoughts centred on this colourful character.

Recognized founder of commercial diving in South Australia, his opinions and facilities were widely sought after. There would be very few diving jobs that he was not called in on, but Mac's diving career had a chancy beginning in old frogman suits and other gear purchased from the war surplus store. Progressing slowly but surely, he went on with it, until today he is rated as one of the most experienced commercial divers in Australia.

His countless jobs, mainly raising lost ships and gear

have not been restricted to South Australian waters only as Mac has carried out important work in Darwin and Fiji as well.

It was Mac Lawrie who first introduced Don McLeay, John Scammell and me to the wonders of underwater sledding, something like flying a glider, when he towed the three of us up and down the Port River.

Mac, also the uncrowned king of the underwater towvane realm had mentioned that whilst in America on a trip promoting towvanes he had learnt of the world endurance record for such craft and my idea in going down to see him was to try and work something out using one to publicize the Champion ships.

Towvanes which come in two types, wet and dry, are towed at speeds of up to five knots behind a surface craft. In theory a person interested in the inspection of the sea bed climbs into the dry model and without the need of any diving experience can sit at atmospheric pressure in the hermetically sealed vehicle and be towed around to his heart's content.

This is in theory as, although he won't admit it, I think Mac has had a certain amount of trouble getting non-divers to go down. I don't exactly blame them, especially after the wild ride he gave me in one once. It was like going over Niagara Falls in a barrel and adding to my discomfort was the knowledge that the last time the vane had been used it had nearly drowned Mac. Apparently the hatch cover had sprung a leak and before he could return to the surface the ballast shifted and the whole outfit rolled over.

This left him in an upside down position with his head in the small water filled conning tower, but fortunately he had a Scuba with him and somehow managed to get the demand valve into his mouth. There, arse up with care and without a mask, he managed to survive in the dirty rusty water until Jim

119

Mac Lawrie takes the heavy towvane hatch cover from me and Jim Paul

Paul righted the vane and got him out.

Mac nonchalantly wrote the episode off to experience, but made a mental note not to go down again without securing the ballast.

However a dry towvane was not what I had in mind for publicizing the Spearfishing Championships. It would have to be a wet one with the occupant using Scuba, otherwise the effect would be lost.

I told Mac my problem and as I'd expected he freely offered his help.

'What you really want is something that would attract Australia-wide interest', he said. 'How about an attempt on the world underwater towvane record? The Yanks told me in New York last month that at present is stands at ten miles. I'll build you an open towvane', he continued, 'if you'll pilot it'.

120

'Good as done', I replied grinning. 'That's what I was hoping you'd say'.

An important point was to decide a route for the attempt and as we knew the previous records stood at ten miles the route had to be a distance in excess of this. The first thought was to make a start at the Outer Harbor and travelling south pass along the line of the city beaches until we ran out of steam.

This although a bit aimless seemed to be the best we could do, until in a flash of inspiration I got the idea of towing across Backstairs Passage from Cape Jervis on the mainland to Penneshaw on Kangaroo Island, the very place we wanted to publicize.

Initially my suggestion was not met with much enthusiasm by Mac. Cape Jervis was over seventy miles from Adelaide and transporting the towvane and a suitable boat down there wouldn't be easy. Then there was Backstairs Passage itself, as nasty a strip of water as you could find anywhere.

Mac shook his head doubtfully. 'It would certainly be better in some ways', he said, 'the distance should be right, but it presents a lot of problems'.

'What about the weather for instance; you can't rely on conditions in the Passage from one hour to the next'.

But only one thing worried me, was the distance more than ten miles? Taking a scale-rule from Mac's desk I crossed his small office to the nautical chart on the wall and measured it off. The rule showed the distance to be a shade over twelve miles on a straight line. As far as I was concerned Cape Jervis to Penneshaw it was.

For the next week or two we became involved in the age-old battle of design versus costs. The towvane would have a limited application after the record attempt and as his gesture was 90 percent philanthropic I was in no position to argue.

When he was ready for the first trial run Mac rang

121

and I went down to the Port to do the testing. The peculiar looking object he proudly uncovered, ingeniously constructed from an old boiler, looked like a stock car from Rowley Park Speedway complete with wings. I remember thinking, 'It's just as well we're looking for performance, not appearance'. But I kept my remarks to myself, as peculiar or not it had taken Mac many hours to build.

Taking the Scuba I'd brought along from the boot of my car we made our way over the series of catwalks and pontoons to the Husky, one of Mac's work boats which was moored out in the river.

Jim Paul and Graham Richardson, who'd both had a hand in making the towvane, were already on board and reversing the Husky back to the bank they hooked on and yanked the yellow painted ex boiler unceremoniously into the river.

When we were out in mid-steam I slipped over the side of the work-boat and swam back down the tow rope to the vane where it lay wallowing half submerged in the wake.

The twin buoyancy tanks had just enough lift to stop it from sinking, which was ideal and swimming carefully into the open cabin I settled into position taking hold of the handles of the vanes.

Vigorously nodding my head, the pre-arranged signal to give her the gun, I hung on and waited. Mac, never one to muck about poured on the herbs and the Husky although no speed boat dug in with her prop and took off.

For the first fifty yards I planed along the surface with the vanes fully retarded, getting the feel of it. Everything seemed OK, so with the idea of taking her down gradually I pushed forward on the handles. She went down all right. As the leading edges of the vanes bit into the water the pressure tore the handles clean out of my hands; with the vanes on full depression we headed

Frank Alexander watches as Mac and I make some
adjustments during the testing of the towvane

Nearly ready
Frank and I climb in before the trip to
Kangaroo Island

straight for the river bottom.

The first thing I lost was my face mask, which ended up round my neck like a collar. This didn't really matter. The river was so muddy I couldn't see anyway and by the time we hit the bottom visibility was inky black with or without the mask. The pressure of the water flowing past was also threatening to tear the demand valve out of my mouth, but by holding on grimly with the set of teeth I'd recently purchased I managed to hang on to it.

The force with which the towvane hit the river bed broke the rope and after hesitating a moment we ascended slowly upside down back to the surface. As I thought about things on the journey back up I snorted with amusement, getting a nose full of water for my trouble. Knowing Mac as I did I should have been prepared for something like this. His methods which are always honest are also a bit rough and ready and the fact that the towvane handled like a badly broken-in horse was a fact I should have been prepared for.

We went on testing for about half-an-hour up and down the river, but when finally my arms gave out we headed back for the slip. The general opinion after the test was that the vanes were too big and also not pitched correctly.

Mac casually commissioned Graham to attend to these items but as we intended to make the record attempt the following Sunday and another trial run seemed out of the question, I had serious doubts if we would make it at all.

Waterlogged and exhausted I made my way back to the car and at that moment it seemed we had a few too many problems. Not only did we have to combat the unpredictable weather and the four-knot tide rips in the Passage, but it was now painfully obvious that the boat I'd teed up to make the tow wouldn't be powerful enough.

Obtaining a suitable boat had been a problem all

along. Several of Mac's would have done the job, but the Port River was seventy miles from Cape Jervis and it would have taken a couple of days just to get one there and back.

What we needed was a trailer-boat that could be carried overland. I fondly imagined we'd covered this by asking Ross Curnow for the loan of his boat. It was an eighteen-footer with a Dodge inboard engine, but after testing the towvane I was forced to realize that, although a good sea boat, Ross's wasn't powerful enough and wouldn't be able to handle the job.

Also in the back of my mind was the disquieting thought that perhaps I wouldn't be able to handle the job either. If I was cold and tired after only half-an-hour in the river, how would I be after three hours which was estimated the crossing would take in the icy waters of the Passage?

Thoughtfully I drove up the Port Road back to town and employed the old technique of evaluation again.

'Right', I thought, 'let's take the problems one at a time'.

First, to overcome the anticipated frigid water conditions I could wear two wet suits. The added warmth of a second suit along with thick gloves on my hands should be enough.

The modern wet suit is an interesting item. Made from cellular neoprene it is designed for a tight fit and the cold water instead of flowing over the diver's bare skin, thus carrying away the body heat, flows over the thick protective rubber allowing the body heat underneath to be retained.

Eventually the diver in a wet suit will get cold as the flowing water finally dissipates the body warmth, but a wet suit does make diving in cold water possible for an hour or two.

The second problem, that of fatigue, could only be overcome by taking a co-pilot. Storing the extra air to accommodate the second diver might prove difficult, but by squeezing up a bit in the cockpit I reckoned two of us should just about fit in.

Frank Alexander was the logical choice for the job. Not only was he reigning State Scuba Champion, he was also president of the Council of Underwater Activities, the controlling body running the Championships.

The third item, that of obtaining another boat for the tow was not so easy. Vaguely I remembered someone telling me that Johnny Johnson had a boat he used for schnapper fishing in the Passage. I'd known Johnny for years and although I had no idea what sort of boat he had I decided he was worth a try.

Next I contacted Frank Alexander and started to tell him about the tow and the trouble of fatigue. Before I'd finished he volunteered as co-pilot and we arranged a test run in the towvane the next day.

Then I rang Johnny Johnson who said he'd be glad to help out. To cap it off his boat, a twenty-one foot sea-going cruiser powered by a 200 horsepower Chrysler marine engine, just happened to be ready and waiting at his holiday shack at Cape Jervis.

The next Sunday the weather was terrible. Down at the Cape we glumly watched the ten-foot high waves pounding in and peered through the rain squalls trying in vain to catch a glimpse of Kangaroo Island in the distance. Obviously an attempt at making the crossing was out of the question and we had no option but to cancel the project until next week.

The towvane was stored behind Johnson's beach shack back on the hill, although it was unlikely that anything short of an earthquake would have damaged it.

During the following week I asked Sir Thomas Playford, the Premier of South Australia to write a letter sending greetings to the people of Kangaroo Island. This we could carry over in a water-tight torch case.

Acting as the Government's official courier carrying the Royal Mail I felt would appeal to the Press and should increase the news value of the effort.

I rang the Premier's office and spoke to Sir Thomas's secretary, a man obviously experienced in the handling of cranks. I explained to him that whilst the whole thing was basically a publicity stunt, we were trying to ensure the success of an official State function and also it was an earnest attempt on a world record.

He patiently heard me out and promised to speak to the Premier, his calm not even being broken when as an afterthought I said, 'Would you mind asking Sir Thomas to make sure that the envelope is no more than six inches long; you see that's the length of the torch case'.

The next Sunday was a beauty, calm and warm. In all there was quite a mob on the beach at the Cape. Apart from the boat owners and chaps from the Press, a few of the boys from the UEC had come down to lend a hand. John Lees, who runs an electrical repair business in town, had rigged up a buzzer system from the towvane to the lead boat. With it we could signal for faster or slower speeds, or in the event of an emergency, stop the tow entirely.

He and Ross Curnow who was acting as safety officer, were to ride in the lead boat with the rest of the chaps in the two boats following behind.

As is usually the case with this type of operation, by the time we were ready to shove off we were running about an hour late. This was pretty serious as it meant that instead of arriving out in the middle of the Passage at slack tide as we'd planned, we would now meet the full force of the rip. Also Frank Alexander was causing me pain by insisting on using a screen he knocked up out of a plank of wood, in an effort to protect himself from the water flow. The screen had two distinct disadvantages. The first was that once it was in place behind me I couldn't get out, which meant that if any one of the four Scubas I was going to use didn't work the moment I needed it, I could drown happily in the knowledge that at least Frank was protected from the cold water.

The other disadvantage was that the screen prevented Frank from reaching round me as was intended and helping out by doing a turn on the controls. This of course made him about as useful a co-pilot as a bag of ballast.

However with all the other frustrations of the morning, plus missing the tide, I was in no mood for these setbacks and realized that the time had come when it was a case of now or never. Climbing in the front of the cockpit I said , 'OK, Frank, stick your bloody plank in and let's get going'.

This he did, jamming me in under the towvane's roof with my face about three inches from the glass screen at the front. My leg was doubled up amongst the tangle of demand valves attached to the cylinders in the bow and it crossed my mind that it was just as well I only had one leg as there definitely wasn't room for any more in that cockpit.

As I waited for Frank to get settled a wave of petty bitterness swept over me at the way things had worked out.

'Damn and blast', I thought savagely. 'After all the careful preparations it's too bad to have to take off like this'.

But I could see Johnny Johnson watching me impatiently from his boat, so deciding to hell with it I took the demand valve out of my mouth and called out, 'Right, let's go'.

Immediately Johnson slipped the powerful Chrysler engine into gear and eased the boat through the shallow water away from the beach. Colin Morphett, standing beside the towvane and caught momentarily unaware by the suddenness of our departure yelled out, 'Hey, don't you want this?' He held out a round metal object which I recognized as the torch case holding the Premier's letter . . . I'd forgotten about it.

'Stick it under me', I said, 'I'll have to sit on it'.

As we cleared the end of the jetty I took my last look at Kangaroo Island clearly visible across the Passage and when Frank tapped my shoulder indicating he was ready I leaned forward on the handles of the vanes and gently coaxed the old boiler under.

I suppose we'd been going ten minutes when suddenly the tow stopped. 'What the hell's happened now?' I thought in exasperation as the towvane, losing steerage, slowly rolled over and hung upside down at a depth of about thirty feet. As Frank and I couldn't move we had no option but to hang there also, suspended in space as it were in our yellow capsule.

To my consternation the torch case carrying the Premier's letter, obeying the laws of gravity was threatening to drop out of the upturned towvane. Grimly I held on to it with the only equipment I had available, the cheeks of my backside. It would have been more than I could bear to have lost Tom's letter in the mud fifty feet below.

Whilst I was concentrating on this tiring task Ross Curnow suddenly appeared. He darted anxiously round us, until finally peering at me through the glass window he went into a pantomime of completely unintelligible hand signals. As the vanes were difficult to recover if let go I had to hang helplessly upside down staring back through the glass at him, as helpless as a herring in jelly.

But if my ability to move was frozen my mind certainly wasn't. 'Bugger off you idiot', I silently screamed at him, 'half a minute more of this and I'll have to drop the torch case'.

Finally Ross gave me the 'Are you Ok?' sign and at my empathically nodded reply he seemed satisfied and swam back up the tow rope.

129

Ross Curnow pays out the rope as we
clear the beach at Cape Jervis to start the tow

The UEC boys steady the towvane at the
Penneshaw Beach

After what seemed an age we eventually got under way again and righting the vane I thankfully relaxed my grip on the Royal Mail. We didn't find out until later of course, but the reason for the delay was that the water pressure activated John Lee's buzzer and made it give off a continuous buzz up in the boat. This was the pre-arranged signal for the emergency stop and Ross, always a worrier and unaware of the cause of the signal, immediately stopped the tow and was over the side and down the tow rope in a flash.

The next three hours were so bad that I can hardly bear to recall them. I think I started to get cold after half-an-hour and my arms, battling the violent vibrations of the vanes, were ready to drop off soon after.

Although I felt that the record attempt was a lost cause it was unthinkable to give it away and go up.

I set myself the task of counting off minutes and in this fashion, minute after minute, staring fixedly ahead passed the first hour mark.

I was aching all over and had difficulty in determining if it was just my imagination telling me that the demand valve was restricting, indicating I was running out of air on the first cylinder. I shouldn't have used up the air that quickly unless and the horrible thought hit me, we were flying too deep.

The depth gauge instead of being on the dash where I could see it, was strapped to my wrist out of my line of vision. I had no option but to let the controls go in order to snatch a quick glimpse.

Immediately the towvane went berserk and rolling over on its back, speared straight for the bottom thirty fathoms down. I had just enough time to note that we were at fifty feet, which was far too deep, then reaching back with my stiff unwilling arm, grappled with the handle of the vane in an effort to get the crazy outfit back on to an even keel.

The only amusement I got out of the exercise was thinking about the fright it must have given Frank, who huddled down behind his plank must have just about been asleep.

When the towvane was back under control I brought it up until by peering through the glass screen I could see the surface, then taking it down again to approximately twenty feet where I wanted it, I gauged our depth from then on by the angle of the tow rope.

In all we rolled over and plummeted towards the bottom three times during the trip, since each time it was necessary to change air cylinders it meant letting go the controls.

Somehow the two hour mark came up and we were still going. I was so tired that I could no longer think clearly and at the last cylinder change had grabbed the wrong demand valve, taking one I'd already used. By the time I'd sorted things out I'd gulped a couple of mouthfuls of water and we'd ended up sixty feet down where retching and coughing I'd finally righted the vane. Also as we'd rolled one of the spare lungs had come adrift and belted me painfully on the knee and in my depression it felt like I'd at least smashed the knee cap.

Wild, rather panicky thoughts started to flash through my mind. 'Why don't you take it up, you fool?' But I knew really I had no intention of taking the towvane up.

I'd never had the occasion to push myself physically to the limit before and in an oddly detached sort of way I was interested to see how far I could go. I'd already surprised myself by lasting this long. I'd never considered myself as much of a stayer and the opportunity to meet a complete physical challenge, an all too rare occurrence in my one-legged world, was too good to be passed over without a 100 percent effort.

Squirming down I hunched my aching shoulders and squinting through my face mask with narrowed eyes bit even harder on the rubber lugs of the demand valve. 'Come on, stick to it. You've only got another half-hour to go'.

Finally we reached the two-and-a-half hour mark and I knew we'd make it. Resisting the temptation to take the towvane up to the surface for a quick look was difficult.

It was out of the question of course; we couldn't have anything go against claiming the record at this stage. Then I started worrying about the Premier's letter; I couldn't find it anywhere and realized it must have fallen out during one of the wild rolls out in the Passage. Dick Hannam wouldn't be very impressed; he owned the torch case.

After a few more burning minutes from the corner of my eye I thought I saw a shadow on the port side and hardly daring to hope that it was seaweed on the bottom, closed my eyes for a few seconds and looked over to starboard. White corrugated sand stretched away into the blue haze. I looked at it dully, not quite comprehending, then the full realization hit: we'd made it, we were at Kangaroo Island.

Leaning back on the vanes I brought the boiler up breaking the surface like some prehistoric deep sea monster, up into the bright sunlight. We were only a hundred yards off the beach and letting go the handles I left the towvane to plane along the surface on its own. Half collapsing back against Frank's plank I spat out the demand valve, too exhausted to do anything but grin back at Curnow and Lees in the lead boat ahead.

Then as I eased my leg a fraction the ultimate happened, the round metal torch case rolled from under it into the bottom of the cockpit. I sat there too tired to even lean forward and pick it up, just looking at it.

After the boys pried me out of the cockpit we made our way through the shallows and I handed the Premier's letter to the Chairman of the District

Council, who was waiting with the entire population of Penneshaw on the beach.

Later up at the guest house where Frank and I were thawing out under the hot shower one of the chaps stuck his head in the door and through the steam called, 'Well Dave, what's it feel like to hold a world record?'

'Hell', I replied, feeling a bit embarrassed, 'I hadn't thought about it'.

Actually I'd forgotten about the record and now that we'd done it, it seemed almost sacrilegious to speak seriously of the trip as a world record, placing it on par as it were with such athletic feats as running a sub four minute mile or climbing Mount Everest.

'Perhaps if you think of it as the world record for the crummiest world record', I told myself, 'it wouldn't be so bad'.

Gratefully straightening my still aching back under the hot water and bearing firmly in mind that all things are relative, I let my imagination run full tilt and hidden from the world by a wall of steam, for a few blissful minutes I breasted the tape with Bannister and stood shoulder to shoulder at the top with Hillary.

★　★　★

Early one morning the phone rang.

'Is that you Dave', the voice queried. 'It's Brian O'Grady here. I think I've got the bends'.

Twelve hours later Darby von Sanden pulled him out of Geosurvey's diving chamber, cured. We'd recompressed him by sealing him in the chamber with a 220 cf cylinder of compressed air, which he cracked open until the internal pressure had built up to four atmospheres. Holding this pressure until his pains eased off, he then slowly over about eight hours released the pressure again by bleeding the air out of the sea-cocks.

12

The magazine article, complete with pictures, featured the Para-Scuba divers of the US Marine Corps.

Apparently specially trained military personnel wearing Scuba, parachute into the sea to assist in the recovery of space rocket nose cones. Their medical training qualifies them in the event of the astronauts being injured, to render immediate first-aid until surface craft arrive. It was an interesting story and after a close study of the photographs I marvelled at how the fellows even stood up, let alone leapt from aircraft, under the mountain of gear they were required to carry.

As I tossed the magazine aside it crossed my mind that one of the parachuting clubs should try to develop the technique in Australia. It had distinct Civil Defence possibilities and as we had the Woomera Rocket Range virtually in our backyard, one day it could well come in handy.

I had all but forgotten about it when a couple of days later a chap wandered in who, of all things, was a skydiver. It was my first contact with a parachutist and I looked at him curiously, for I'd always considered they were slightly crazy.

To move the conversation along I mentioned the article on Para-Scuba. He was interested enough from the parachuting angle, but to my surprise gave the thumbs down to landing in the sea.

'Not on your life', he said emphatically. 'If you don't drown when you hit the water, the sharks are a moral to get you'.

Seeing the picture from the diver's angle I couldn't agree. 'Ease up', I said jokingly, 'landing in the water should be the easiest part'.

The fellow looked at me with that unfortunate holier than thou attitude adopted by some parachutists and smugly said, 'OK, then, why don't you do it?' The uneasy feeling I felt at this suggestion worried me. Perhaps I was the one to do it.

Apparently the problem was not the parachuting, it was the landing in the water. This should be easy for a diver, no worries. All he had to do was make himself leave the plane, lots of worries.

Looking across the desk and trying to hide my rising apprehension at what I was letting myself in for, I said in answer to his question, 'I reckon I will at that'.

The skydiver's laugh lacked warmth. 'You must be kidding', he said, 'you haven't made a jump on land let alone one in the sea and anyway you'd never get the Department of Civil Aviation to approve it. Nobody in Australia has done a water drop'. He rambled on, but I was no longer listening. Already I was planning the next move.

★ ★ ★

There were about twenty chaps at the meeting in our office. They presented the South Coast Skydivers, South Australian Sea Rescue Squadron and the Underwater Explorer's Club. It had been agreed that the Skydivers could carry out the necessary training, obtain DCA permission and arrange for the aircraft. The Sea Rescue Squadron were to provide the boats to form a Drop Zone and the UEC would man each boat with fully equipped divers ready to go over the side if the need arose.

Everything had been covered with the exception of my nerves, but all concerned were happy with the arrangements. As the plan of action unfolded the dreadful sinking feeling I felt told me how committed I was to this thing, but I guess I must have been happy too, for long before the end of the meeting I found myself, even without provocation, having fits of giggles.

Every Tuesday night for the next couple of months I turned up at an old church hall in North Adelaide for training.

I was taught how to pack 'chutes, climb out under imaginary aircraft wings and how to jump.

My instructor, a red-headed youth named Fred, took himself and his parachuting very seriously. 'A skydiver has to have that something extra', he said to me one night. 'Unless you've got it, when you get out on the wing you freeze and can't jump'.

'Thanks a lot Fred', I said as the old mental picture mechanism started working. I could see myself hanging from the wing strut in the tearing slipstream, hands clutching and refusing to let go. The chaps inside the aircraft cursing and attempting to release my frozen fingers with the heels of their heavy boots. As a psychologist, Fred had a lot to learn.

One night he was giving me a run-down on the reserve chute procedure.

'When jumping with a static line deployment', he said, 'after you have cleared the aircraft, count three. If the main 'chute hasn't opened by that time, say 'malfunction' and then reach across the body with the right hand and pull the reserve 'chute ripcord.'

I couldn't help smiling. I thought, 'No, Fred old boy, make no error, if that happens to me I won't be saying 'malfunction'; what I'd say may relate to a body function but it would be a word much shorter, much cruder and much more explicit'.

★　★　★

I felt a bit of a dill as I lugged the heavy parachutes through the doors of the West Beach Airport Terminal. On crutches and dressed in a rubber wet suit, I caused

137

many raised eyebrows among the smart set who were seeing people off to Melbourne and Sydney. To make things worse a plane had just come in from Surfers Paradise, with the entire Port Adelaide Football Club on board. They had just returned from their end of season holiday trip and along with the mob who had come down to meet them, the place was in a turmoil.

Doing my best to hide in a corner, I offered a silent prayer that I wouldn't see anyone I knew. Eventually Max Chaplin one of the South Coast Skydivers and Brian Brown another parachutist who was to act as jumpmaster, arrived. The three of us, wending our way between the huge jets, straggled across to the small plane bay on the far side of the tarmac. The pilot of our plane walked a little to one side in an effort to mislead any of his friends, who might have been watching, into thinking he was associated with us. As a rule pilots can't abide parachutists. They consider them to be rank exhibitionists and if it wasn't for the money involved there'd be little or no contact at all.

Our plane, a Cessna 210 with the off-side door missing was ready for take-off and after double checking our gear we all climbed in.

As I settled down in my seat I tried not to think of our last effort a few weeks previously. On that occasion it had rained and the wind had howled in from the South-West.

When we arrived over the DZ there were no boats to be seen, only white capped grey waves and we had no option but to return to the airstrip at Aldinga without jumping.

At the time I didn't know whether to be pleased or sorry. The psychological let-down after weeks of mental and physical preparation was frustrating. But apparently not as frustrating as the events that befell the boys in the boats.

It had been decided on the first day to launch the boats in the Onkaparinga River, the nearest point to the DZ, drive them down the river to the mouth and then out into the open sea. Unfortunately the information on the tide conditions was incorrect and the boats ran out of water long before they made the river mouth. Everyone had hopped out and pushed but it was hopeless and they had no option but to stay where they were, stranded on the mud until the tide came in.

It was probably all for the best. It was blowing so hard outside that if I had jumped I more than likely would have ended up on Mount Lofty.

However today was different, the sun was shining and we had arranged to put the boats in at Christie's Beach which although a bit further away, was a safer launching spot.

After a minor delay the pilot received a clearance to take off and taxied the plane out of the bay.

I remember looking out the gap where the door should have been at the bitumen runway flowing past. It looked solid and familiar and for the first time I really had qualms as to my ability to see the job through.

Up until then I had mentally ducked the issue whenever the thought of jumping had arisen in my mind.

'You'll be right when the time comes', I kept telling myself. But now my reflection in the side window said otherwise and in an effort to build up morale I smiled gaily at it. The reflection must have been feeling even worse than me. It returned my bright smile with a weak sickly grin and I decided not to look at it any more. I don't mind admitting that I had a bad time for the next ten minutes, for as the Cessna took off and soared into the air my enthusiasm for the whole deal nose-dived back to the ground and hit rock bottom.

I started to worry about the boats. 'What if they hadn't made it', I thought, 'the chaps might have got the days mixed. I haven't seen some of them for over a week'.

Thoughts of Mike Reilly came rushing out before I could close the mental door on them. Reilly, a top British skydiver and veteran of hundreds of jumps was drowned only a few weeks previously doing a water-drop in the Channel.

Whilst I was still busy trying to put poor Mike out of my mind, my thoughts leapt ahead to the bloke in Sydney recently whose main 'chute hadn't opened. He'd pulled his reserve 'chute ripcord but because he was tumbling as the canopy came out of the pack he'd wrapped himself up in it. As my loneliness and resolve reached their lowest ebb I cursed myself for a fool.

'You should have handed the whole thing over to the Army and let the Paratroopers handle it', I told myself bitterly.

Perhaps the thought of the Paratroopers was the turning point. It reminded me of that day in the office months before when it had come to me that this was a diver's deal not a parachutist's.

Nothing had happened that should make me change my theory and it was with a stab of guilt that I realised the direction my thoughts had been taking.

As normal conversation was out of the question due to the noise of the engine through the open door, I accepted the opportunity to mentally lock myself in and give my nerves a very much-needed peptalk.

'Righto boy', I started, settling back. 'Let's look at the position. You're well trained, the boats will be there and the boys will pull you out if anything goes wrong. You knew it wouldn't be easy and you've had your little attack of nerves. Now, how about getting your mind on the job!'

Hunching forward with arms folded over the reserve pack attached to the harness at my waist, I narrowed my eyes and looked as mean as I could.

'You're tough and fit', I told myself. 'This job's tailor-made for you'.

Somehow it worked. Deep down within me the determination started to flow back.

To get the adrenalin really working I leant over and punching Max Chaplin roughly on the shoulder to attract his attention, yelled as loud as I could in his ear, 'it won't be long now'.

We came in low over the cliffs.

As we roared past I searched the upturned faces of the crowd barely having time to pick out Ona, with our eldest girl Jane jumping up and down beside her, as we circled and swept on out to sea.

About half a mile out were the boats. 'You beauty', I thought, spirits rising and loneliness forgotten.

There were five of them in a tight circle already forming the DZ and as we approached we again came in low.

I had no difficulty in recognising the chaps in each boat. My friends Don McLeay and Brian Cornish were waving their arms off from Ron Tickle's Sea Rescue Squadron Cruiser and behind them was Don Douglas, one of the UEC boys in his eighteen foot runabout with Bruce Berry and Don Mitchell on board.

As the circling plane heeled over I looked straight down on them and they all looked mighty good to me.

With McLeay and Cornish, who were both doctors, on hand to revive me and Bruce Berry, who worked with me in the skin diving shop, all geared up to pull me out of the water, I couldn't go wrong. As the Cessna spiralled its way up to jumping height this time my spirits went up with it and by the time we reached the 2200 feet of altitude required I was rarin' to go.

Brian Brown, the despatcher, reached over and tapped the pilot's shoulder. 'Cut', he yelled and turning to me nodded. 'This is it!' I thought, watching for a second whilst Brian checked my static line snap-hook,

141

then pulling my wet suit hood up over my head, I slid forward out of the seat.

Reaching for the handgrip inside the doorway, I probed around with my foot outside the cabin until I found the landing wheel. Standing on it I leant out and forward, grabbing for the strut under the wing with my right hand. After a second or two spent adjusting my balance to the slipstream, I let go the handgrip and brought my left hand out on to the strut.

By this time I roughly resembled the position a small boy might be in if he was holding the handlebars whilst seated on a large motor bike.

Glancing down between my outstretched arms I caught sight of the boats far below and decided very swiftly that the sight wasn't good for morale I quickly looked back inside the cabin. Brian Brown was still directing the pilot in positioning the plane, but after a few seconds he turned, and I saw rather than hear him yell, 'Go!'.

Without stopping to think I pushed off from the strut with my hands and leapt backwards into space.

The first thing that hits you when jumping from an aircraft is the shocking initial drop. Nobody seems to have measured the exact distance, but when jumping on a static line and using a deployment sleeve, the parachutist drops hundreds of feet before his canopy opens fully.

This may be a piece of cake to an experienced skydiver, but to a novice it's a bit disconcerting.

The second thing and just as dramatic, is the complete and utter silence. After being practically deafened by the noise of the engine for the best part of an hour, to suddenly have it cut off is such a relief that it greatly subscribes to the ethereal sensation parachuting gives. However I had too much to do to hang around philosophising and looking up I checked my canopy. It was a twenty-eight foot diameter C9

American sporting 'chute with LL modifications and was ideal for this type of work. All was in order with the canopy and I was pleased to see that it was distinctively marked with alternate red and white panels, the colours of the North Adelaide Football Club.

Below me I could see the sleeve fluttering down towards the sea. I hoped the boys in the boats would also see it and send someone to pick it up before it sank. Sporting 'chutes are different to those used in the Services in that they use a deployment sleeve.

With an Air Force 'chute the canopy develops or opens first and then the rigging lines deploy. With a sporting 'chute using a sleeve, the rigging lines deploy first and then the canopy develops relatively slowly as the sleeve is drawn off it by a small pilot 'chute. This reduces the opening jar.

Also with a C9 it is possible to steer in any direction, by making use of the modifications. These are actually wide slits in the canopy and the action of the air being forced through them as the parachute descends gives a jet like thrust of about 5 mph forward driving speed.

Para-Scuba

Direction is controlled with two rigging lines attached to each side of the canopy. If the left one is pulled, that side of the canopy collapses and the parachutist turns left; the same applies to the right.

I was having a high old time steering round the sky when I happened to look up as I pulled on the left-hand line and witnessed the disconcerting sight of half the canopy deflating. As I was still a 1000 feet up, I saved any further efforts at steering until I was closer to the sea.

By this time, I could hear Joe Mutch, the safety officer in one of the boats calling out landing instructions and I knew that it was time to undo my reserve 'chute and put it in the plastic bag I'd brought along to stop it getting wet.

So engrossed did I get in the job that I didn't realise how low I was getting and it was with somewhat of a shock that I saw the sea rushing up to meet me. There was no time to reverse and drive back into the wind as I should have done, landing backwards and I barely had time to throw my hands over my face as I drove in. The shock of hitting the water wasn't too bad, in fact I'd hit harder at times off the tower at the Pool.

After a moment's hesitation when I hit, the canopy which was still under control of the wind, took off again at terrific speed dragging me with it.

Just as I was disappearing under the wall of water that my momentum built up, I caught a fleeting glimpse of Bruce Berry leaping over the side of the speedboat that ranged alongside. He was a comforting sight for at the time I was just swallowing my second mouthful of salt water and was in need of a little help.

Bruce, performing a sort of underwater rugby tackle held on grimly round my waist and with his extra weight we slowed the racing parachute. However it was still necessary for one of the boats to run the billowing canopy down, deflating it like a burst balloon, before

Bruce Berry and Ron Tickle carry
me in from the submarine

Bruce and I came to a water-logged halt.

Laughing and spluttering we disentangled ourselves from the mass of rigging lines, whilst on board the boat that had run into the parachute the crew were fighting their way out from under the mass of clinging wet nylon.

This undignified and balled-up finish represented the conclusion of the exercise.

It was clear to all concerned that the effort which was meant to be a familiarisation jump, had served its purpose well. It was obvious that we still had a lot to learn and before we could hope to do the jump wearing Scuba. I'd have to iron out a lot of mistakes I'd made. Secretly though, I was happy enough. I'd survived the bloody thing and the experience gained would be invaluable for the planning of the next one wearing full diving gear.

After the first jump we had a meeting and carefully went over every point. We covered 'chute control, the time-consuming task of putting the reserve away in the plastic bag and minor problems with the boats.

I asked Dick Hannam, a UEC member who does the lung repairs for our shop, to build up a special light Scuba from a single 40 cf German cylinder.

It was most important that it should be small, in order to go under the parachute harness. Dick was just the boy for the job and came up with a beauty. It was light and compact, which was just what we wanted.

For some time I'd been racking my brain for an idea to prove in a tangible way, our point that it was possible to usefully transfer a man from the aircraft to the sea. To just get him from point A to point B aimlessly was not enough and I badly needed a practical or useful task to perform after I hit the water. Without doing anything other than landing in the sea the whole thing seemed to lack purpose and virtually proved nothing.

This point concerned me as the operation aimed at attracting the attention the Civil Defence Authorities to the possibilities of Para-Scuba would be wasted if it was written off by them as just a foolhardy stunt. The answer came to me whilst driving to the office one morning.

'Of course', I thought, wondering why it hadn't occurred to me before, 'Kym Bonython's submarine'.

Kym, a well known Adelaide sportsman had recently imported the two-man submarine from Italy, but after the initial novelty had worn off it had been gathering dust, half-forgotten at Rowley Park Speedway where he kept it.

By the time I arrived in town I'd worked out a neat plan that would give the Para-Scuba jump all the purpose it needed.

I rang Kym and asked if he'd mind waiting in his sub under the boats forming the DZ. After landing in the water I intended to release the parachute harness and using the lung Dick Hannam had knocked up, swim down and meet up with the waiting Bonython fifty feet down.

Once inside the sub which was an open wet type, we would then cruise back the shore under water.

I felt that if we could successfully transfer a man from an aircraft to a submarine in a matter of minutes, our point would be well proven.

The day of the jump dawned clear and calm. All was in readiness, the chaps, the boats, the plane and the submarine.

The UEC in honour of the occasion had arranged a barbecue on the beach at Port Noarlunga and we had just finished lunch. It was nearly time for me to leave and drive over to the airstrip at Aldinga about ten miles away and pick up the plane, so I gave Bob Main the nod to get his car.

As Bob walked off Brian Cornish wandered over and half embarrassed that it might upset me and half casual as was his usual style, mentioned that he'd brought along an oxygen reviver outfit.

'Just in case you get one too many mouthfuls of water this time', he said.

'You're a bloody cheer-up', I ribbed, laughing. 'Anyway you probably don't even know how to work the thing'.

Cornish, equal to the tilt at his professional ability, replied, 'True, but there's an instruction book inside and I'm going to read it during the trip out to the DZ if I get time'.

Ona must have been anxious, but as usual she didn't show it, other than being a bit sharp with the kids. Our four daughters not really understanding what it was all about, wanted to go back on the beach and play. They didn't appreciate having to hang around to say goodbye to Dad, who after all was really only going for a swim and they were trying to urge me to go down and swim

Plotting the submarine's proposed position
before the second jump with
Jim Simpson and Kym Bonython

off the beach like everyone else.

Perhaps Ona showed how concerned she really was, when she offered me the last cup of tea in the thermos. Acts of mercy such as this are generally reserved by wives for special occasions only.

Telling her to hang on to it and that I'd have it when I got back I climbed into Bob's car and slowly we took off through the small band of well-wishers and headed for the airstrip at Aldinga.

*   *   *

'But can't you lengthen the shoulder-straps a bit more?' I said, starting to get desperate. Gloomily Max Chaplin studied the parachute harness. 'They're let out as far as they can go now', he said and over my shoulder I could see he was right. Disaster had struck!

148

We couldn't get the parachute harness to fit over the Scuba. Weeks before after Dick had built the lung, I'd borrowed a spare B4 back-pack to make sure everything would fit and it worked fine. Now here we were, already an hour behind schedule due to a mix-up with the plane and the blasted thing wouldn't fit. My frustration was such that if there had been a wall handy I would have walked straight up it.

However nothing could be gained by crying over it, or for that matter standing around fiddling.

It was obvious I couldn't jump with the lung on so trying not to think of the boat crews, no doubt waiting impatiently for me to appear, I tried to evaluate the situation.

'Right', I thought, 'first things first. I can't wear the lung so take the damn thing off'.

Savagely I stripped off the parachute harness, then my skindiving weight belt and the small Scuba.

My patience was fast running out but as calmly as possible I turned to Bob and said, 'Shoot back to the beach and contact the boats on the two-way radio. Ask them to have a lung ready for me when I hit'.

Bob Main, always the amiable one replied, 'Good as done dad', and climbing into his car made off like Jack Brabham.

All Max and I could do was return the mutilated parachute harness to its original condition and after seemingly endless delays Max was finally satisfied.

Picking up my weight belt I whipped it on and then shrugged into the parachute harness. I was as ready as I'd ever be. Trying not to show my despair at the way things had worked out, I nodded curtly to the pilot who had been standing aloofly on one side and snapped, 'Let's go'.

It was then I realised that I'd left my crutches in Bob Main's car. This was about the last straw. In my anger I became furiously independent. I'd be blowed if I was going to ask anyone to help me. 'Starve the Lizards', I thought in exasperation, as I eyed off the distance between me and the plane. 'With all this gear on you'll never make it'.

But the stubbornness wouldn't be denied and although I blasted myself for being all kinds of a fool I hopped the thirty yards with paracutes flapping up and down, like some ridiculous fat bird trying for a take-off.

As I bounded past the pilot the startled look on this fellow's face told me that he thought I'd finally flipped and that he was sure I was all set to have a go at flying to Port Noarlunga on my own, without assistance from him or his plane.

I was still in a rage when I jumped, but the drop before the 'chute opened soon sobered me up.

I didn't think I'd ever get used to that plummet through space and this time if anything it seemed worse than before. In fact it seemed to last so long that I thought my main 'chute hadn't opened and I tentatively reached for my reserve ripcord, at the same time berating myself for not concentrating, for in my anger I realised I hadn't been counting. But just as I was taking a firm grip on the ripcord D-ring the main 'chute opened and all was well.

The celestial silence of the parachutist's domain made the frustrations of the last hour seem paltry and in the couple of minutes that my eighteen-feet-per-second descent allowed before hitting the water, I forgot my problems completely.

'That's it, a little more to the right. Steady now'. Joe Mutch was calling me in over the last few hundred feet. 'Now reverse and drive back into the wind', he yelled as I came in to land 'that's it, a bit more, that's it, bloody luverly'.

As I went backwards towards the water I adjusted my face mask and started undoing the parachute harness.

I'd already put my flipper on and by the time I hit, this time correctly coming in backwards, it was just a matter of slipping out of the shoulder-straps.

Over the side of the first boat to come alongside Bruce handed me a twin-hose Aquamaster and after struggling into it the conversation from skydiver to skindiver was complete.

'Where's Bonython's marker?' I asked, looking up at Bruce. He laughed, 'You're a lousy navigator, you overshot him by about thirty yards. Hang onto the back of the boat we'll tow you over to it'.

We had decided earlier to put a marker on the sub. Not only would it make it easier to find, but the boats could follow the bobbing float in to the shore like sheep dogs in case Kym strayed off the mark.

We were soon back at the marker buoy and giving the boat crews a wave I dived down the shot line.

Under water the visibility was poor and it wasn't until I was about ten feet off the sea bed that I made out the first outline of the yellow sub.

Kym, standing alongside like a chauffeur at attention, gave me a smart salute and we solemnly shook hands. His hand felt like a block of ice and I realised what the hour delay must have meant to him.

As I swam past him into the front cock-pit he climbed into the back and when we were set he started up the electric motor.

As we took off for the shore, first circling to pick up our compass bearing, I hoped Ona hadn't knocked off that last cup of tea.

★   ★   ★

I'd come back up on to the jetty to get another mask out of my bag and was crouched over searching for it as she walked past with her husband.

She was obviously keenly interested in skindiving,

151

no doubt having read thrilling accounts of the Navy Frogmen during the war. Her husband didn't notice me and went to walk on, but leaning forward and insistently pulling at his sleeve she said in a stage whisper for all to hear, 'Look Harold, there's one of those frogskin divers'.

13

One of the more dangerous dives in which I was involved was the time we did a survey for the Mount Gambier Council in the Englebrecht Caves.

These caves are part of the vast underground volcanic system at Mount Gambier in South Australia's South-Eastern district, and are a product of the volcanic upheavals of 90 000 years ago.

The caves, sinkholes, shafts, blow-holes, call them what you will, of the system are the frozen aftermath of the lava channels, which all those years ago spewed the white hot liquid bile from the very bowels of the earth.

Now, being under the present water table, they are flooded and the air-clear water slowly filtering through the system provides some of the most spectacular inland diving to be found anywhere. The Piccaninny Ponds, which the Mount Gambier diver Mick Potter first discovered in the early 1960s, are now internationally famous and start in a deceptively innocent-looking open water-filled chasm some ninety feet deep, but continue on down through shafts and splits in the rock for hundreds of feet.

The system can be dangerous and unfortunately in the early days many quite experienced sea divers drowned in its confusing labyrinths, but now controls are tight and only qualified divers are legally permitted to enter the holes.

Sinkhole diving demands different techniques to open sea diving, as most of it is done either in horizontal passages or at least on the underlay and a diver cannot crash straight up out of a dive in the event of an emergency, as he can in the open sea. Consequently if divers enter a water-filled tunnel they have to bear in mind, that in the event of trouble, they have to make it back to the tunnel's mouth before they can start to ascend.

I suppose it is understandable that the thought of being trapped forty feet up a tunnel, with torch or set failure, can have an inhibiting psychological effect and some divers never really come to grips with it.

Oddly enough another problem can be caused by the water clarity. It is so clear that it all seems too easy and novices tend to be lured to depths far beyond their capabilities and possibly for the first time enter their, as everyone has different levels, nitrogen narcosis or rapture of the depths zone.

Narcosis is a not yet fully understood condition which is psychological and partly physiological when the diver, due to the rapid build up of nitrogen on the brain, becomes confused and disorientated and can, as if mesmerised by the beam of his torch, keep on going down.

The biggest problem, the one that has caused most of the deaths, is the fine black volcanic silt which lies inches thick on the bottom of the caves and tunnels. This silt, when disturbed by the turbulence created by a passing diver, builds up into a visually impenetrable black cloud behind him and unless a guide line is being paid out on entering an area, he can have a real problem in finding his way out.

When the Mount Gambier Council asked me to survey the Englebrechts in 1963 we were still very much in the learning stage of this type of diving and my first move was to contact Mick Potter. I'd already dived with Mick in the Piccaninny Ponds and several other places around Mount Gambier, including a clandestine effort in the cities water supply — the hallowed Blue Lake itself and as Mick was one of Australia's most experienced sinkhole divers it seemed like a good idea to invite him along.

Also Ross Curnow and John Lees wanted to come so with these boys on hand to act as standby divers we had a team and a week or so later Ross, John and I set off from Adelaide on the 300 mile trip to Mount Gambier.

I was glad we had arranged to meet Mick there for the car was laden down with the usual collection of divers' gear. Lungs, suits, ropes and torches, all necessary to complete the survey, plus our camping gear. Mick and several councillors were already at the site of the caves, which were marked by a forty foot dry crater. At the bottom of this crater was a split in the rocks forming an opening into a natural tunnel-like cleft which in turn led down to the lake a further sixty feet below. To reach the water it was necessary to worm our way along and down this tunnel, which was probably a blow-hole in the old volcanic days.

At times the ceiling was so low that we had to slide on our stomachs and as it was pitch dark as well I was pleased enough when it opened up into a huge cathedral-like cave. With the lake acting as a floor this impressive area was about one hundred feet long, thirty feet wide and forty feet from the water level to the ceiling. Lit up by the powerful lights we'd lugged down it looked magnificent and I could well understand the council's desire to find out if there were any more such caves close by, for if there were the plan was to open the whole thing up and with steps and lights turn it into a tourist attraction.

The domed ceiling sweeping down in the unbroken line to the water gave no indication of any further caves and our job was to search around under the water-line and see if any tunnels ran off. If there were it was intended to follow them and see where they led. The water was so clear at the bank where we were standing that if it hadn't been for some patches of dust on the surface it would have been hard to tell it was there at all. So leaving my scuba on the bank, I took a torch and

155

snorkelled around the perimeter of the lake looking for tunnels.

I'd nearly completed an underwater sweep of the walls without finding any lead-off and was on my way back feeling mighty disappointed when the probing beam of the torch picked up an opening about ten feet down. Taking a couple of deep breaths I duck-dived to the tunnel's entrance and steadying myself against the roof of the opening with one hand, carefully inspected the passage with the aid of the torch. As far as I could see the passage, which angled down at about forty-five degrees, led into another cave and I decided it was certainly worth investigating. Returning to the bank I worked out a plan with Mick and we decided, using our scubas, to follow the tunnel as far as we could whilst John and Ross waited outside.

Mick had wisely rolled the nylon shot line round an old electric cable spool, for previous experience had taught him that it is better to pay the rope out as you go from the diver's end, rather than have someone paying it out from the surface. So anchoring the end of the rope to an iron spike driven into the ground, we asked one of the councillors to hold onto it as well.

Taking two torches myself, I tied a third on to Mick's belt as an added precaution and with me leading he paid out the shot-line from the spool as we swam down through the tunnel. Coming out the other end through the roof of the flooded second cave we entered a world of fantasy. The water was so clear that I felt it must surely be too thin to hold us and I had the uncanny feeling that at any moment we'd fall right through it on to the rocks forty feet below.

From our vantage point up near the roof I played the torch round the eerie scene. Across on the far side wall near the floor the beam picked out yet other another passage, so giving Mick a nudge, we dropped through the air-like water down to this new opening. We

156

continued on in this fashion winding and twisting down passage after passage, carefully paying out our shot-line until finally we ran out of rope. This meant that we were 300 feet from where we started and a glance at my depth gauge showed we were also fifty feet deeper than the water level in the first cave.

There wasn't much more we could do and I'd just given Mick the signal to pack it in and return back to the others, when it happened.

Quite suddenly everything went completely black. For one terrible moment I thought somehow I'd gone blind. I just couldn't see anything.

Then to my great relief for a few fleeting seconds Mick appeared again in the beam. Through what appeared to be lazy swirls of black mist I could just make out his eyes staring back at me from behind his face mask and I realised what had happened. Apparently in the Englebrecht system, like many of these deep volcanic fissures, the springs channelling the water in were reasonably slow, so slow in fact that the thick volcanic dust on the floor of the tunnels had lain hardly disturbed for thousands of years. But the turbulence caused by Mick and me swimming down had stirred up this now fine silt, which following us in a dense black cloud enveloped us completely when we stopped after coming to the end of the rope.

In the few seconds we had between the temporary clearance and final total darkness I gave Mick the 'Are you OK?' sign and jerking my head in the direction of the main cave, indicated, 'Let's go'.

Mick was in the act of acknowledging the sign when the black mist once more curled in and he disappeared altogether.

'Steady now,' I told myself as an uneasy stab hit me in the stomach, 'the first thing is to check your air'.

Feeling for the tactile gauge on my high pressure hose I estimated the quantity of air left as shown by the indicator needle then carefully reaching across to where I knew Mick must be I quietly felt around him until I located his gauge; like mine it showed three-quarters full.

'That's OK,' I thought, 'at least we have plenty of air'. Whilst searching for Mick's gauge I could tell he was taking up the initial shot-line slack on his cable spool and realised what a mess we'd have been in if the rope had been paid out from the other end. I also appreciated having a cool-headed bloke like Mick for company. If there'd been the slightest panic it could well have meant the end for both of us. The old Potter, always the quiet one, doesn't say much as a rule but as a diving mate he'll do me any time.

I suppose 300 feet doesn't sound far, but when it involves winding your way blind through a labyrinth of tunnels it seems like 300 miles and I was very much aware of the danger we were in.

For if either of us accidentally clouted our regulators on the uneven walls and ceiling which in the dark was quite on the cards, we would have run the risk of immediately losing our air supply, or if the shot-line, sawing back and forth at a hundred places against the sharp volcanic rock happened to break under the strain, we would never have found our way out. It was a case of sustaining slow calculated movements and concentrating on following the shot-line which had now virtually become a life-line, for to have lost contact with the rope would have proved equally disastrous. Letting the now useless torch go and leaving it to hang from the cord round my wrist I took a firm grip on the rope and inching along fed the line back to Mick who rolled it up as we went.

Due to the tortuous nature of the passages the shot-line had pulled into cracks and fissures in the broken ceilings and walls and several times we came up against solid rock with the line seemingly feeding through a minute split in the wall confronting us.

On these occasions holding the rope in one hand I would then endeavour to trace the split back to the main tunnel with the other hand, feeling around in as large an arc as possible.

If this proved unsuccessful I'd repeat the performance on the other side. Four times this happened and four times I had to remind myself that as we'd got in there must be a way out. Also I remember feeling easier if I closed my eyes instead of staring into that black nothingness. There must have been something psychological about it and I always meant to discuss it with my cobber John Litt, who like most psychiatrists can logically explain anything away.

During these times when we were held up, Mick who seemed to sense what was happening would wait patiently somewhere behind me until I'd sorted out our new course, until finally we swam back up into the main lake and made our way across to the bank.

The Mount Gambier Council, after hearing our report, eventually decided to abandon the project and although Mick and I haven't talked about it much we both know that our dive in the Englebrecht Caves was a close one. The slightest mishap or mistake could well have resulted in us staying down there — permanently.

14

Lowering myself carefully down inside the cockpit I eased into the bucket seat and taking hold of the small steering wheel, stretched my foot out and placed it lightly on the huge accelerator.

It was really quite a moment. 'Boy, you certainly get yourself into the oddest places,' I thought.

I was at the controls of the most famous speedboat in the world, Donald Campbell's Bluebird. The time was December 1964 and the place Lake Bonney at Barmera, in South Australia's Upper Murray River district.

After three weeks of frustration waiting for the rough surface on the wind-swept lake to return to its normal placid state, it appeared that Campbell would at last have his chance to break the world water speed record, for today conditions looked favourable enough for Bluebird to make her run.

We were there, Ross Curnow and I, in answer to the urgent phone call I'd received the night before from the project manager, Graham Ferrett. He needed a couple of divers on hand in case Bluebird came to grief and sank, for if this happened at a speed in excess of 200 mph it would be necessary to pull Donald Campbell out quickly.

Peter Warman and Colin Williams of the Police Underwater Recovery Squad, who had been standing by at the lake as a security measure for the past three weeks, had been recalled to Adelaide since the bad weather looked like continuing, prohibiting an attempt for at least a few more days.

Suddenly, however, the wind had died and the lake started to flatten out. Immediately all stations were on go and as Graham found after an urgent phone call to Adelaide that the police divers were unobtainable, being off somewhere on another job, he rang me. I told him I'd be pleased to help out and when he said he wanted two divers I gave Ross Curnow a ring. By four in the morning we were on our way.

After arriving at Barmera, Graham introduced us to Campbell and his master mechanic Leo Villa who had been on hand at no less than twenty-eight world record speed attempts, both on land and water, assisting Donald and his famous father Sir Malcolm.

Taking Ross and me down to the shed on the bank of the lake where Bluebird was housed, Leo Villa explained how important it was to be on the job quickly if anything did go wrong. Unlike John Cobb's Crusader which dug in nose first at 205 mph on Loch Ness in Scotland, the Bluebird's design was such that in the event of an accident she would like as not flip over backwards, making it necessary for us to work on the boat upside down. He showed us how to release the cockpit canopy, assuming it wasn't damaged and how to bust it open if it was.

Everyone was a bit tense as the overall project which was aimed at breaking both the world land and water speed records in the one year, was fast running out of time. They had the land record, 403.1 mph on Lake Eyre in South Australia's Far North under the belt, but in order to pull off the double had to do better than 260 mph on water before midnight on 31 December, less than a month away.

I asked Leo if it was OK for me to climb into the cockpit of the boat. I wanted to get an idea of what obstructions there may be to a man's legs if we had to pull him out in a hurry. He gave me the go ahead, so there I was, no doubt at the peak of a million schoolboys' dreams, in Donald Campbell's seat at the controls of the Bluebird.

The Bluebird

A little later we were squatting on the bank waiting. It seems you do a lot of this when breaking records. Leo was explaining how when she's up and planing the whole two tons of the Bluebird rides on eighteen square inches. 'Breaking the water barrier is the difficult part,' he said. 'This is somewhere round 200 mph plus and the boat vibrates violently up until about 230, but once she's passed that she really takes off.'

Behind Leo's back at this remark I raised an eyebrow at Curnow. His only reply was to silently shake his head. Obviously Ross's boat, flat out at 25 mph was fast enough for him.

* * *

With an awesome roar at 210 mph she seemed to be coming straight for us, the almost imperceptible swell making her snake and leap.

'If he goes a mile an hour faster,' I thought, 'Curnow and I are a moral to go over the side of these pick-up boats'.

162

It seemed she was all but out of control and we were mighty relieved when Campbell finally heeded Leo Villa's repeated requests over the radio to give it away. The swell caused by the flooded river flowing into the lake had beaten them again.

That was the last try on Lake Bonney, for shortly after the whole crew plus the boat left for a last-ditch try on Lake Dumbleyung, over 2000 miles away in Western Australia and there they got the ten minutes of calm water they needed.

At 3.40 on the afternoon of 31 December, with less than eight-and-a-half hours' time left, Donald Campbell set a new world water speed record of 276 mph and completed the double.

* * *

I've found that being grey and bald doesn't help your image much. I was about twenty-one when I noticed the first grey hairs around my ears and it wasn't too many years later that those disheartening bald patches started to appear. One chap that I met thought it was my son who was towed across Backstairs Passage underwater and for years people have been asking me if I still dive, the unsaid inference being 'at your age!!'

But probably the most crushing comment was made when I was in my thirties and Ona and I were holidaying on the Barrier Reef. We took a day trip on one of the inter-island cruise boats and among the attractions on board was riding the boom net and aquaplaning. The safety precautions provided by the crew were to say the least casual and I had already fished an elderly guy, half drowned and naked, out of the boom net, when we noticed a girl fall off the aquaplane behind the boat.

By the time the helmsman's attention was drawn to the fact that he'd lost a passenger and the large boat came round in a leisurely sweep to pick her up, a full five minutes had elapsed.

Ona and I watched the rescue operation from the top deck and as the boat approached the girl in the water it was obvious to me that with the strong cross current, we were going to miss her by about fifty yards.

That the kid looked white and frightened was understandable, as she was only about sixteen and didn't have a lifejacket on. Also the knowledge that she was out in the middle of the Whitsunday Passage, miles from land in several hundred fathoms of water, wouldn't have helped. By this time the character at the helm, who should have been reported for not having his learner's plates showing, also realised that he was going to miss her and casually called out, 'Hang on, we'll have to go round again', which meant the girl was on her own for another lonely five minutes. I glanced around the boat but as nobody seemed very concerned I looked at Ona and shrugging resignedly said, 'I suppose I'd better go and keep her company' and trying not to think of all the strange creatures that cruise the waters of the Whitsunday Passage, I climbed the rail and dived the twenty feet into the sea. It was an excellent dive and would easily have rated 9½ points in open competition, but it was wasted, as Ona told me afterwards, as wives are happy to do when they know you are showing off, that everyone was looking at the girl in the water and my dive had unfortunately gone unnoticed.

It didn't take long to swim down current to where the girl was treading water in the choppy sea and it was probably just as well I did dive in as she was getting a bit nervous. But we had a little chat and finally we were both picked up and the boat headed back to shore.

Of course I knew that my heroic act in saving the girl's life was no big deal. I mean how could I not know. Ona kept telling me it wasn't. But unfortunately for Ona most of the people who take day trips on cruise boats are not very adventurous and to them the whole thing was high drama and I was getting plenty of attention.

No doubt she groaned as she could see a long boring night coming up with me recounting to her each step of the rescue, for by the time we berthed my wife's insight recognised all the signs that her husband was feeling pretty good and that whilst outwardly he was modestly brushing aside the 'Well dones' and 'Good on yers', inwardly his ego was at full puff.

But as Ona started down the plank, carrying all our gear, the long boring night along with my inflated ego went straight over the side in a package deal. As she turned to see how Wonder Boy was managing on his crutches, to her delight a young deck hand called out for all to hear. 'You go on ahead miss, I'll help your father'.

15

The original HMAS *Perth*, a modified Leander Class Light cruiser of some 6800 tons, was a formidable fighting unit.

She was armed with eight six-inch and eight four-inch guns, on her port and starboard sides were twenty-one inch torpedo quads and strategically mounted on other sections of the ship were lighter calibre anti-aircraft weapons and depth charges.

Between her twin funnels, perched high on its catapult, she carried a single-engined Walrus biplane. Known as the 'Pussers Duck' by the Senior Service, not always sympathetic to this intrusion by the RAAF, the Walrus however proved to be a worthy forerunner to her sleeker faster sisters, the Sea Furies and Sea Venoms, of Fleet Air Arm which was yet to be formed. The collective thrust of the *Perth's* four engines which developed 72 000 horsepower between them, could drive her at speeds in excess of thirty knots over a range of 2500 miles. Her length overall was 555 feet and her beam 55 feet. At the time *Perth* was lost the ship's company numbered 682 officers and men.

She began service with the Royal Navy in 1936 as the HMS *Amphion*, but in June 1939 was renamed *Perth* and commissioned in the Royal Australian Navy. The outbreak of war in September 1939 found her in the Caribbean under the command of Captain Harold B. Farncomb, RAN and after service there and in the Western Atlantic she came home to Australia and for the next eight months carried out convoy duties in the Pacific.

In December 1940 *Perth* joined the Mediterranean Fleet as a member of the 7th Cruiser Squadron. Now commanded by Captain Sir Phillip Bowyer Smythe, RN she took part in the Battle of Matapan, the evacuation of Greece and Crete and many other patrols and escorts in the area.

In August *Perth* returned to the Australian Station and after a refit again took part in convoy and escort duties.

Now her commander was Captain Hector L. Waller, DSO, RAN, who had already distinguished himself with the 'Scrap Iron Flotilla' in the Mediterranean, where as captain of the destroyer HMAS *Stuart* he had won not only the title of 'Hardover Hec' for his dashing and skilful seamanship, but a permanent place in Australian naval history as a gallant and resourceful officer.

Early in February 1942 with Captain Waller in command *Perth* again left Australia, this time for the East Indies where she joined the ill-fated ABDA (American, British, Dutch, Australian) Fleet. There in company with such ships as *Houston, Exeter* and *De Ruyter*, she fought in the disastrous Battle of the Java Sea. This battle was so disastrous in fact that when it was over, of the fourteen allied warships involved only *Perth* and *Houston* were left still in a fighting condition. These two ships, under orders from the Allied Command in Java, reformed at Tanjong Priok, the seaport of Batavia to refuel and prepare for a desperate dash through Sunda Strait in an effort to escape the rapidly closing Java Sea trap.

For in February 1942 as the Japanese swept down from the north, the allied position was chaotic. Singapore had fallen. The *Repulse* and the *Prince of Wales*, pride of the Royal Navy, had been sunk off Malaysia by enemy aircraft. To the south New Guinea was being overrun and Darwin had been bombed.

Vital information in Batavia regarding enemy movements was sketchy and what was known was bad. Only one clear fact emerged from it all: it was obvious

H.M.A.S. PERTH, July 1939
SCALE: 1 inch = 40 feet

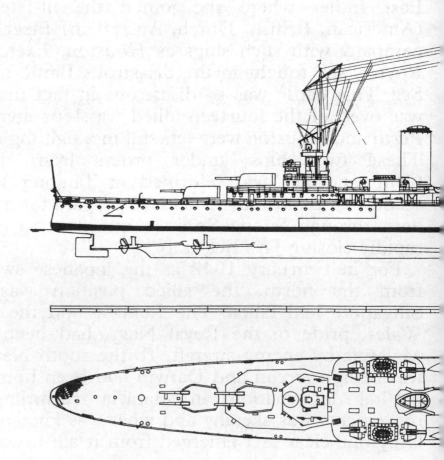

Modified 'Leander' Class Light Cruiser. Ex-H.M.S. Amphion, transferred from Royal Navy, 29 June 1939.

Displacement:	6,890 tons, standard (9,130 tons, full load).
Armament:	Eight 6-inch (4x2), Eight 4-inch A.A. (4x2), Twelve 0.5-inch A.A. (3x4), Four 3-pdr. (4x1) guns, Eight 21-inch (2x4) torpedo tubes, 15 DC.
Armour:	Main belt: 4-3½-in. Deck: 2-1¼-in. Turrets: 1-in. DCT: ½-in.
Dimensions:	530-ft. (p.p.) 559-ft. 6-in. (o.a.) x 56-ft. 8-in. x 15-ft. 9-in. (mean) 19-ft. (max.)
Machinery:	Four Admiralty 3-drum boilers. Four-shaft Parsons geared turbines. 72,000 SHP = 32.5 knots.
Oil Fuel:	1,760 tons.
Radius of Action:	7,400 miles at 13 knots. 1,920 miles at 30.5 knots.
Builders:	H.M. Naval Dockyard, Portsmouth.
Laid down:	26 June 1933
Launched:	27 July 1934
Completed:	21 July 1936
Fate:	Sunk in action with Japanese cruisers and destroyers, Sunda Strait, 4 miles NE of ST Nicholas Point, Bantam Bay, 1 March 1942.

that in order to escape and fight again somewhere else, the allies had to get out of Java . . . and fast.

As the crews of the *Perth* and *Houston* hurriedly refuelled their ships, alongside in the go-downs on the wharves Air Force personnel destroyed stores and equipment which had been destined for Singapore and before they sailed some mighty solemn handshaking took place, between the men of the ships and the men left behind in Tanjong Priok Harbour.

The latest report from Sunda Strait, seventy miles to the west, advised that it was still clear of enemy shipping. Consequently it was felt that if *Perth* and *Houston* could make the Strait, they would have every chance of passing through this narrow stretch of water separating Java from Sumatra and reach the relative safety of the Indian Ocean. There was no way of knowing that as they left Priok in the early evening of 28 February these two ships, like David and Jonathon, were heading straight into the path of an enemy invasion fleet steaming down from the north in support of the Japanese troop landings in West Java. As the allied cruisers were approaching St Nicholas Point, the northernmost tip of the island, with Sunda Strait and freedom almost within reach, they made contact with the enemy when from out of the black tropical night Japanese ships appeared on every quarter.

The realization that the end was only a matter of time must have come to the captains of *Perth* and *Houston* after the first few minutes, for outnumbered and outgunned by the numerically superior Japanese fleet the two cruisers had no chance of breaking through. Accepting this their crews immediately set to and in the true tradition of their respective navies, started in to slug it out and sell themselves as dearly as possible.

Perth, who took the initial onslaught lasted just over an hour. At the finish, having expended all her six-inch ammunition she was firing starshells and practice

170

bricks. *Houston* lasted a little longer. At the end she was also out of ammunition for her eight-inch guns, but was still defiantly firing .50 calibre tracers as she too disappeared beneath the dark Java Sea. Along with 800 of their men the captains of both *Perth* and *Houston* went down with their ships.

16

As soon as I'd finished reading the newspaper article it seemed that something had to be done ... by an Australian ... about finding the *Perth*. This was back in 1963 and the local Press report stated that the Japanese, some twenty years after they had sunk the ship, were interested in salvaging her for scrap. Apparently they had approached the Indonesian Government for permission to salvage the *Perth* along with some of their own vessels which were sunk in Indonesian Territorial Waters, to help pay their war repatriation debts. But the Australian Government outraged at the thought of any desecration to this, an Australian War Grave, had vigorously resisted the move and the Japanese bowing to public opinion promptly dropped the matter.

However it did mean that the ship must be at a depth that could be reached; for the Japanese are very good at this type of thing and must have made some preliminary enquiries. As I read on I wondered if the significance of the report would be apparent to other divers. If the information were noted in some quarters the *Perth's* days of lying unmolested could well be numbered, for unfortunately in this everchanging world of ours what is politically expedient today is not always so tomorrow. Also with the rapid advance of diving techniques, it soon may no longer require the wholehearted efforts of a government-sponsored team to reach her. For whereas the dive using present day diving methods could be considered pretty dicey, it might not be long before using improved methods, it could well be treated as commonplace. If this happened it would leave the ship wide open to be preyed on by all and sundry, including those competent but very unethical fellows, the diving pirates.

Mainly outlaw divers, these characters for the sake of the quick quid are always willing to take a calculated personal and legal risk to recover nonferrous metal from sunken ships. Completely ruthless, they blast and rip with explosives and underwater cutting gear and are quite oblivious to the desecration and ruin they leave behind. Diving pirates are shunned by most commercial and sporting divers around the world, but nevertheless many are the historically priceless artifacts that have been melted down and sold to the scrap merchant by these looters.

While the very real possibility that the *Perth*'s bell could end up as a brass ingot was totally unacceptable to me, I was at a loss to know what I could do about it. The ship lay thousands of miles away in foreign waters on the fringe of one of the world's trouble spots; no doubt the depth she was in would be extreme and to cap it off the currents in the Sunda Strait were reported to run at up to eight knots.

'Hardly a Sunday afternoon dive,' I thought as I tossed the newspaper aside. 'It's more than I could handle'.

But strangely the idle act of throwing the newspaper away immediately made me feel uneasy, as if with it I was throwing away some new-found responsibility to the men of the *Perth* and almost guiltily I quickly reached down and picked the paper up again. This unexpected reaction surprised me as I hadn't considered becoming involved, but the odd feeling that it was I who was morally accountable to first find this ship persisted and even then I knew I was committed.

In those early days the knowledge of the commitment was of the comforting kind, perhaps best described as the type of feeling a young boy has when suddenly he decides one day he is going to be a jet pilot. All he sees is the end result, with no conception of what he must go through to achieve it.

It is a time of day-dreaming and in my case as I slipped easily into this Walter Mitty world I could see myself returning home proudly bearing the *Perth's* bell. Then with the bell safely back in Australia, installed in some suitable place such as the War Memorial in Canberra, I could rest easy in the knowledge that whatever the future held, be it foreign powers or pirates, at least part of the ship would be here permanently commemorating the *Perth* and the men who had died with her. Like all would-be Walter Mittys I conveniently filtered out the harsh realities that such an ambitious project presented; how I was to afford the time or money — gain the necessary experience — or even start to plan it. But at that time, the time of dreaming, these things didn't matter; the time for action when they would matter was still to come. Sufficient at this stage was that the seed had been sown.

For the next four years while I certainly did not forget the *Perth*, I didn't do anything positive about finding her either. There was always some other project taking up my time and it seems strange when I look back, but all the skindiving stunts and projects in which I was involved during those intervening years must have been preparing me for the *Perth* venture when it came.

Then, when the powers that be decided that the time had come and that I was as ready as I was ever likely to be . . . it was almost as if they opened a door.

★ ★ ★

The Reid's party was well under way when we arrived. It wasn't a large turnout perhaps twenty or so, mainly a family affair in honour of Alan Reid.

Alan, a friend of mine since schooldays, was making one of his rare appearances in Adelaide from his property at Deniliquin in New South Wales and his parents had asked a few friends in to mark the occasion.

We knew most of the people scattered around the large drawing-room and Ona and I drifted around talking to people. After a while I noticed a chap in a wheelchair whom I hadn't met before and I asked Alan who he was.

'Haven't you met Gordon?' he answered, surprised. 'He's my cousin, Gordon Reid. He was in the *Perth*. Come over and meet him.'

I downed the last of my drink and placed the empty glass on a small table near by, pausing a moment to light a cigarette before following Alan over to where Gordon was sitting. As I did so I smiled at myself as I recognized the signs — the sudden butterflies in the stomach — the slight tremble of the match flame in my hand. These were signs that I had grown to know only too well. It wasn't exactly fear, although this sometimes came later, but a peculiar feeling, a mixture of acknowledgement of the inevitable and a keen almost awesome anticipation of a forthcoming physical and mental challenge.

I'd felt it the day I realized that my leg had to come off and again, when I knew that I'd have to parachute into the sea. There were other occasions perhaps not so dramatic, but in their time equally important and I didn't need a ton of bricks to let me know that for my rendezvous with the *Perth*, the days of dreaming were over. The time for action had come.

As I hadn't mentioned what I had in mind to Gordon, he must have been irritated at the way I monopolised his time at the party. Unfortunately for him, being confined to his wheelchair, he found it difficult to escape me and all evening I followed him around bombarding him with questions about his old ship.

Later that night I did some heavy thinking as I faced making a decision about attempting to find the *Perth*.

175

The more I thought about it the greater the problems seemed to become and realizing that trying to plan it from start to finish in one go was beyond me, I decided to just take each hurdle as it came. First I had to obtain approval for the project from the Ex-Perth Association. Morally she was still their ship and without the association's permission to dive on her I couldn't even start to think about it.

As Gordon Reid was the President the best approach was through him and next day I rang him at his office and asked if he could see me. We arranged a meeting for later that afternoon by the racecourse and there, away from the noise of the city traffic, I told him of my plan.

Gordon's initial reaction was understandable I suppose, the way I sprang the whole thing on him. But nevertheless I was saddened to see that he obviously felt I'd lost most of my marbles.

'For a start', he asked rather coldly when I'd finished 'how do you expect to survive in the currents of Sunda Strait?' When I didn't readily reply he went on, 'Now look, I don't know much about diving but I do know that the night the ship went down the current swept men — American, Australian and Japanese alike — down through the Strait like corks in a storm water drain'.

I was a bit embarrassed as it was apparent he considered my whole scheme irresponsible, but I pressed on. 'I know there are problems', I said, 'but all I'm asking at this stage is for the moral approval of your association to go into the possibilities of it'.

Gordon immediately looked relieved. Obviously he considered there were no possibilities. 'All right', he said, 'I'll bring the matter before the attention of the members. I'll let you know their decision'.

As I waited impatiently for word from the Ex-Perth Association, I studied up on their ship. From the public library I obtained the book, *Age Shall Not Weary*

Them. It was published during the war before the story of the *Perth's* final battle was known and while it gave a good coverage of the ship's earlier exploits in the Mediterranean, it ceased abruptly at the period in which I was most interested. The second book, Ronald McKie's *Proud Echo*, was more helpful for not only did it give the *Perth's* last-known bearings but also the depth of water in which she sank. Buying an Admiralty Chart of Sunda Strait and using the bearings given in *Proud Echo* I plotted *Perth's* position. This position could only be approximate, but it did give me something to work on. The depth of water at forty-two fathoms was a problem, for although I had dived deeper than this the dives had taken place miles off shore where the currents had been relatively slight. Also, as with the bearings, the reported depth could only be regarded as approximate. What if the ship lay deeper? At forty-two fathoms, or 250 feet, she was already nearing the limit of compressed air breathing. At that depth the associated problems very nearly outweigh the scuba diver's ability to cope with them.

The main danger is divers' bends, for down round the 200 foot mark in the half-real world of nitrogen narcosis, the possibility of contracting the bends is ever at hand to claim the unwary.

While studying the battles of the Java Sea and Sunda Strait, I learnt of the USS *Houston* and the part she had played. According to the reports although *Houston* had sunk near *Perth*, she had gone under rather closer inshore and if this was the case it should make her the easier ship to find. I decided that if I did make it to Indonesia I'd attempt to find *Houston* as well and return her bell to the people of Houston, in Texas. With this addition to the project I felt the objects of the venture rang clear enough.

A few weeks after the day I spoke to Gordon Reid by the racecourse he rang and invited me to the Perth

177

Association's annual dinner. The association met infrequently as a complete group and Gordon felt that the annual dinner presented a good opportunity to tell the members of my proposition. I'll never forget that night, not that anything really dramatic happened, but it was a rare privilege to be invited to sit down at the same table with chaps like these.

I outlined my plan, such as it was, stressing the possibility of future salvage of the ship by governments other than ours. After I'd finished and after I'd answered many questions, the members although doubtful as to the chances of the success, gave permission for me to go ahead and try. This was particularly pleasing as I'd realized all along that it was quite possible the survivors might not want me to dive on their ship.

Before officially giving me the okay, the South Australians considered it best to gauge the feelings of *Perth* survivors in at least one other State and with this in mind a letter was sent to the Ex-Perth Association in Melbourne to test the reaction of the Victorian Branch. In due course the Victorians also indicated their approval and with the moral issues cleared I went on to the next step, that of obtaining legal permission from the Indonesian Government to dive in Indonesian territorial waters.

This was a delicate matter. Since the confrontation with Malaysia, Indonesia's attitude to foreigners had been a bit touchy to say the least and on top of this I was told the domestic situation in Djakarta, following the attempted Communist coup in 1965, was somewhat sensitive. While the political problems of Indonesia were personally no concern of mine, I realized they must have a strong bearing on the success or failure of the project. For to attempt to enlist a country's aid, when its people are still preoccupied and angry over a bitter civil war, was a job that would have to be handled carefully.

To equip me for this task in international relations I

178

was relying heavily on my previous experience, which was limited to once having made three friends in Fiji. This effort didn't exactly fill me with confidence, for as everyone knows the Fijian must be rated as about the friendliest person on earth.

After considering the problem the only solution I could see was to write directly to the Indonesian Ambassador in Canberra, tell him my story and ask his advice. As I didn't know the Ambassador's name I rang and asked Jim Forbes, a chap with whom I'd gone to school. Jim was the current Minister for Health in Federal Parliament and although he gave me the information I required he was fairly cautious about it. I think the old Forbes was concerned that I'd use his name and if this assumption were correct his concern was well founded, for I was aware of the weight it would give to any request I made. Not that I compromised him, but with great care I dropped his name into the opening paragraph of my letter to the Ambassador, knowing full well that although it would probably incur Jim's displeasure, it must assist in obtaining me an audience at the Indonesian Embassy.

* * *

'His Excellency will see you now.' The Naval Attache's voice was soft and combined with the marked accent difficult to follow.

Taking a deep breath, which I hoped was disguised in the act of bending down to pick up my briefcase, I straightened up and walked past the Attache into the Ambassador's office.

General Kosasih was shorter than I'd imagined, but both the authority and dignity of office were there. He stepped forward and shook hands, then waved me into a chair.

'Well, Mr Burchell,' he said with a smile, 'we meet at

last. Now tell me about this diving you want to do'.

It had taken longer than I planned to meet the General. Not that it was his fault, for he had answered my letters politely and promptly through his Naval Attache. But Canberra is a long way from Adelaide and I'd had to work things a bit in order to get there.

I told the General of my plans and although he listened pretty much in silence, by the time I'd finished I sensed I had won a valuable ally. First a soldier, with politics coming second, General Kosasih was naturally interested in military history and any attempt to honour ships and men was to him praiseworthy enough to warrant encouragement.

When I started to explain my motives for wanting to find *Perth* and *Houston* he stopped me with a quick movement of his hand.

'I have visited your War Memorial here in Canberra', he said, 'and I need no explanation of why you want to dive, but I am certainly interested to know how you propose to do it. Also I wish to know what assistance you require from my government in Indonesia.'

Among the papers in my briefcase was a list of items I considered as essential to pull off a dive of this nature. Its size was embarrassing. Finding the list, I handed it to the General.

'Of course Your Excellency,' I added awkwardly. 'I am not expecting your government to provide all these things, but in case some are already in Indonesia and could be loaned it would save my having to take them.'

Feeling decidedly uncomfortable, I watched him scan the list and as I mentally ticked off each point with him I found myself wincing, as I knew very well that most of the items couldn't possibly be taken up with me.

The list, which spelt money, time and manpower, read:

1. A vessel from which to dive and operate.
2. Recompression chamber.
3. Echo sounder.
4. Assisting divers.
5. Winches and lifting gear.
6. 50 lb weights, ropes for shot-lines and buoys.
7. High pressure air compressor.
8. Scuba cylinders.

It went on to include such things as queries on diving conditions, depths, current flows, availability of stores, etcetera. By the time he reached the end of it we were both wincing.

Desperately I cast around for the right words to say. I wanted to explain that this was not the presumptuous request it appeared and that although some of the items could possibly be provided by the Indonesians, I appreciated that it was pretty cheeky to bob up like this and just expect them to produce the goods. Yet if they didn't the whole project was in trouble.

I needn't have worried too much; the General was a man of great understanding. He listened intently, then cut off my clumsy attempt at explanation with the same quick gesture of the hand.

'That's all right Mr Burchell,' he said. 'I am sure our Navy has many of the things you have listed and I will recommend that they assist you. But as most of your questions are of a technical nature, my advice would be for you to go to Djakarta and carry out a survey. Talk first-hand with our Diving and Salvage Command in Surabaya and see what help they are able to give you.'

I hesitated at this suggestion, as I'd been hoping the whole thing could be arranged from Canberra before I left. The thought of just turning up, unheralded and unknown and being faced with the job of trying to influence the impersonal Indonesian Navy to become interested in my plan was not exactly what I'd had in mind.

Realizing I was in no position to argue, I decided not to burden General Kosasih with my problems. I told him that I'd have to give the survey trip some thought and we arranged that while I did this he would write to Djakarta seeking the necessary approval from the Indonesian Government.

Before leaving Canberra to return home I asked Martin Hinson, a friend of mine who lives in Canberra, to drive me up to the War Memorial. Like most Australians who have visited this place, the memorial always has a profound effect on me. This day was no exception. As my time was short, I made straight for the Naval Gallery and spent my half hour wandering round just letting the feel of it sink in.

I'm not much of a one for making vows but that day in the quiet loneliness of the War Memorial, in front of the painting of the *Perth*'s Captain, Hec Waller, I made a promise and although I realized I was not yet fully aware of the size and complexity of the job in front of me, it was a promise that I knew it would take a lot to make me break.

Shortly after returning from Canberra I could see I'd have to take General Kosasih's advice and do the survey trip. There were so many questions to which answers couldn't be obtained that I was stalemated — the survey was the only solution. Once the decision was made, I immediately plunged into a pre-embarkation whirl of visas and vaccinations and while the bouts of smallpox and cholera raged within me, I did my best to explain to the few people who were interested that my journey was really necessary. Apparently I didn't do much of a job of it as I noticed I was far from popular in some quarters.

When the time came to catch the plane for Sydney, Ona came down to the airport to see me off. Actually, I wasn't sure if she came down to see me off, or to drive the car home. It was one of those days . . . I was still feeling lousy from the last batch of needles, my wooden leg was giving me some trouble and my wife was feeling sarcastic.

'Goodbye, Marco Polo,' she said. 'Don't worry about me and the children, just try and enjoy yourself.'

Something told me that this wasn't the time for a smart reply, even if I'd been capable of one. So feeling anything but the great adventurer, with my crutches in one hand and tatty suitcase in the other, I limped across to the luggage desk and silently booked in my gear.

17

The Qantas jet heeled over in preparation for its approach into Djakarta airport and through the cabin window I caught a glimpse of the city below and wondered again about the kind of reception I would receive. The plane rolled to a stop and collecting the few belongings I had with me I walked down the steps into the blast of heat which was Djakarta.

Up in my room at the hotel I undressed, took a shower and flopped on the bed. 'Well, you're here boy', I told myself, staring at the ceiling. 'What now?'

It was a good question and while pondering it I groped for my briefcase beside the bed and took from it a folder of papers. There wasn't much in the file, just the copies of letters I'd written to the Indonesian Embassy along with the replies and it was the last of these that I wanted now.

The letter had arrived just before I left home and it was important, for it formed my introduction to the Indonesian Navy. Taking it from the file I settled back and under the imposing letterhead read the typed words:

'Sir,
> Diving on the wreck of H.M.A.S. PERTH

1. Since my letter to you on the 4th of April, I have received a letter from the Naval Department in Djakarta concerning your plan.
2. The Indonesian Navy will put at your disposal a boat, free of charge. However, I doubt whether the boat is equipped with an echo sounder.
3. Besides this equipment the Navy will also attach some divers to you.

4. The cost of all the operations will be your responsibility.
5. On arrival in Djakarta you are advised to contact the Assistant for Naval Intelligence at the Naval Department through the Australian Naval Attache in Djakarta.

> Yours faithfully,
> *M. Poerbonegoro*
> Colonel ALRI, Naval Attache.'

Deciding that if I could find the Australian Embassy I would also find the Australian Naval Attache, who I kidded myself had heard all about me and was probably right now anxiously awaiting my call, I placed the file back in the briefcase. 'First thing in the morning,' I said with a yawn, 'it's the Australian Embassy. Right now it's a feed and early to bed'.

★   ★   ★

'Sherborne,' he said, sticking out his hand. 'I'm the Naval Attache. You wanted to see me?'

'Burchell,' I replied smiling modestly and returning his grip, at the same time watching with interest for his eyes to light up in recognition of the name. Nothing happened.

'Er — Burchell,' I repeated, frowning slightly. 'You haven't heard of me?'

He shook his head, 'No,' he said, politely puzzled, 'afraid not. Why, should I have?'

Hell I thought, groaning inwardly and wondering where I was going to start. 'General Kosasih,' I suggested hopefully, like a patient father prompting a forgetful child. 'Indonesian Navy — Perth — Houston.'

At the mention of the ships' names the awaited flicker of interest came. 'Ah yes,' he said, 'now I remember,

185

you're the diver fellow. I must say I haven't heard of you through our Embassy, but the Indonesian Navy contacted me about you. Perhaps you'd better come up to my office.'

Upstairs in his office Freddie Sherborne, Captain, RAN, like General Kosasih before him, listened to my story in silence. When I showed him the letter from Colonel Poerbonegoro he glanced at his watch.

'Colonel Sugito is the Assistant for Naval Intelligence,' he said. 'I know he is attending a parade this afternoon. If we don't catch him before that you'll have to wait until tomorrow.' He stood up and crossing to this desk picked up the telephone. 'I'll give him a ring and ask if he will see you now.' He spoke briefly into the phone. I was in luck . . . Colonel Sugito would call at the Embassy within the hour.

'You're fortunate in having Wal Sugito for a contact,' Sherborne said. 'He was the Naval Attache at the Indonesian Embassy in Canberra for a couple of years. He knows the ropes pretty well.'

While we waited I went over the points with him that most concerned me. One thing I particularly wanted to clarify with the Indonesians was my financial obligation. 'It'll just be great,' I said, 'if they hand me a bill at the end that I can't pay.'

He agreed that this would not exactly help cement Indo-Australian relations and promised to assist me to establish the costs involved. As we talked I started to realize the tremendous help Freddie Sherborne was going to be. Not only was he an influential ally at the Embassy itself, but being navy he shared in the camaraderie that personnel of all navies seem to reserve for one another, already evidenced here by Colonel Sugito's prompt response to the phone call.

When the Indonesian Colonel arrived Fred introduced us and after the usual preliminaries we started in on our discussions.

Djoko Suyatno, Walugo Sugito,
Freddie Sherborne and me at Naval HQ

Waludjo Sugito, a slim, dark chap in his early forties, had doubtless been assigned to the project because of his Australian experience, but as he knew very little of what I wanted I found myself having to go through all the explanations again. He also listened to my story without comment and by the time I'd finished I was beginning to realize why they called the Navy the silent service.

Somewhat casually he scanned the formidable list of essential gear, but this time there was no need for me to worry. For Colonel Sugito, not being a diver and not particularly wanting to become involved anyway, was more than ready to palm me off on the Diving and Salvage Command at Surabaya.

'They have all kinds of equipment down there,' he said. 'I'll make the necessary arrangements for you to meet Lieut. Colonel Suyato, the OC. He's the one to whom you should talk. When can you make the trip?'

As Surabaya was 400 miles away in East Java, the arrangements took some organizing, especially as hard core Communist elements were still active in the Eastern Sector, but after a few phone calls it was fixed and I was booked on a Garuda Airways flight the following Tuesday. There wasn't much more Wal Sugito could do, so after wishing me luck he left.

'Well,' said Fred, after the Indonesian had gone. 'You're doing all right. I don't think a foreigner has been invited into the Naval Dockyards at Surabaya since the coup.'

I'm sure he meant the remark to be both complimentary and encouraging, but I had an uneasy feeling that somehow I had missed the point.

That afternoon Fred invited me home to meet his family, comprising his wife, Bobbie and Kristen, their youngest daughter, the two older children being at boarding school in Sydney.

After lunch we went on a tour of Djakarta in Fred's car. Like all Diplomatic Personnel the Sherbornes included in their staff an Indonesian driver. This is standard procedure and depending on your point of view has several distinct advantages. For not only does it keep up appearances, but it provides steady employment for an Indonesian, discourages the local kids from letting your tyres down if the car is left in the street and most important, saves the foreigner from being lynched by the mob if he becomes involved in an accident. These are not uncommon in the dense Rafferty's Rules Djakarta traffic, where young children play along the roadside, inches from the greatest collection of wheeled vehicles imaginable.

We wound our way through Djakarta then through the historic seaport of Tanjong Priok and on into the old city, known to the world for 300 years by its Dutch name of Batavia, but now called Glodok by the Indonesians.

Glodok these days is not much more than one of Djakarta's suburbs and for many years a Chinatown, is now in a state of advanced disrepair. Much of the obvious charm of this once great city has faded. The water no longer flows in the choked canals and the narrow winding streets are littered with refuse and rubble. It can be a dangerous place and is frequently the scene of mayhem and murder, of burning overturned cars and police blocks. But we were not looking for trouble and on that bright holiday afternoon I found the place fascinating.

Asking Fred to stop the car and disregarding the stony stares of the locals I got out to just walk in its streets. This was my first contact with an ancient city and it didn't take long to learn the trick of looking past the moulding unpainted exteriors of the buildings to see the classic line of the Dutch architecture. It was easy to visualize the same buildings as they must have been hundreds of years before, when Captain Cook called in to Batavia to refit his unseaworthy *Endeavour*.

Or perhaps Bligh, still coldly fuming at his treatment by the Bounty mutineers strode down this very street, rudely brushing past rich Dutch traders as he impatiently waited for a ship to take him home to England. I could have spent the rest of the day there and kicked myself for having left my camera behind.

Early the next morning with photography in mind, I hired a taxi and armed with the camera set off to capture old Batavia. But the police at the road block turned us back. During the night there had been a riot with several people injured and as the driver hastily turned his car I glimpsed a blazing motorbike lying on its side . . . dark knots of people heatedly arguing. As we sped away I thought that perhaps it was just as well, as the camera lacking the aid of human imagination can record only the present and consequently was a few hundred years too late. Batavia, that place with the nostalgic name, along with Captain Cook and the old Dutch merchantmen was forever gone. That which remained, Glodok, ugly in title and ugly in character, like so many of our contemporary scenes probably wouldn't have shown up too well on film.

Thanks to Freddy Sherborne I was introduced into a round of Embassy parties that were being held to farewell a chap named Bob Rigney, an Air Force Major from San Antonio, Texas. Bob was on his way home after two years as the Assistant Air Attache at the American Embassy and as he was a popular fellow, there was a different turnout on each night in his honour. Coming from Texas he was naturally interested in the plan to find the *Houston* and offered to fly me up to West Java so that I could study the diving conditions in Sunda Strait from the air.

Spontaneous offers of assistance like this were typical of the Americans. One night I was talking to the American Ambassador and after we had chatted for a while he asked me if I knew the *Houston's* last-known bearings. When I told him I didn't, the Ambassador knowing what a help the bearing would be called Wilbur Kellogg, his Naval Attache over and instructed him to cable Washington and request the information. Also Joe Swarz, the US Embassy doctor, a young Naval Lieutenant and keen student of his country's military history offered to accompany me as medical officer and observer. With this and other offers all looked well at the Djakarta end, but the big hurdle, that of enlisting the aid of the Diving and Salvage Command at Surabaya, was still the one that caused me concern.

★　★　★

'Don't tell me you're gonna dive in that?' Bob Rigney bawled in my ear as he circled the plane over Sunda Strait and although I managed a grin I had to admit that the view from a thousand feet was distinctly depressing.

The fast-flowing water, apart from giving an impression of eerie depth, in some places had whirlpools on the surface that were ten feet across. But

190

I noticed that most of these were caused by the currents sweeping round the islands at the head of the Strait and although the ships were reportedly sunk as they approached this area, they were not supposed to be near any islands. Perhaps it would be easier in the deeper water . . .

I asked Bob to fly south down Sunda Strait so that I could photograph Toppers and Sangiang Islands, as sailors from both *Perth* and *Houston* had tried to swim to them for shelter after the battle and I knew that the survivors who had made it would be interested to see them again.

We took some good shots, some of which included the infamous volcanic island of Krakatoa which had caused a major catastrophe when it blew up in the late 1800s. With the mission completed we headed for home, first across the mountains and then over the paddy fields that between them go to make up West Java.

The next day in the Australian Embassy's Landrover Freddie Sherborne and I drove back to the same area to study conditions from the shore. As it was Sunday Bobbie and Kristen came with us for the ride and we had a picnic lunch on the beach in Banten Bay. Wal Sugito assigned an Indonesian Navy Major to accompany us as interpreter and guide, as some of the areas we intended surveying were remote and rarely visited.

It was a terrible trip, rough, hot and dirty and while not a great distance by Australian standards, the 150 miles took us nearly twelve hours to complete. Ox drays, cyclists, pony-carts and pedestrians swarmed over the road in colourful profusion and here in the rural areas as in the city I was struck with the same impression — people . . . people everywhere.

To the visitor coming direct from a place like Australia where the population per square mile is 3.5 to Java where the population per square mile is something like 1120, a comparison of the relative population densities must be inevitable. Day or night, city or country, it made little difference, there were people everywhere, at times almost claustrophobic in their numbers.

One soon becomes used to it and when I first returned home to Australia I missed them and even Sydney seemed half empty.

We slowly threaded our way when the traffic was thick, speeded up when it wasn't and stopped altogether at the occasional road blocks, although the presence of the Indonesian Major, combined with the Diplomatic Corps plates on the landrover were usually enough for the police to wave us through.

We called on the Port Authority in Merak, a seaport at the northern end of Sunda Strait and obtained permission to travel up the rough stony coast road to St Nicholas Point.

To me it was all pretty exciting stuff, for not only were the people and the scenery completely absorbing, but I knew that when we reached the Point we would be within a few miles of *Perth* and *Houston*, for it was here that the battle of Sunda Strait had been fought. At the Point we stopped and I walked down to the rocky beach to take a closer look at the water conditions. As far as I could see from the shore they weren't too bad. The current was running strongly, but the water seemed clear enough.

Deciding that the conditions would just have to be all right, I sat down and looked out over Sunda Strait. Being there gave me the same feeling I know I'd have if I visited Gallipoli — The Kakoda Trail — or the thousand other places that will always have a special meaning for Australians.

Somewhere out there under the sparkling seas were the ships. Perhaps now more cemeteries than ships and especially because of this it was time they were visited by the living even if only for this once, so that the report 'All's well' could be taken back to those who still remembered.

18

My concern that things would not work out with the Diving and Salvage Command proved to be groundless. However during the flight from Djakarta to Surabaya, at that stage not knowing how I'd be received, I did some homework in preparation for an anticipated hard sell.

First, I repeated Djoko Suyatno's name over and over until I'd memorized it, as the gesture in getting his name straight was about the only thing I had to offer in return for the requests I wished to make of him.

Next, after re-studying the tiresome list of essentials, I decided against asking for the loan of scuba cylinders and the high pressure compressor. These I'd have to bring up from Australia somehow. This decision, admittedly partly based on a feeling of embarrassment at asking for too much, was also partly based on the psychological point of not wishing to appear to the Indonesians as a complete freeloader. True, the difference between the two was pretty fine and the cylinders and compressor would be a nuisance to freight, but the effort involved in producing them would show that at least I was prepared to try to pull some of my own weight. Also by having my own scuba cylinders and compressor I'd be independent as far as actual diving equipment was concerned and as past experience had taught me not to rely too heavily on other people's gear, I felt it would be unwise to take the chance even with the Indonesian Navy.

Carefully I went over point after point on the list, thinking about them for the hundredth time . . . size and capabilities of the diving tender, how many people could live on board, would we require a base camp on shore, number and experience of the assisting divers, availability of stores and fuel. There were twenty-three major items, all more or less vital to the success of the venture and again I was conscious of the seeming presumptuousness of the requests. All I could do was hope that the man waiting for me in Surabaya was as understanding and in the same position to be as helpful as General Kosasih had been in Canberra.

Lieutenant Colonel Djoko Suyatno was at the plane steps when I arrived and after introducing ourselves we moved across to his new Holden car which was nearby on the tarmac.

He was small, even for an Indonesian and although I'm only six feet I towered above him.

We climbed into the car and slowly made our way through the crowded Surabaya streets towards the Naval Dockyards. At the main gate, as the guards snapped to attention, I heard the shrill whistle of the Bosun's pipe as we passed through and I remember feeling very lonely and momentarily a little overawed. But by making a conscious effort I shrugged the feeling off, as this was no time to start feeling sorry for myself.

Waiting on the steps at the Diving and Salvage Command Headquarters were three of Djoko's officers and after he had introduced us we all set off on a tour of inspection. The Command was a huge place and Djoko, who was very proud of it, was determined I was going to see the lot. We inspected the thirty- five foot high diver-training tanks, which were equipped with Davis escape apparatus for simulated ascents from submarines. The British Seibe Gorman recompression chambers, the rows of scuba and conventional hard-hat gear and then on to the compressor rooms and other miscellaneous sections that go to make up a command of this nature. It was all of great interest to me and fortunately over the years I'd had some experience with nearly all the types of equipment the Indonesians were using. This allowed me to make the occasional intelligent remark which of course is a great morale booster to the man who senses he is on trial.

Finally, the tour completed, we ended up in the Wardroom and while a steward poured out glasses of cold Surabaya beer I made a last minute mental check before doing battle for the loan of the equipment I needed.

Sitting down next to me Djoko broke my train of thought. 'We are interested to know,' he said, 'why you, an ex-air force pilot and officer, are interested in naval ships.'

It was not the first time his direct questions had shown he knew more about me than I'd told him, but on this occasion he'd been misinformed, for being an LAC in the Ground Staff was a far cry from a dashing Squadron Leader fighter pilot.

Suppressing a smile at the mental picture I had of myself in the unglamorous fuzzy blue uniform of the Leading Aircraftsman, I nevertheless kept silent about the fact that I hadn't exactly won the Battle of Britain singlehanded.

'Actually finding the ships has nothing to do with the different service,' I replied carefully. 'I'm a diver and I'm interested in our military history. To Australians the *Perth* is a very famous ship and we are very proud of her and her crew. It's the same thing with the *Houston* in America.'

Continuing, I told them of the War Memorials in Canberra and Texas and of the attempt to dive to recover the ships' bells so that they could be sent home for safekeeping. 'I feel that we as divers' and I glanced around to include them all, 'have a responsibility to do these things, but as you can see I'll need some help.'

A further glance at the faces of the Indonesians told me that my worries were over and that I could rely on the support of the Diving and Salvage Command.

After some discussion Djoko offered me a 300-ton sea-going diving tender complete with echo-sounders, recompression chamber and six 'A' class Indonesian Navy divers to assist and act as standbys.

He was so receptive that I was almost tempted to ask for the scuba cylinders and compressor — but didn't. We talked the project out and finally arranged that they should meet me in Tanjong Priok harbour with the ship and divers at the end of May, allowing me a month to organize myself and my own gear.

I was highly elated at the result of the meeting, for these chaps were divers, they understood the difficulties and their practical assistance would be invaluable. Also with Djoko's aid the tricky navigational problems of picking up the *Perth* and *Houston* with the echo-sounders would be minimized.

During the flight back to Djakarta I felt for the first time reasonably confident about the outcome of the project. Admittedly there were still the currents and a few other things, but they could wait. At this stage the venture was looking good and while not yet underwater, I considered it was definitely off the ground.

Back home, the inevitable crises of the next four weeks were overcome. A chap from Melbourne rang and said that four or five years before he'd seen the *Houston*'s bell in a private museum in Manila and asked what did I make of that. I said I didn't know what to make of it. There was the difficulty involving the transportation of the scuba cylinders and compressor from Australia. Shipping them to Djakarta was too slow and commercial air freight was too expensive. One day in the street I told Dick Colley my problems and he suggested I try the Air Force. 'They sometimes have transport planes going through that area on their way to Vietnam,' he said. 'Give Geoff Giles a ring, he might be able to help you.'

'Hell,' I said, initially unimpressed with the idea. 'I

can't do that. Geoff has nothing to do with the Air Force.'

Also I might say I was a bit wary of taking Colley's advice as he experienced great delight in playing on my naive nature and several times over the years he'd set me up with his suggestions. But on the other hand he did seem to know about these things and as I was getting desperate and couldn't think of anything myself it was probably worth a try.

Geoff Giles MHR was at a meeting when I rang his Canberra office but his secretary said she would ask if he would speak to me. When he came on the line, being over-anxious, I must have given it to him a bit quick for somehow he got the impression I wanted to fly a party of Indonesians to Perth to pick up an air compressor.

From somewhere near the beginning I started the story again . . . this time more slowly. We had several conversations after that, the upshot being that the RAAF did have a Hercules going to Vietnam and for the first time in eighteen months it was stopping off at Djakarta en route. Also by some minor miracle the plane wasn't fully loaded and there would be room for my gear. When the okay from the Air Force finally came through it only left two days to road-freight the diving equipment to Richmond RAAF base in New South Wales, nearly a thousand miles away. There wasn't much time.

Gordon Wilson, the Sales Manager of the Commercial Case Co., came in and free of charge made up the crates to hold the gear and two young Customs officials made the trip from Port Adelaide in their lunch hour to carry out the necessary Customs inspection. As Gordon nailed down the lids of the crates I wrote Freddie Sherborne's address on them. The Customs chaps then made out the papers and the carrier loaded the boxes on his truck. In what seemed like a flash they were gone and hoping that the driver fully understood the

197

complicated delivery instructions I was left standing in the empty street, seriously wondering if I'd ever see my gear again.

Apparently there was some truth in the report that the bell of the USS *Houston* had been seen in Manila. Walter Allen, my contact in Houston, Texas, in reply to the news that the bell may have been sighted, wrote advising that a reporter from the *Houston Post* had located a former citizen of the Philippines who had actually touched the bell.

The Texas newspaper story ended by stating a possibility that was now also alarmingly apparent to me . . . perhaps someone had already dived on the ships, perhaps they weren't there anymore. I didn't know what to make of it. One encouraging thing was that the survivors of the *Houston* were enthusiastic about the search and that they would be pleased to receive any part of their ship that was recovered.

Walter Allen also sent some photographs of the *Houston*. These showed the bell's position on the main-mast just aft of the bridge and in the event of the ship being found would be of tremendous value.

Several nights were spent with the South Australian *Perth* survivors discussing the layout of their ship and again we mainly used photographs. They told me that the *Perth*'s bell could be in either of two positions. Generally in port it was hung just forward of X Turret on the open quarterdeck, while at sea it was stowed inside the deck housing in the quartermaster's lobby. But no one was certain where the bell was on the night the ship sank. Even ex-Chief Petty Officer Harry Knight, although he commissioned the ship, wasn't sure. He had gone to some trouble to draw the quarterdeck to scale for me and although this would be a great help, I still really needed to know where the bell had last been seen.

Harry felt that if anyone should know it would be Ray

Parkin, a fellow CPO and friend of his who lived in Melbourne. Ray, who had also commissioned the ship, had been her quartermaster and was at the wheel when she went down. He was a recognized authority on matters of the *Perth* and during his captivity in the ungentle hands of the Japanese and while a hundred of the original *Perth* survivors died around him, Ray sketched scenes and wrote the basic drafts of two books. Subsequently published after the war as *Out of the Smoke* and *Into the Smother*, the original manuscripts were smuggled from camp to camp under the very noses of the Japs for three-and-a-half years.

Harry Knight rang him from Adelaide and asked if he knew the bell's position, but Ray wasn't sure either, so it looked as if I'd have to search for it.

Because of international interest, minor though it was and because I thought he should know something about the project in case it was successful, I wrote to the Prime Minister. The letter covered the granting of legal permission by to Indonesian Government and the ready offers of assistance from General Kosasih in Canberra and the Indonesian Navy in Surabaya. Reading it through before posting it, I had second thoughts about sending the letter at all, realising that the Prime Minister would have one or two more important things on his mind. But I sent it off.

Several offers of assistance came from friends in Adelaide. Brian Fricker considered I shouldn't have to pay my own fare. Not that he intended doing anything practical about it, like paying for it himself, but he insisted on arranging an introduction to his friend Bert Kelly, MHR, a South Australian who at the time was Minister for Works in the Federal Parliament. Brian felt Mr Kelly might be able to help, but I wasn't too keen as I didn't feel inclined to front up to a Federal Parliamentarian and ask for a free airline ticket. However Fricker arranged the meeting and Bert Kelly, who patiently heard me out, promised to see what he could do. He was as good as his word and eventually I received a refund of nearly two-thirds of the air fare.

John Martin, the President of the Underwater Explorers Club, gave me a quantity of UEC Club Lapel badges and some blank membership certificates. John Scammell asked if he could accompany me on the trip and help out. I told him I'd think it over, but had little hesitation really in accepting the offer. For although I appreciated he wouldn't be much help underwater, as deep diving wasn't in Scammell's bag of tricks, he was a friend of long standing on whom I knew I could rely and this alone made him a valuable acquisition.

Finally all that was left was the last minute rush, camera, special underwater film, flashbulbs that would stand the pressure of 200 feet, an Indonesian/English dictionary, visa problems and finding room in my bag for a large parcel of nuts and dried fruit that Chappy Charlesworth gave me to keep up my strength.

19

We were flying high over the Bali Strait. Below and to the left the volcanoes of East Java poked their coned heads through the heavy cumulus cloud indicating that at last Djakarta was close by.

Nudging Scammell, I nodded at the peaks and he stirred and groped round his feet for his camera, at the same time keeping his eyes firmly fixed on the volcanoes like a hunter watching his prey. I understood how he felt, for the peaks contained an unreal, almost ethereal quality which gave the impression that if you looked away, even for a second, they must surely disappear. Soon the jet swept in over Tanjong Priok and looking down I noted a grey naval ship at anchor in the harbour. 'Good old Djoko', I thought, 'right on time'. Turning towards John I said confidently, 'That'll be ours, boy', and I could hardly wait to land and get started.

The next morning the phone in our hotel room rang. It was a clerk from the reception desk advising us that a car was waiting to take John and me to the Australian Embassy . . . I recognised Freddie Sherborne's thoughtfulness. True to form, he was right on the job and as we rode the lift down the ten floors to the ground I had a distinct feeling that this was going to be a good day. In Fred's office at the Embassy were the two crates of diving gear and as far as I could tell without opening them the compressor and Scubas appeared to have survived their trip well enough. I was anxious to service and start the compressor but there wasn't time — it would have to wait until later aboard Djoko's ship.

Leaving the airconditioned Australian Embassy we battled our way through the heat and bustle of Djakarta this time to the Indonesian Naval Head- quarters for a conference with Admiral Harijono Nimpuno, head of the 3rd Naval District, which included Sunda Strait. Wal Sugito and Djoko Suyatno were to be there also and I was looking forward to seeing them and to making the final arrangements so that we could put to sea.

Freddie, John and I, received with due ceremony in the foyer, were ushered through to the Intelligence section by a petty officer, but as soon as introductions were completed and we'd all sat down it was apparent that something was very wrong.

Djoko, in contrast to my enthusiastic greeting appeared ill-at-ease and furtive, while Wal Sugito could have been likened to Pontius Pilate looking for somewhere to wash his hands. We took some time to uncover the reason for this unexpected embarrassment, but finally we found that Djoko, on thinking things over, had reversed his decision and had officially recommended that the Indonesian Navy not become involved in the diving at all. Also his survey ship, which had engine trouble, was still in Surabaya.

At first I couldn't believe it and quite seriously thought with the language problems that I wasn't hearing properly. But it was true enough. With alarming clarity in a letter to the Admiral, Djoko had explained his reasons to veto the dive . . . the depth was too great . . . the currents were too strong . . . the dive was far too dangerous.

'Imagine the repercussions', he'd asked, 'if this man who is virtually a guest of the Indonesian Government, while using Navy equipment got the bends, or because of the currents, drowned himself?' He went on to say that in his opinion this was a distinct possibility and that he wasn't prepared to be a party to it.

His main concern was the depth, calculated to be from 230 to 245 feet. Apparently after we had parted in Surabaya a month before he had worked out the dive theoretically, using the Haldane decompression tables as a basis for his computations. He found that the dive was impracticable.

The Haldane tables, designed to obviate diver's bends have been recognized as an authority for many years. But they are conservative to the extreme and along with many other divers who have had the opportunity to purchase one, I prefer to use what is called an automatic decompression meter. Of Italian origin, the decompression meter is carried by the diver, registering the actual depth in which he is operating and generally, using a meter, the time underwater can be doubled against the time allowed by basing a dive on tables. While I'd had some dives beyond 250 feet with them, I could hardly tell Djoko in front of everyone that he was behind the times and a point that made me hesitate further was the frustrating knowledge that he honestly thought he was doing me a favour. However, as Officer in Charge of Diving and Salvage Command his opinions on matters involving underwater activities were accepted without question and it was painfully obvious that without Djoko in my team I was in trouble.

But how best to get him back on my side was a psychological problem for which I wasn't equipped and I never really found out just what made Djoko change his mind.

Whether the depth put him off, or that his ship was more seriously incapacitated than he cared to admit, I couldn't establish. I tried hard to get through to him, using every approach I knew, but none was successful and although he sat in on a couple of subsequent meetings Djoko Suyatno gradually eased out of the picture, finally returning to Surabaya to go on leave. I never saw him again.

The brief popularity that I'd enjoyed before Djoko torpedoed my plans disappeared as fast as he did. In its place came a cold front, subtle at first, but becoming more and more obvious. I almost expected to see a sign on the gates of Naval Headquarters reading 'Burchell Go Home'.

The situation at the Australian Embassy was much the same. There I'd become a nuisance and it seemed that my only supporters were our Service Attaches and the Americans.

Freddie did all he could and somehow arranged for a private ship, the *Samudra*, to take John and me to Sunda Strait for three days. Unfortunately the *Samudra* had been engaged in carrying copra and was infested with lice and cockroaches. These we didn't mind so much, but the first day out when finally we arrived over the marks, her echo sounder broke down and I was reduced to trying visual sweeps riding the anchor chain. The visibility on the bottom was poor and as there was quite a sea running the chain whipped five or six feet with every wave the ship rode on the surface. These

With John Scammell and Somantri
on the *Aries* forecastle

violent rides caused me to lose several bits of gear, including a specially made prising tool and my weight belt. The tool I could do without, but the weight belt's loss would have been serious, so I had no option but to leave the doubtful security of the chain and go back and look for it. Finding the belt, I slipped it on and caught up again by following the grooves left in the mud and sand by the bounding anchor. I lost no time, as the chain was my only link from this eerie green wilderness to the ship high above.

After five sweeps we gave it away. This was last-resort-desperation searching at its worst, with the odds stacked against any possible success and although I realized we may have to fall back on it again later, there were one or two other methods that were worth a try first.

I asked the young Navy Captain, Sumantri, who had been assigned to us as an interpreter, if he thought some of the local Bantenese fishermen might know of wrecks. Seeking the help of fishermen was a technique we often used back home as they always seem to know where the wrecks are. Sumantri agreed it was worth a try, although he said the local fishermen used traps and nets in the shallow water and may not be familiar with the area seven miles offshore. Also the Bantenese were a pretty unsophisticated crowd, mostly not even speaking Indonesian and Sumantri not knowing their dialect, could see difficulties in talking with them.

That night Ming the Merciless, the name John had bestowed upon the Captain of the *Samudra*, took us ashore in one of the ship's boats. Ming, a real character with his half-closed slanting eyes, high cheek bones and drooping Mandarin moustache, claimed to have picked up his knowledge of English in the saloons of San Francisco and the bars of Kings Cross. The project to find the *Perth* and *Houston* left him cold, as he reckoned it lacked percentage, but he was a good

205

seaman and worked his ship expertly during the search sweeps.

Once ashore John, Sumantri and I started walking. First along the built-up earth marinas stretching across the mud flats and then on to the dirt road which wound its way through the jungle linking the coastal fishing villages. We walked for miles, slogging along in silence with the humidity bringing out the sweat and at each village Sumantri would engage in long pow-wows with the headman, asking if anyone knew of wrecks. This was always a complicated procedure, as certain protocol had to be observed and with the triple language problem aggravating things it was with great relief that finally we found a couple of fishermen who said they would help.

They also offered to paddle us back to the *Samudra* which interested me, for even though my hands were toughened after years of walking with crutches, they had so softened with sweat during the long trek that the palms were blistered and raw.

West Java can be incredibly beautiful. That night as we glided over the bay in the soft moonlight, with the lights from the cooking fires on shore and the occasional shouted call coming across the calm sea, it was at its best. My stinging hands became a minor discomfort and I relaxed back in the warm bilge of the dugout canoe and let them make phosphorous trails over the side. I realised at that moment how fortunate we were just to be there.

At 5am the next morning we put to sea and Ming, following the overawed fishermen's signals manoeuvred the *Samudra* to a point some six miles offshore. I thought it was too far to the east for the *Perth* or *Houston* but being in no position to argue and perhaps hoping for a miracle, I dived.

There was nothing but the colourless mud and sand. Back on deck we conferred again in sign language with the fishermen . . . they pointed a hundred yards to port

. . . we shifted and I dived again . . . still nothing. All day it went on, even long after we could see that the fishermen were obviously confused. Eventually we were forced to stop. My diving time for the twelve-hour period was gone and the *Samudra* had to return to Djakarta.

On the trip back to Tanjong Priok I discussed the situation with Sumantri. Somehow I had to acquire a ship, one that was available for three to four weeks and one that was equipped with efficient sounding gear. To carry out a box pattern search, the accepted procedure when looking for wrecks in deep water, the ship would also have to be highly manoeuvrable to combat the currents. Box pattern searching is done by placing four buoys in a square, the area then being methodically swept up and down with the echo sounder. If the wreck is not found in the square, the buoys are shifted across to a new position and the sweeps start again. It is slow and laborious but is successful if the initial bearings are reasonably accurate. Sumantri promised to help in any way he could and started off by offering John and me sleeping accommodation on his ship the *Bergamahl*, which was temporarily out of commission in Priok Harbour. This was accepted with alacrity, as we had already noticed to our cost that the tariff at the hotel was as high as ever. Sumantri also promised to speak to his Commodore about a ship, although he wasn't very hopeful.

The next two weeks were among the most depressing I've ever put in and although Scammell started off well enough, after a few days of my snarling he ended up feeling pretty lousy as well.

In the quest to obtain a ship I rang Admirals, pleaded with Commodores and argued with Colonels. Each morning Sumantri would turn up at the Yacht Club wharf in his Russian jeep and hail us across the 200 yards of water to where the *Bergamahl* was moored.

This was the signal to start another hot, grubby day, being duck-shoved from one Naval Department to another telling my story and as each of these days passed, the people who were prepared to listen diminished and I started to become desperate.

Finally one night, nearly three weeks after John and I had arrived in Java, unable to sleep I surrendered the stifling cabin to the bugs and cockroaches and went out on the open deck. It wasn't much cooler, but at least there was air and I spent a couple of hours miserably staring across the stagnant water of Priok Harbour at the blinking lights ashore. Always having been a firm believer that things happen for the best, my faith was being sorely tried for if I couldn't get a ship the next day from Sumantri's chief, Commodore Wardiman OC Hydrographic Command, I didn't know what I was going to do.

When Sumantri and I arrived at Commodore Wardiman's office, having left John behind on the *Bergamahl*, three or four others were already present Waludjo Sugito, sitting at a table in the corner was moodily scribbling with a pencil, the Commodore was talking with an Aide and Freddie, who was faithful, to the last, stood up when we entered and shook hands.

'I suppose you're sick of the sound of my name, Wal', I called apologetically to the dark figures at the table and Sugito, showing that some Australian had rubbed off on him during his two years as an Attache in Canberra, replied, ' I'm sick of the whole bloody thing'.

He went on to say that he wasn't blaming me for what had happened and even that morning in an effort to help he had been trying to acquire the President's barge, but he had just received advice that it had engine trouble and wasn't available. 'Hell', I thought, 'Soekarno's own launch, that would have been all right'.

It crossed my mind to say that half the fleet seemed to be having engine trouble but decided it was not the time, so sighing with frustration I turned my attention to the Commodore.

Wardiman and I were by now good friends, having already discussed the problem of a ship on several occasions, but today I planned a much bolder attack.

'Commodore Wardiman', I said looking him straight in the eye, 'here is a letter from Colonel Poerbonegoro, your Naval Attache in Canberra' and then reading from the letter I quoted the clause in which the Indonesian Navy had promised to put a boat at my disposal. Glancing at him again I continued, 'Now Commodore, I'm sorry but I want that boat'. Wardiman like most Indonesians was a charming fellow, endowed with much humour and understanding.

'David', he admonished me with mild reproach, 'you don't seem to understand. This is not my responsibility. I didn't promise you anything. I've told you before that if there were a suitable ship and it was available you could have it'. We both knew he could have gone on, pointing out that with Djoko's veto the Indonesian Navy could no longer be held responsible for the promise and that consequently the clause from the letter was completely out of context. I realised that he had purposely spared me in front of the others by not making these points and this knowledge made what I was about to say all the harder. 'I'm afraid I can't accept that Commodore', I said, the embarrassment and rising despair making my voice sound harsh. 'As far as I'm concerned you are the Indonesian Navy, you have made a promise and I must ask you to produce a ship. I'll settle for anything that'll float'.

In the shocked silence that followed I noticed that Wal Sugito had stopped doodling. Freddie looked somewhat aghast, Sumantri had his head in his hands and a dirty great frown had appeared on the face of the Commodore. I'm not sure now what I'd hoped to achieve with these means, as Wardiman at any time

209

could have verbally cut me to bits. Perhaps I thought he may have been impressed with my resolute approach, I don't know. All I did know, as I sat there not knowing what next to say with the sweat running down my face, was that I'd muffed it.

But I hadn't reckoned on the Commodore. As fast as the frown appeared it left him and he began to chuckle with genuine amusement. As the tension inside me started to break I giggled along with him, at first not knowing why and then with the growing realization that to him I was like a pane of glass. An exterior that he could see right through to the poor worried character inside, one who might never make a diplomat, but who if given half a chance might make a diver.

'So you want a ship', he said. 'Anything that will float'. And with a last chuckle that should have warned me he turned to Sumantri. 'Captain', he said, 'as you seem to be so interested, I'm assigning you to the position of liaison officer for this project and as far as a ship is concerned take David and show him the *Aries*. He can have that'.

20

We had quite a job finding the *Aries*, but I was so elated I didn't mind and as Sumantri and I bumped along the overgrown tracks that threaded the Tanjong Priok backwaters I didn't even notice how quiet he was.

Sumantri had proved to be a tremendous addition to the team. Aged about thirty, he represented the new breed Indonesian Naval Officer, for he was alert, well trained and well informed. But the one thing that probably most endeared him to John and me was his humour, for this, like his loyalty, never flagged. He spoke excellent English.

Almost reluctantly, in answer to my questions he told me about the *Aries*. A ninety-foot Russian sloop, she had once been engaged in regular survey work. However her sister ship had sunk with all hands somewhere off Sumatra three years before and the *Aries* own seaworthiness had immediately come under suspicion, hence her being on the beach. I also rather gathered that as far as Sumantri was concerned she could stay there.

We found her resting on a mudbank in a disused canal and my short-lived elation died at the sight, for even from a distance it was obvious . . . the *Aries* was a derelict.

Scrambling over the canted and rusted steel deck to the small wheel-house I squeezed inside. She'd been stripped. There was no wireless, no compass, there were no navigational aids at all. Down in the engine room sulked an ancient Russian diesel . . . it didn't work . . . the instructions were all in Russian . . . no one could read them.

I must admit that with this sudden letdown my

211

morale did a nose-dive and sprawling dejectedly in some meagre shade on the quarter-deck I bitterly reviewed the position. From every angle it looked hopeless. On top of this the Indonesians were embarrassed to the extreme; the Americans although sympathetic, thought I was crazy; and my own Embassy would have been very pleased to see me fly out on the next plane.

But previous experience in similar ventures had shown that they were never easy and that they seldom went to plan. Also I don't know of anyone who has done something personally difficult who wasn't tempted to give it away at some stage.

After awhile I wearily propped myself up on an elbow and toed the prostrate form of Sumantri with my foot. 'Come on Admiral', I said, trying to rouse him, 'it's time we got this bucket of bolts to sea. Remember what Churchill said, 'This could be her finest hour'. But Sumantri, disgusted, tired and unwilling to see any glory in the moment of our lowest ebb, could only reply, 'Stuff Churchill'.

Two days later, with the aid of most of Commodore Wardiman's engineers, the Aries moved, not much, but she moved. Another half a day spent recleaning injectors and she was ready for her sea trials . . . fifty yards up and down the canal . . . These she passed and we had a ship. But as no echosounder was available to carry out the box pattern searches we still had a problem and the only solution as far as I could see was the fishermen. Sumantri agreed that if left alone in their own boats the fishermen could do better, as we both felt that working from the bridge of the Samudra had confused them.

It meant another long trip into West Java, but there appeared to be no alternative. As Sumantri's jeep was not capable of tackling the journey to Banten Bay, we drove into Djakarta to borrow one of the Australian Embassy Landrovers. Freddie was away in Sumatra so in his absence I asked the Consul for a Landrover. To my surprise and dismay he flatly refused. 'These are Government vehicles', he said 'and you have absolutely no authority to ask for one'. My explanations and arguments were in vain, he wouldn't budge and although I could see his point the situation called for desperate measures.

With no Freddie to help, I went over the Consul's head and asked Dick Warren, our Military Attache, to requisition a Landrover for me.

This move didn't exactly please the Consul and I was sorry, for I can't stand smart bastards myself and I'm sure that this was the category in which he immediately placed me.

Back in Banten Bay we went through the rigmarole with the village headmen again, only this time they were different headmen in different villages. There seemed to be no end to it, but after some hours of verbal approaches, discussions, and withdrawals, laced with strict protocol and lukewarm tea, we found a village whose headman had actually witnessed the Battle of Sunda Strait.

He was extremely reserved and not at all inclined to help, but eventually Sumantri wore him down and he promised to send some fishermen out the next day in an attempt to place buoys over the wrecks.

I gave him some money to buy the necessary ropes and weights and promised to pay each fisherman for every wreck they could put a line on, irrespective of what the ship was. This interested the Bantanese who, while they lived reasonably well, were still financially pretty close to the rice line.

Although the deal appeared to have been made I was still loath to leave. I was worried that the fishermen might not appreciate the importance of their contribution and so I made Sumantri go through it all again. We had to remember that these people were extremely insular and that in the main they were unaware of events happening as little as five miles away. None of them had been to Djakarta and in general could only speak their local dialects. I wasn't even sure that they knew what we were talking about, but finally I had to be satisfied. Telling them that we'd be back in two days with a ship, we left.

★ ★ ★

Inland from Banten Bay is the West Javanese town of Serang, known only too well by the survivors of the *Perth* and *Houston* for it was here in the notorious Serang gaol that most of them after their capture by the Japanese had started their terms as POW's. Some had died there, the rest after an anxious few weeks were transferred to the Bicycle Camp, as the gaol in Batavia was called, for eventual distribution to various other hell-holes all over Asia. The road back to Djakarta passed through Serang and I wanted to photograph the prison as I knew the *Perth* survivors would be interested to see it again.

Sumantri wasn't at all keen on the idea, as apparently in Indonesia entering a gaol is not considered to be very smart, even if one goes in voluntarily and when I first suggested stopping he rolled his eyes in despair . . . it had been a long day and this was about the last straw.

Scammell, who had been tremendous during the past three weeks — unobtrusive, but always there when wanted — also thought I was being too ambitious. He was quite blunt about it. 'Hell boy', he said, 'you wouldn't even be allowed into the Adelaide Gaol, especially with a camera, let alone up here. They'll probably think you want to stir up trouble with the political prisoners and we'll all be invited to join 'em".

But it seemed worth a try, so prodding the unwilling Sumantri into action we drove round to the District

Director's office to have a go at obtaining the necessary permission.

The District Director turned out to be a reasonable chap who, once he understood the reason for us wanting to enter the gaol, immediately gave the okay, but back at the prison gates it was another story, for the Warden, a suspicious character, took some convincing.

Finally he let us in, but only after he had relieved Sumantri of his .45 automatic and posted half a dozen armed guards around us. There was some doubt about whom they were protecting, us or the prisoners, so rather quickly we took the photographs of the grim interior and then set off again on the slow hot trip to Djakarta.

It was well after dark even by the time we reached the outskirts of the city and driving to the Embassy we picked up Sumantri's jeep, but before going on to our own prison, the *Bergamahl* in Tanjong Priok Harbour, we called at the hotel to see if there was any mail.

Walking through the huge plate-glass doors into the air-conditioned luxury of the pub was like entering another world. It seemed incredible that this had been

Inside the Serang Gaol

Our daughters
Jane, Amanda, Susan and Cassie

ours only three weeks earlier and standing dirty and tired by the reception desk John and I felt almost belligerent towards the clean well-dressed businessmen who drifted from the dimly lit bar to their expensive evening meals in the restaurant alongside. At the desk there was a letter for each of us, plus a note to me from Freddie and a telegram. The telegram, from George Collett and my friends at the Norwood Apex Club, read 'Remember it's Bells not Belles in Sunda Strait'.

My letter which was from Ona, also contained messages from our four daughters.

Jane, the eldest, started off:

Dear Father,

I hope you are very successful in your search to find the bells of the HMAS *Perth* and the *Houston* . . . for your sake and ours.

Mandy, the second eldest, asked me to bring her home a tape recorder from Singapore for her birthday and Cassie, the youngest, just hoped I'd get the bells. It was our third daughter, Susan, whose message depressed me the most. She wrote:

Dear Daddy,

I hope you are feeling well. I have not had a bad day

at school. Please try hard to get the bells. We are all depending on you, so get the bells please. Sorry it is not a long letter but I cannot think of much.

Goodbye for now,

Yours truly, Susan.

P.S. Remember we are depending on you.

'Starve the bloody lizards', I thought, 'that's just great'. But it got worse.

John's letter, also from his wife, informed him that his son Mark had broken an arm at school and Freddie in his note, written before he left for Sumatra, suggested I write to the Indonesian Government relieving them of any responsibility in case I drowned myself.

Although not great drinkers Scammell and I decided it was about time we socked a couple. Collecting Sumantri we were half-way to the bar when I realised we didn't have any money. I'd given all I'd had on me to the village headman in Banten Bay.

We straggled dispiritedly towards the door but as we were about to go out we ran into Geoff Giles and John McLeay, another South Australian MHR on their way in.

This unexpected meeting was the cause of much celebration and not only did we spend an hour or two in the bar at the parliamentarians' expense, but it was like blowing a safety valve to relax for awhile and talk of things other than our own particular problems. Geoff Giles and John McLeay were on their way home after several weeks in Vietnam and as they also came from Adelaide there was plenty to talk about.

Later that night we bade them a rousing farewell and feeling quite rejuvenated, Scammell and I sang bawdy Australian songs to Sumantri all the way back to the ship.

★ ★ ★

As I understood it, part of my contract with the Indonesian Navy was to provision the *Aries* for her three to four weeks' voyage and as she had a crew of twelve, plus John and myself, the provisioning represented quite a project in itself.

I brought up the matter with the Commodore Wardiman, intending to ask his advice on what to purchase for the Indonesian sailors, but he wouldn't hear of it. 'You don't have to feed the crew' he said, 'that's our responsibility. But unless you want to eat rice all the time you're out there you had better obtain some food for yourself'.

I'd found out when buying food for our trip on the *Samudra* that the only place to purchase suitable tinned stores in Djakarta was from the Embassy canteen, but this had posed no problem as Freddie Sherborne was President of the Canteen Committee and had let me use his account.

Thanking the Commodore for his generosity and agreeing that John and I wouldn't want to survive on rice for a month, I asked him for the loan of his jeep so that I could go into the city and buy food from our Embassy. This didn't exactly thrill the Commodore as he wanted to use the jeep himself, but he let me have it on the condition that I was back within the hour. It didn't leave much time, as we could easily spend half an hour stuck in a Djakarata traffic jam, so with all haste I grabbed a driver and took off.

* * *

'You can't use the canteen without a Diplomatic Passport', he said. 'The trouble is you chaps come up here and think you can take over the place'. In Freddie's absence I was running foul of the Consul again. I sighed. He was probably right, no doubt there were rules and regulations that governed these things and in a way it embarrassed me to have to push him like this, for he was really a decent enough fellow.

'But can't I use Captain Sherborne's account?' I asked 'I'm sure he wouldn't mind, you see I've used it before'. But the Consul's reply clearly indicated that I was wasting my time. 'Not without his authority', he answered primly and I could feel the anger start to stir.

I knew most of the Embassy staff gave me no show of finding the ships and that to them I was just a bloody nuisance causing unnecessary trouble. This was fair enough and as much as possible I'd tried to keep out of their way, especially as it could put Freddie on the spot and after all he had to live there. In retrospect one realizes that no party is all right or all wrong and that in the black and white of the picture there must be some shades of grey. But unfortunately the Consul was my countryman; in fact he even came from South Australia and because of this I felt the restraint, which I'd been forced to exercise towards my Indonesian hosts during the past weeks, did not apply to him.

I could contain my frustration and anger no longer and like most people who lose their temper I proceeded to make a fool of myself telling the official a few home-truths and for a grand finale, although I forget now where I suggested he put it, I rudely told the Consul to 'stick his canteen'.

Back in the jeep I lit a cigarette and morosely contemplated the position in which I'd placed myself. It boiled down to the fact that while there had been certain satisfaction in my talk with the Consul, I still didn't have any stores and unless I thought of something pretty quickly, Scammell and I would be facing up to some fairly uninteresting meals.

There was really only one alternative worth trying, so giving the slumbering driver a nudge I asked him to take me to the American Embassy.

'Lieutenant-Commander Carr, please', I said to the

219

girl at the desk and as she turned away to ring him I did my best to smooth out my crumpled and not very clean shirt.

Jim Carr, the American Assistant Naval Attache, had been very good to John and me, asking us over to dinner a couple of times and generally taking an interest. He now represented my last resort on the food front.

'I'm sorry', the girl said coming back to me, 'but Lieutenant-Commander Carr is in conference and won't be able to see you for some time'.

'Bloody hell', I muttered, but the thought of eating nothing but rice pudding for a month urged me on.

'Would you tell him it's Dave Burchell', I said, forcing a smile and trying to make the name sound interesting, 'and it's most urgent'. I could see she was unimpressed, but reluctantly she rang again. This time Jim Carr said he would see me.

Up in his office Jim introduced me to his two visitors. One was a chap from State Department Washington, the other was a submarine Commander from Vietnam and as I sat down with them Jim handed me a cup of beautiful American coffee. 'Do you know what this crazy Australian is trying to do?' he said with a laugh and went on and told them of the diving in Sunda Strait. 'Tell me', he concluded, 'have you got a ship yet?' I explained the *Aries* as best I could and how because of the lack of echo-sounders we had made arrangements with the fishermen in Banten Bay. 'Don't discount the value of the fishermen', the Washington fellow said. 'It was fishermen who found the atomic bomb that was lost off the coast of Spain, even after the Metal Anomaly Detectors and other modern searching gear had failed to locate it'.

'Also keep an eye out for oil slick', the Commander added. 'There is still fuel oil coming up from the *Arizona* in Pearl Harbour and she was sunk over a year before the *Perth* and *Houston*.

This encouragement, although not much, represented about a 100 percent improvement on what I'd been getting and I thanked them. However being conscious of the limited time left with the Commodore's jeep I thought it best to come straight to the point.

'I have to provision the ship, Jim', I said, 'and it's only fair to tell you that my own Embassy won't have a bar of me, but can I buy some stores from you blokes?'

Carr laughed again. I could see I was making his day. 'Is that all you want?' he asked with a grin. 'Sure, help yourself, book it up to my account, you can fix me up when you get back'.

21

Although we had been up for over an hour, it was still dark when the ropes that moored the *Aries* to the *Bergamahl* were slipped and we slowly made our way past the brilliantly lit Pilgrim ships that formed the roads into Priok Harbour. In a way it was just as well, for the rusty unpainted old *Aries*, with twenty-seven lifejackets tied to her rails, would have presented a sorry picture in the daylight. As far as I could see the only reason we had twenty-seven lifejackets was that there wasn't room for twenty-eight, for I'd got the distinct impression that the crew were not over-confident in their ship.

Scammell, whose cautious approach to nautical matters back home had won him the title 'Captain Tuna . . . the Chicken of the Sea' made no bones at all about how he felt and for the first week he even slept in his lifejacket.

Also, although we didn't know of it at the time, Commodore Wardiman's conscience got the better of him to the extent that he detailed an officer to follow us along the coast in a jeep, his job being to view our progress continually through field-glasses and to report back immediately if the *Aries* disappeared.

As we cleared the harbour Sumantri mustered all hands on the small fo'c'sle as I wanted to tell them what was going on. There were two officers, three petty officers and seven seamen and as none of them could understand English Sumantri spoke for me. As he warmed up to the subject, he got a bit carried away, but perhaps it was a night for the dramatic. For this was Tangong Priok, one of the most historic seaports of the world and our course, set to thread initially through the

I make our two Bantenese fishermen
— Salim and Makri — Honorary Members
of the Underwater Explorers Club

vast Bay of a Thousand Islands, was following the long gone wakes of those two other ships whose unmarked graves we were now about to try to find.

Sumantri told the men that the eyes of Australia were upon them and that it was their duty as Indonesian sailors to assist in every way possible to make the search a success.

Listening, I looked around at the dark intent faces dimly reflected in the light from the wheelhouse and it seemed that John and I were a long way from home, not only in miles but in time as well. It was very moving and to me not over-dramatized at all, for although our boat was old and ill-equipped and we were relying on the memories of a few simple fishermen, somehow I felt confident and I knew we would succeed.

Late that afternoon we arrived in Banten Bay and as the *Aries* moved in behind Pandjang Island several dugout canoes, or prahus as the Indonesians call them, came out to meet us. First aboard the *Aries* was the

223

headman. He told Sumantri that his men had located a wreck and that in the morning they would take us out to where they had placed the buoys. From what he said the position seemed too far to the east, but it was a start.

None of us slept much, for it was hot and steamy close inshore where we'd anchored. To me the night appeared interminable. Lying on a mattress on the *Aries* foredeck I lay awake and worried. Still wound up from the effort of getting here at all, I felt I couldn't relax even though we were back at the diving area. True the ship had made the seventy mile journey, but how long would she last? Already there was an uneasy growling noise coming from her gearbox and we'd found that most of her other equipment was either badly worn or broken. Finally, telling myself I was worrying about things that were beyond my control anyway, I thought, 'Ah well, to hell with it, if the ship breaks down, it breaks down. We'll worry about it then.'

As it turned out, although plenty of other things broke, the old *Aries* engine with its groaning gearbox at no time let us down and not once during the three weeks we were out there did the Russian diesel miss a beat. Part of the credit for this phenomenon must go to the Russians, who designed the engine in the first place. But part must also go to the two Indonesian engineers who, sweating it out in the claustrophobic hot box that was the *Aries* engine room, alternatively coaxed and bullied the revs out of her.

* * *

Cautiously the helmsman edged the *Aries* up to the fishermen's buoy. Looking down from the comparative safety of the deck I felt a strong affinity for the yellow painted drum as it strained half submerged against the current, for it reminded me of a tired swimmer struggling to keep his head above water.

'Well, what do you think,' Sumantri asked as he squatted down beside me. 'Do you want to leave it for awhile? The current may ease up in an hour or so.'

I knew this was possible but it was also on the cards that it could even be stronger, as this was our experience on the *Samudra* when initially we'd tried working to the tide tables. Either we couldn't calculate them correctly or the tables were wrong, for each time the current was meant to be slack it invariably was running a banker. I'd already decided to disregard the currents as much as possible and couldn't see any point in hesitating now.

'No,' I replied, 'we won't wait, let's see what they've hooked.' Putting on my wet suit was a minor ordeal in itself. I couldn't remember ever having been so hot, the humidity was intense, the thick nylon-lined rubber of the suit suffocating and by the time I was geared up, complete with boots, gloves and hood, the sweat was running in rivulets. The reason for the full wet suit was not for warmth, its usual function, but for protection against coral and sea wasps, whose sting can be fatal. Also a full wet suit has a buoyancy factor of about ten pounds in salt water which is handy if an accident occurs and the diver has to swim on the surface for a prolonged period, for by dropping the weight belt you can float indefinitely. Along with the usual standard equipment I was also using an SOS decompression meter, an oil-filled diaphragmtype depth gauge, a Rolex Submariner watch with lapse time bezel and a heavy diver's knife which was in a sheath strapped to my leg.

The three Scubas we'd brought up from Australia were 72 cf 'Seabees', fitted with tensile type pressure gauges on the regulators so that I could tell at anytime, by sight or feel, the remaining air pressure in the cylinders. As we always used the dinghy when diving, we took one of the spare Scuba sets with us. The third was always kept on board the *Aries*.

Wasting no time once over the side of the dinghy I started the haul down the cable, which because of the current angled at about forty-five degrees and quivered like a piano wire. The water was dense with vegetable matter and plankton, which not only cut the visibility back to about ten feet but also made the cable slippery and difficult to grip. At a hundred feet by the depth gauge I was winded and my arms were so tired from pulling that I started to wonder what would happen when I'd have to let go. Levering forward I managed to rest after a fashion by hanging with my arms over the cable and there I was stuck, too weary to go up or down.

After a minute or two the hanging by my armpits became so uncomfortable that I had no option but to move and I pulled on down, slowly passing the 120 foot mark, then 130 with another brief stop and on again. At 160 feet a ship started to materialise around me from the grey fog.

I'd been so engrossed that I'd moved right into her without noticing the usual sign that a wreck is near, generally evidenced by the school fish attracted to the food provided by such an artificial reef.

Momentarily confused I scrabbled for a footing on her canted deck and as my foot came down something large and slimy clawed from under me. It was a four-foot Green turtle and as it frantically sculled away into the gloom, although there was no chance to discuss the point, it would have been a toss-up who had received the biggest fright.

The ship, which was a freighter, was lying on her starboard side and because of the shell holes and other visible damage, it seemed likely that she was one of the Japanese troop ships sunk by the *Perth* and *Houston*.

Letting the current take me, I skimmed across the deck up the bridge. It was burnt out, with the still

226

visible scars graphically indicating the fury and pain of her sinking. From the bridge I swam over her foredeck to the bow and then worked back aft. Even after all these years there was still evidence of the hasty departure of the crew. Her lifeboats were gone, with the exception of one whose smashed remnants were still hanging from the twisted davits. The anchors were still in place and the holds were packed with trucks and equipment.

Moving along the guard rail I went over the stern and swam down to her single propeller. It was a big skinny looking screw with blades about seven feet long and looking at it I couldn't help wondering again about that night when this propeller, along with so many others, had stopped its turning forever. I was struck with a feeling of sadness and would have liked to stay on and investigate this unknown ship, perhaps identifying her, as no doubt someone would be interested but there was no time. Gliding with the current I made my way back to the midships section and the shot line.

On the way I did manage to salvage one of her porthole rims and although the glass was gone, being solid brass it seemed to weigh a ton and was difficult to carry.

At the shot-line I started working to free the weight at the end of the cable, but found it was inextricably caught deep inside the ship. This presented several problems, for it not only meant the loss of one of our precious weights and about forty feet of cable, but as I had nothing with me to cut the wire I would have to go back up to the *Aries* and get a hacksaw. I wasn't overjoyed at the thought of the return trip, but there was no option as we couldn't afford to abandon the 200 feet or so of cable from the wreck to the buoy on the surface. Also instead of just tying the porthole to the weight and letting the chaps in the dinghy pull it up I'd have to carry it, as once the cable was cut and the strain released, the severed end could fly anywhere. I gave the wire a couple of savage jerks, but it wouldn't budge. Carefully I placed my arm through the rough marine growth encrusted porthole and hoisting it up onto my shoulder, started the angled haul back to the surface.

The second trip with the hacksaw wasn't much better than the first, but apart from nearly being decapitated when the cable suddenly parted after I'd all but despaired it ever would and a lonely blind swim back to the surface, the job was done.

On reaching the top I found that the current had swept me some distance from the ship. Fortunately my old mate Scammell was awake, he being more interested in what had happened to me than the crew who were engrossed in unravelling the tangled cable, but in spite of his prompt action by the time they picked me up I was exhausted and quite content to lie gasping on a matress on the *Aries* foredeck.

Sumantri, whose already evidenced interest in mattress bashing had moved John to nickname him the 'Kapok Kid', flopped down beside me. He lit up a cigarette and stuck it in my mouth. 'Well, Daddy,' he asked, 'what did you find?' He'd called me 'Daddy' ever since I'd shown him Susan's letter saying she was depending on me.

'It's a freighter,' I replied, puffing on the clove-scented Indonesian cigarette, 'probably a Japanese troop-ship. Would you thank the fishermen and tell them this is not the ship we're looking for. Ask them what else they've got.'

He ambled off aft with the message, engaging in a brief scuffle with John as they passed each other in the narrow waist of the *Aries*.

Scammell had been working on the porthole recovered from the freighter and as he carried it forward I could see he'd already cleaned most of the marine growth from it. Closer inspection showed why I was

228

able to break the rim away from the ship's bulkhead so easily. About half the circumference was sharp and jagged where the heat of the fire had melted the brass and fortunately the mountings securing the frame to the ship were nearly gone.

We entered the dive in the log, noting the bearings and describing the ship as an unidentified Japanese troop-ship of about two or three thousand tons.

'The fishermen say there is a big ship further to the east,' Sumantri said, collapsing again. 'Do you want to move over to it?' 'To the East,' I exclaimed, experiencing an uneasy feeling at the increasing enormity of the search. 'Hell, that will place us miles from the *Perth*'s reported bearings. Haven't they anything a bit more to the west?'

Sumantri shrugged. 'That's all they seem to know of,' he replied with a yawn.

'Okay, let's go,' I said, sitting up and stretching, 'but don't hurry. According to the decompression meter I won't be able to dive again for about five hours.'

22

The Bantanese fishermen never ceased to amaze me the way they could drop onto a wreck with visual bearings. Over the years I'd had enough experience at it to know just how difficult this medium can be, where the slightest error can mean ending up hundreds of yards off target, especially when the cross bearings are a mountain or a headland twenty miles away. However to these chaps it was a piece of cake and full of confidence they manoeuvred their dugouts to the required spot.

After about half an hour of battling with the current, the second wreck was hooked with one of my spare weights attached to a thin nylon line and when all was ready I again went over the side of the dinghy. The current had increased to an estimated five knots and as much as I tried I couldn't pull down against it. The thin nylon line kept slipping through my hands and finally I was forced to give it away, not even being able to get under the surface.

Winded, I hung onto the side of the dinghy and talked the situation over with John. He was suggesting we leave it and come back in the morning when the current should be less strong, but I was all for trying again with a thicker rope.

At that moment the weight of the loaded dinghy proved too much for the light line and with a twang it parted. At this sudden release the dinghy took off down Sunda Strait with the *Aries*, after a slow start as she had to turn around, in hot pursuit.

By the time we arrived back over the wreck everyone was pretty sick of the deal, but I badgered Sumantri into asking the fishermen to try again as I was anxious to identify the ship which I felt was another freighter so that we could leave it and work more to the west. After some trouble manoeuvring the fishermen again hooked the wreck, this time using a half-inch diameter rope and a ten-pound shot. The day was very hot and even underwater it wasn't much better, for the sea was warm and thick with the porridge-like plankton sticking to the rope, making it slippery against my rubber gloves.

At about 150 feet the school fish started to appear and I knew I was nearly there. The fish, which were grey with yellow backs and tails and about eighteen inches long, hung in thick clouds. I stopped to check my instruments and made a routine survey. All was well and I started off again, cautiously, eyes probing ahead and around for signs of the wreck.

For awhile nothing, then from out of the grey mist a ship started to take shape under me. At first it was just a confused pattern of steel plates and rivets, and I couldn't recognise any more or form a mental picture of how she was lying. Moving on I realised the ship was on her port side and that the weight at the end of the line must have caught on something beyond her.

The visibility was improving now, more than twenty feet and I could make out the shape of her propeller with the rope leading straight to it. This was better than I'd hoped, for once on the propeller it should be easy enough to find hand-holds to work back to the hull.

The last few feet were like a nightmare, the propeller wouldn't seem to come any closer no matter how hard I pulled against the current and I was just about finished by the time I moved in behind the protection of the huge blade.

After awhile I stood on the drive shaft and inspected the propeller. It was larger than the one on the freighter we'd found that morning, with the blades more clover shaped. Taking hold of the edge I peered out into the current, immediately springing back, in my haste almost losing my footing. There was a shark pack gliding along in line astern making straight for me!

They were heart-stoppers and I don't mind admitting that the sight of them chilled me to the marrow.

Pressing back against the blade of the propeller I watched as they circled, counting them. There were six and each one looked lean and fast and had cold swivelling eyes. I reckoned that I was safe enough where I was, but I couldn't stay there. The only escape from the sharks seemed to be the rope, stretching away into the fog across the hull. It looked awfully open and unprotected and after first checking my air supply, I looked around quickly for possible alternatives.

It was then, almost at the limit of visibility, that I saw the second propeller. I experienced a chill far more sudden and severe than that brought on by the sight of the sharks. This was no freighter! Twin propellers on the starboard side could mean only one thing . . . This was a four-screw ship, a warship and the only warships in the area were the *Perth* and *Houston*.

For a moment my mind was numbed and crouching down on the shaft I stared at the metal without really seeing it, rubbing at it with my hand and blinking unbelievingly. It was all too quick to comprehend. I was like a boxer who had mentally conditioned himself for a hard fifteen round bout, only to find that he'd won by a knockout in the first.

As my mind cleared there came a feeling of almost overpowering awe at the knowledge of where I was, together with a strong sensation of trespass which made me doubt my right to be there.

But this was a natural reaction and was as it should be, and I knew that if I were going to finish the job this psychological hurdle had to be overcome like any other problem. I looked again at the drive-shaft, this time seeing it in detail. Which one was she? The question seemed to leap at me. Was this the *Perth*'s outer starboard prop I was on, or was it one of the older but larger *Houston*'s? I had to know the answer. A check of my air supply and instruments showed I had another ten minutes. With luck there was time.

There was still the shark pack, but my attitude towards it had now changed. Having found one of my ships somehow gave me courage. The sharks were the intruders, not I and by the time I was ready to move I'd worked up a hate against them.

To reach the hull I had to cover ten feet or so of open water, so waiting for a break in their picket line, I leapt across. Unfortunately one of the sharks had got out of sequence with its circling and as I sprang from behind the protection of the blade we very nearly collided. My karate-like yell was a hundred percent fright, despite my new-found courage, but it served its purpose and the shark nearly slipped a disc in its effort to avoid contact.

Working slowly up the hull, using anything I could find for hand-holds against the current, I noticed the sharks' interest was much less aggressive and by the time I'd reached the deck line they had disappeared altogether.

Grasping the edge of the deck, I peered through the porridge-like sea at the superstructure. It was eerie and ghost-like in its stillness and difficult to identify. Although realizing that because of its size and complexity a quick identification may not be possible, I started to moe aft in the hope of finding something specific. After moving about twenty feet I looked upwards and for the third time that morning I froze. Above me, like two dark outstretched arms were the guns.

I knew the *Perth*'s guns were twin six-inch and that the *Houston* had triple eight-inch. From where I was I

233

H.M.A.S. *PERTH*

As she now lies sunk in Sunda Strait

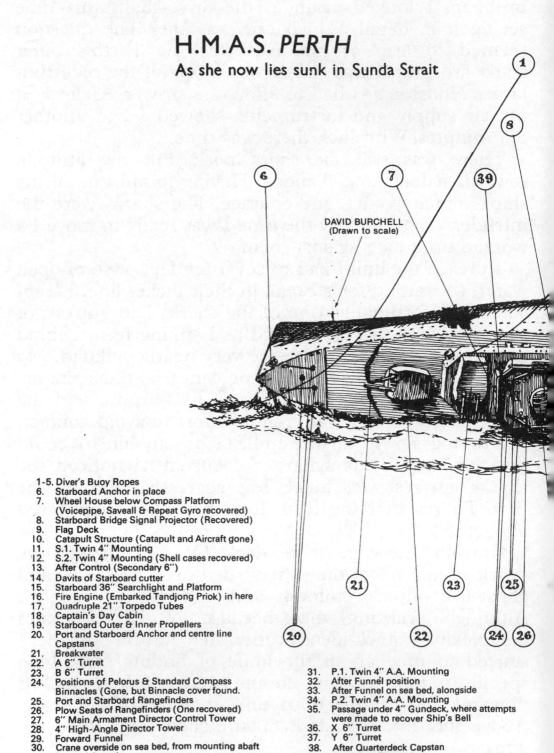

DAVID BURCHELL
(Drawn to scale)

1-5. Diver's Buoy Ropes
6. Starboard Anchor in place
7. Wheel House below Compass Platform
    (Voicepipe, Saveall & Repeat Gyro recovered)
8. Starboard Bridge Signal Projector (Recovered)
9. Flag Deck
10. Catapult Structure (Catapult and Aircraft gone)
11. S.1. Twin 4" Mounting
12. S.2. Twin 4" Mounting (Shell cases recovered)
13. After Control (Secondary 6")
14. Davits of Starboard cutter
15. Starboard 36" Searchlight and Platform
16. Fire Engine (Embarked Tandjong Priok) in here
17. Quadruple 21" Torpedo Tubes
18. Captain's Day Cabin
19. Starboard Outer & Inner Propellers
20. Port and Starboard Anchor and centre line
    Capstans
21. Breakwater
22. A 6" Turret
23. B 6" Turret
24. Positions of Pelorus & Standard Compass
    Binnacles (Gone, but Binnacle cover found.
25. Port and Starboard Rangefinders
26. Plow Seats of Rangefinders (One recovered)
27. 6" Main Armament Director Control Tower
28. 4" High-Angle Director Tower
29. Forward Funnel
30. Crane overside on sea bed, from mounting abaft
    forward funnel

31. P.1. Twin 4" A.A. Mounting
32. After Funnel position
33. After Funnel on sea bed, alongside
34. P.2. Twin 4" A.A. Mounting
35. Passage under 4" Gundeck, where attempts
    were made to recover Ship's Bell
36. X 6" Turret
37. Y 6" Turret
38. After Quarterdeck Capstan
39. Coral "tree" growth

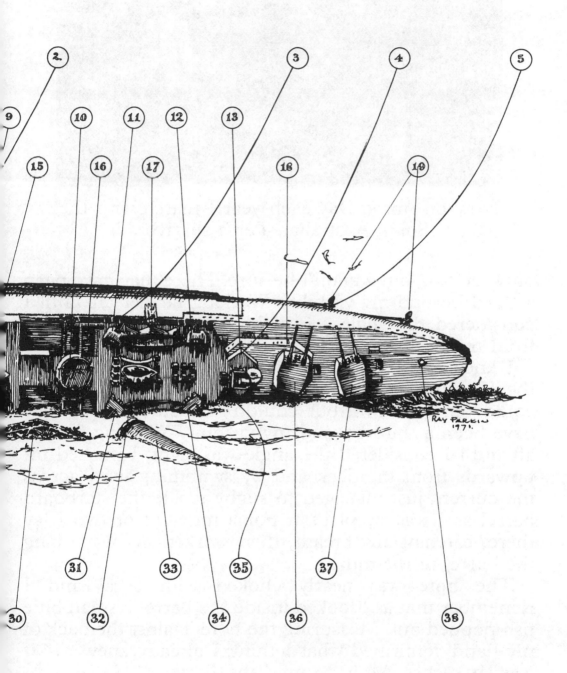

RAY PARKIN
1971.

Now on Anzac Day each year I march with the
South Australian *Perth* survivors

only see two, but couldn't be sure. There may have been
a third beyond my visibility. Working farther aft until I
considered the angle was right, I pushed off upwards
from the deck and by swimming hard across

I knew the *Perth*'s guns were twin six-inch and that
the *Houston* had triple eight-inch. From where I was I
could only see two, but couldn't be sure. There may
have been a third beyond my visibility. Working farther
aft until I considered the angle was right, I pushed off
upwards from the deck and by swimming hard across
the current just managed to rugby tackle the starboard
barrel as I was swept past. For a moment or two I lay
there, catching my breath, then worked my way along
the barrel to the muzzle.

The bore was nearly choked with coral and I
remember that as I looked inside the barrel a small blue
fish popped out. Measuring the bore against the back of
my hand confirmed what I think I already knew . . . it
was six inches. We had found the *Perth*.

23

During the next ten dives I made surveys, using the knowledge gained to form a mental picture of the ship. The huge bulk of her made this task difficult, for being nearly 200 yards long and 100 feet from keel to compass platform the *Perth* was about the size of a city block and with the visibility down to twenty feet I found it hard at times even to work out where I was.

But we kept at it, first placing several buoys along her whole length, finally ending up with five. These were spaced at about 100 foot intervals and when each new one was in place I'd dive and survey that particular area.

It was slow and frustrating work. The ropes we were using for shot-lines were old and rotten and the first two mornings we found that during the night the ropes had broken and that the buoys were gone. The fishermen would obligingly find the wreck and we'd start again. After finally deciding that the ropes were useless, we spent time unravelling the steel cable used for the dive on the freighter. That held all right and we started to build up the row of buoys again.

Eventually the completed mental picture showed that the *Perth* was lying on her port side, with her bow strangely enough pointing east back towards Djakarta and away from Sunda Strait and the freedom she was so desperately seeking.

Deep in the starboard side of her hull, approximately under 'A' turret, there was a gaping hole about forty feet across, but the rest of her visible side was undamaged with even most of the glass still intact in the scuttles.

The six inch turrets were all in place, with 'A' turret's guns trained forward, the starboard gun elevated and the port gun depressed. 'B' turret was trained hard to port with the gun muzzles stuck in the sand and on the quarter-deck 'X' and 'Y' turrets were pointing about forty-five degrees to starboard. Up forward, her anchors were in place and the characteristic cruiser bow still swept down in one clean unbroken line. The Walrus aeroplane had gone, but the retrieving crane with its open-web steelwork was lying on the sea bed beside the ship.

On the four-inch gun deck the barrels pointed in all directions, with 'S2' turret at least having received a direct hit, as several live rounds bent at right angles were lying inside.

The port torpedo quad was under the ship and I couldn't reach it, but on the starboard side the four tubes were empty with the muzzles slightly trained out and in some of the places I rubbed with my glove, the brasswork was still shiny under the thin film of calcified marine growth that covered it.

On the deck near the aft control was a vehicle that I first took to be a truck, but which turned out to be some sort of fire fighting unit. I inspected its tyres, they were Dunlops and still seemed to be inflated.

On the upper bridge the damage was more evident. The standard compass and most of the other navigational instruments were gone and there were several shell holes in the deck.

Along the front of the bridge the groups of voice tubes showed shrapnel damage, but the stainless steel handles for winding up the weather screens were untouched and glinted dully through the grey green water.

The bridge held a strong fascination for me and I never tired of spending time there, visualizing the scenes that must have taken place on it. The spit and polish of the peace-time days, when as HMS *Amphion* she was one of the most up-to-date cruisers in the Royal Navy.

The desperate times, when as a member of the 7th Cruiser Squadron she had distinguished herself so well in the Mediterranean in the battles of Matapan, Greece and Crete. The less hectic period of convoy duty in the Pacific and final days and nights in the Java Sea. In my imagination I could see her various Captains and other personnel, who had lived, fought and at the last died, on this small patch of deck.

On the starboard side of the bridge, growing from out of the guard rail and defying the current, was a magnificent spray of Gorgonia coral. It was over six feet across and because of the depth it looked grey in colour, but in fact was probably orange or dark red. I was always careful not to damage it, for although the ship is now still and the mortal remains of the men she took down with her have long since gone, I felt the coral spray represented a living tribute to the memory of both the ship and the men.

After the survey dives were completed we began a serious search for the bell.

The position in which the ship was lying meant that the Quartermaster's lobby, in which the bell was meant to be kept, would be right underneath her and the first approach was to try to move in under the port side of the quarter-deck and find the door leading inside the ship.

With this in mind, I swam down over the four-inch gun deck to the sea bed and then worked aft along the quarter-deck housing. There was a gap about three feet high between the built up sand and what had been the top of the quarter-deck superstructure and swimming through this I entered a restricted cave-like area right under the ship.

Inside it was dark and still and I was conscious of the 7000 tons of ship on top of me. Also I missed the bustle and company of the current. However, when my eyes had grown accustomed to the gloom, I could see there was company of a different kind and I warily watched the three or four large groper whose home I'd invaded.

Contrary to popular opinion tropical groper, while being big and ugly, are not normally dangerous. But they are unpredictable and it would have been unwise to upset them in the confined area we were sharing, as they were bigger than a man and probably weighed well over 300 pounds. Waiting quietly, I watched as one by one they moved away into the black recesses of the ship and when finally satisfied that they had gone I turned over and started a close inspection of the quarter-deck housing, which was now acting as a ceiling to the cave.

Being out of the current's cleansing influence the weed growth was more prolific under the ship than on the open areas outside, making the search for the door in the lobby difficult. Working carefully over each square foot I slowly moved deeper and deeper under the ship, not realizing that my progress was being watched with interest and no doubt, growing alarm by yet another resident of this quiet eerie backwater. During a routine check I glanced over my shoulder and found I was practically eye to eye with a very agitated octopus.

Unlike the groper which can be almost stupidly curious, the octopus is generally extremely timid and if given half a chance will jet smartly off when disturbed. But unwittingly I'd backed this chap into a corner and he had nowhere to go. For a moment or two we regarded each other. He was big and evil-looking and from the tentacle that was nervously flicking out I estimated he was all of fifteen feet across. There was never any question as to who was going to give way and cautiously I backed off, deciding that the door to the lobby wouldn't be in that direction anyway.

In the attempt to find the bell I made six separate dives in under the ship. The groper soon became accustomed to the intrusion, finally taking no notice of me at all and at times in the cramped area I even

240

bumped into them. Only at my touch would they move haughtily away, their huge down-turned mouths registering disapproval like a group of dowagers disturbed at their afternoon tea. I didn't see the octopus again but I knew he was there and in my imagination I could feel him watching and wondered if I worried him as much as he did me.

The area was lonely and claustrophobic and not without danger and it was always with a feeling of relief that I'd leave when my time was up and swim through the narrow opening into the relative brightness outside.

I found the door on the fourth dive. It was closed tight with all the locking handles dogged. I tried time after time to open it, using a hammer and a crowbar, but couldn't and finally I was forced to accept the fact that as far as I was concerned the *Perth*'s bell was irretrievable.

To get so close, almost within a few feet and not be able to reach it was a great disappointment. But we had no option and reluctantly I decided to leave the quarter-deck to concentrate on other areas, in hope of finding suitable artefacts to take back home.

John was pleased enough at the decision, for although he too was disappointed about the bell, he was never keen on the dives under the ship. His only indication that I was okay during his anxious waits up in the dinghy was the sight of my bubbles hitting the surface. But when I was under the ship these would be trapped and he would have no idea for ten minutes or so how I was going and if in his opinion I stayed a bit too long I was always sure to get a verbal blast as he hauled me back on board.

For the first week or so, after the diving for each day was completed, we would return inshore and anchor in the small bay fronting the village of our two fishermen. Gradually the villagers' initial shyness disappeared until finally John and I were accepted as part of the scene. We found they were friendly simple people, but they had their own strict code of ethics, evidenced the day Sumantri told me that our fishermen, Salim and Makri, wanted to leave us and go back to their fishing. As we didn't need their help anymore, the *Perth* being now securely buoyed, I said 'Okay, ask them how much I owe them?'

Sumantri grinned, as if anticipating the question. 'They don't want any money', he said. 'They say that as you have worked so hard on this they want to be part of it as well. They have talked it over with the headman and that's their decision.'

I was mighty impressed. Although the money was not a large sum by our standards, it was more than the fishermen could hope to save in twelve months. We had given them small gifts and cigarettes, but not knowing their language had made it difficult to communicate. I think the fact that they realized the importance of the dive pleased me more than anything else, for I knew that with this knowledge the appreciation to them of their own contribution must naturally follow.

'Hell, that's tremendous', I said to Sumantri, 'but they can't afford to do that. Tell them I appreciate their thought very much and that without their help the *Perth* would never have been found, but that I insist on paying them.'

Feeling that the fishermen's departure warranted some recognition we dressed the ship, draping the red and white flag of the Republic of Indonesia across the front of the wheelhouse and set up the compressor crate as a table on the foredeck. All the boys turned out in their number one uniforms and with Sumantri acting as interpreter I made a speech of appreciation to Salim and Makri.

After giving them the money, which I'd discreetly placed in an envelope, I also presented them with an old pair of Fletcher Jones pants, my spare pair of dark glasses, fifty kilos of rice and some soap. By the time John dobbed in a couple of shirts and a tube of Golden Eye Ointment for Salim's conjunctivitis, they thought they were made. To round it off I made them both members of the Underwater Explorers Club, taking great care to write their names correctly on the certificates.

Salim replied, thanking us for the gifts and stating that he and Makri would always be ready to help us and amid much hand shaking we put them ashore on the beach at their village.

South from St Nicholas Point down Sunda Strait is the large seaport town of Merak which we made the home base for our operations. It was here that we refuelled, maintained contact with Djakarta over the Port Authority's telephone and purchased fresh provisions from the well-stocked markets. Merak is also the turn-around point for the two ships that daily ferried the thousands of travellers crossing the strait between Java and Sumatra. I could never find out just what caused this mass commutation of people, but guessed that with a population of over 120 million a few would always be on the move.

One ferry, the *Bukit Barisan*, named after a mountain in North Sumatra, arrived every morning and the other the *Krakatoa* would arrive in the afternoon.

They were both sizeable ships of about 2000 tons and were invariably loaded to the gunwhales with passengers. As there was only half an hour allowed for the turn around it didn't leave much time to unload six hundred people and freight and reload for the return trip. But everyone lined up three wide in a cheerful queue and in no time it seemed they were all loaded and the ferry would be gone.

At the wharf in Merak one day the ferry *Krakatoa* had loaded her human freight and was ready for the trip across the strait to Sumatra. She gave the usual blast on the foghorns indicating that she was about to cast off and apart from wincing at the noise as we were tied up in front of her, we took no notice.

It was only at the unaccustomed second two blasts that we looked up from our work on the *Aries* and saw that a prahu, which had been heading down Sunda Strait for Merak, was now at anchor with sails furled and was lying across the entrance to the small harbour. She was blocking the *Krakatoa's* path and the Captain, who was an impatient man, was telling the crew of the prahu to shift.

But they took no notice and her decks remained deserted. Up on the bridge of the *Krakatoa* the Captain produced a heavy sub-machine-gun and without any fuss or further warning started firing bursts into the water a few feet from the prahu's stern. To this there was an immediate response and as the crew swarmed all over her, the prahu's anchors were up and the sails unfurled in the blink of an eye. But even then she didn't move fast enough to suit the Captain and as she slowly got underway, in an effort to assist, he kept boring it up her with the machine-gun.

As the bullets whizzed over our heads, Scammel and I along with the rest of the crew lay flat on the *Aries* deck. We caught each other's eye and Scammell grinned. 'Hardly the Manly ferry leaving Circular Quay,' he said.

The travellers on the ferries intrigued us and John and I never tired of watching them as they filed past. Generally we were refilling the Scuba cylinders on the *Aries* foredeck and I suppose with our diving gear lying around we were of as much interest to them as they were to us. Sometimes they asked a question of our crew, obviously inquiring who we were and the sailor on watch would answer in Indonesian with 'Australia' being the only word we could pick out.

★ ★ ★

244

I was sitting on the wharf at Merak patching the knee of my wetsuit one day when Sumantri sat down opposite.

'Do you live here?' he asked politely. I nodded.

'Yes', I replied. 'My name is Daddy. I was born in Merak. It was many years ago, even before the little yellow men came.'

'I suppose you think I'm just a simple fisherman', he continued idly, throwing pebbles into the water. I agreed that he certainly looked simple, but he carried on as if not hearing at the same time drawing his right leg up under him.

'Actually, I'm 007 Dave, the famous one-legged Australian skin diver,' he said, 'no doubt you've heard of me.' He could continue in this vein indefinitely and we were always changing identities.

Another time as I was recuperating after a particularly hard dive, he came to where I was lying on the mattress and swooping down plucked a clump of hair from my chest. Oblivious to my surprised yell he inspected the hair closely.

'What's this?' he asked, puzzled. 'Australian wool?'

Resignedly I relaxed again. 'Yes', I said, 'and what's more it's AAA quality.'

'Is that so', he exclaimed in an interested tone, then selecting one of the few hairs growing on his shin he pulled it out and offering it to me proudly said, 'Well this is Indonesian nylon.'

He had also invented a percentage system to mark our degree of success, or lack of it, in the attempts to recover the bell. When we first found *Perth* he gave me a fifty percent chance. This improved to sixty percent after the first few relics came up, but as the days went by and no bell appeared my ratings dropped steadily.

★   ★   ★

We soon settled into a routine on board the *Aries*, this being timed around the two dives a day that I was able to make. Early each morning after leaving Merak we'd head up the Strait to the diving area, the idea being to get the first dive in by seven o'clock so that the second could be made at about one or two. Then in the mid-afternoon, with the diving for the day finished, we would return to Merak and while the crew refuelled the *Aries* from one of the ferries, John and I would fill the Scuba cylinders with the compressor and prepare for the next day's work. Generally our first indication that another day was about to dawn was when the cook's offsider placed a mug of thick Javanese coffee on the deck by our heads. One sip of this and the eyes involuntarily snapped wide open. Once I made the mistake of drinking some at night, paying for it by lying awake for hours until the effects had worn off.

The meals that John prepared from the American stores were pretty terrible. It wasn't entirely Scammell's fault although I don't think he'd win too many Oscars as a chef, but rations were short and we had to augment them with large dollops of rice to eke things out.

In an effort to give the rice a bit more kick, but to the horrified fascination and disbelief of the crew, he would mix apricot jam with it and spinkle cut up bananas on top. We didn't think it was too bad, but to the Indonesians this bastardisation of perfectly good rice, the staple diet of countless millions of Asians, was beyond the pale and although we offered them some on numerous occasions, not even Sumatri would touch it. We sent one of the *Aries* officers, Lieutentant Abdul Kahar, to Djakarta with the news that the *Perth* had been found. Apparently I had been forgiven by the Australian Embassy, for upon his return we found that with the congratulatory messages were two tins of condensed milk.

Sumantri also left us for a few days, as he had been

recalled to Djakarta by Commodore Wardiman to report on our operations. This left us without an interpreter as no one else in the crew could speak English, but with the Australian-Indonesian dictionary that I'd bought before leaving home we got by.

The main problem I found was in the pronunciation of words, for while the Indonesian is very staccato in his speech, Australians, although we deny it, tend to drawl and use the broad 'a'. I'd already had a couple of instances of this. Once was when Djoko Suyatno asked me my first name. When I told him it was Dave he said delightedly, 'Well, that's appropriate, Dive the diver.'

Another time was during my first trip to Djakarta, when ordering a meal in the restaurant at the hotel I introduced myself to the chap sitting opposite, adding that I was an Australian.

'You didn't have to tell me where you came from', he said in a heavy American drawl. 'As soon as you ordered your 'styke' I knew you were an Australian.'

While I gave the Yank a big cheerio for his trouble, I was forced to accept the fact that apparently we do have an accent and to make the crew of the *Aries* understand me at all I had to change my pronounciation dramatically. A word like Djakarta for instance, that in Australia we would pronounce Ja-car-dar, the Indonesian pronounce Ja-co-ta. They also fool around with their 'ues' and 'oes' and mostly the 'd' is silent altogether.

Every afternoon the men would gather on the tiny foredeck and with the aid of a dictionary and many drawings I'd tell them what had happened during the dives that morning down on the *Perth*. By the time Sumantri came back we were getting quite good at it and he was rather put out when we jokingly told him he wasn't needed anymore.

The *Aries* and her crew

24

The first dive down the number one buoy cable revealed that the shot at the end of the line had pulled clear of the ship and was resting on the sand some ten to fifteen feet off the *Perth's* bow. Kneeling on the sea bed I heaved at the heavy weight in an effort to shift it back. It wasn't that the weight itself was so heavy, but the current dragging at the buoy on the surface and the attached 300 feet or so of cable made it difficult to handle.

Finally I decided to leave the shot where it was and turning my attention back to the ship curiously studied the unfamiliar head-on view. I remember being struck by her enormous bulk. For the bow, rearing up from the sea floor like some huge canted cliff, disappeared out of sight in the fog above completely dwarfing me.

On impulse I decided to try to swim the complete length of her. The current was right and if the distance proved too great and I ran out of time I could ascend any one of the four buoy cables between me and the stern. Then once on the surface it wouldn't be difficult to attract the attention of the crew in the dinghy, who could abandon their position at the number one buoy and pick me up.

Pushing off from where the *Perth's* bow dipped into her keel I worked diagonally across the hull, skirting the torpedo hole under 'A' turret and making the deckline at a point just aft of the starboard anchor. To the left ran the neat row of scuttles along the ship's side and following these I moved on aft. About the position of the seamen's mess deck I started peering into each porthole, but the inside of the ship was dark and still I couldn't identify anything specific.

249

I thought of Perc Partington a real character, who now lived in Adelaide. He had been a bandsman in the *Perth* and just before I left home he said, 'If you do find the ship, go to my locker on the mess deck. There's a hundred quid in notes in it.'

I didn't think there would be much left of the money by now, although when Mac Lawrie dived on the USS *Peary* eighteen years after she was sunk in Darwin Harbour, he brought up all sorts of things. Included in these were some old 78 rpm phonograph records featuring the Andrew Sisters and although the records were warped and a bit scratchy they still played.

Leaving the row of portholes I swam up past 'B' turret, pausing a moment at the turret's open door to reflect on who perhaps had been the last to use it a quarter of a century before, and to wonder further if this unknown sailor had survived the holocaust that must have met him as he stepped outside. From 'B' turret, with the current behind me, I soared up the front face of the Bridge structure past the open scuttles of the wheelhouse, up and over the compass platform weather screens and onto the bridge itself.

As I sat down on the brass plow-type seat of the starboard rangefinder I noticed that it moved slightly and I made a mental note to come back on a subsequent dive to see if it could be recovered. But realising that I'd have to keep moving as I'd only covered about a third of the ship's length, I let go of the rangefinder and the current picked me up again. Together we swept the length of the bridge and then over the flag deck from where I angled down across the flow, and again stopped by grasping one of the two davits that once had held the starboard cutter but which now stood empty from out of the ship's side.

Moving on past the mid-ship section where the forward deck line steps down on to the waist of the ship, I made another quick inspection of the fire-fighting unit which was jammed in behind one of the characteristic lattice-like supports for the deck above. From this point I crossed back over the upper deck to see if there was any trace of the Walrus aeroplane that had once roosted there, for I'd promised Jock McDonough the pilot of the *Walrus*, that I'd try to find his plane and if possible bring part of it back for him. But although I searched the area where it should have been, there was no sign of the gallant old crate. It must have been swept away by the force of the water pouring and tearing over the hull when the *Perth* made her last plunge.

However, the heavy recovery crane, used for retrieving the *Walrus* from the sea after her chancy flights, was lying on the sea bed beside the ship and I swam the length of it in the hope of finding some small part that I could take home for Jock. But the crane's construction of open-web steelwork offered nothing readily removable and I had to leave it empty-handed.

Just as I was about to swim back to the main hull my attention was attracted by a large smooth object to the right, which not only towered above me but disappeared out of sight in both directions along the sea floor. Moving towards it I approached with caution, for somehow its very shape and smoothness made it appear foreign, causing me for some reason to become suspicious.

It was not until I was right up to it that I recognised what it was and snorted with amusement at letting my imagination run away with me, for the ominous looking object was nothing more sinister than the aft funnel.

Following the funnel out along the sand to its end, I grasped the rim and peered inside. It was surprising to see the mass of pipes that nearly filled it, as I'd always thought of a ship's funnel being a hollow tube like a factory chimney. It now provided a home for dozens of small fish, which darted nervously back at my unexpected appearance and as I watched them swim

251

around in their snug apartment I thought of the workmen on the Clyde who had originally made this thing of rivets and steel. Even in their wildest imagination they could not have had any conception of its ultimate use.

Making my way back along the top surface of the funnel I was surprised to see that a large spotted ray was accompanying me. He was about ten feet across and although his sudden appearance gave me a start, I couldn't help but admire the grace and ease with which he moved. The ray, soon bored by my slow awkward pace as I battled with the cross current, left me to plod on alone and I was thankful enough to reach the ship again and make use of the handholds her superstructure offered.

Passing over the four-inch gun deck I inspected the torpedo quads underneath it, noticing that the four tubes still retained a certain look of deadliness which even the encrusted covering of coral failed to hide.

Reaching the quarter-deck I drifted with the current, looking upwards until the guns of 'X' turret came into view. It was here that I'd first joined the ship when I came up over the side from the propeller and which ironically was the same place that Harry Knight told me he'd left her twenty-five years before.

On the starboard side of the quarter-deck is a door leading into the passage which once serviced the Captain's cabin and the wardroom. The door is open and the passage, now more like a lift-well because of the angle at which the ship is lying, is dark and choked with debris. I didn't realize it at the time, but this door corresponds with the one for which I spent so much time searching on the port side.

Apparently the two doors are linked by the passage, for although it angles around in places and involves a couple of water-tight bulkheads, it does run from one side of the ship to the other.

Perhaps it is just as well that I wasn't aware of this as I would have been tempted to use the passage in an effort to reach the bell and although I could have possibly cleared a path down and taken a shot-line with me to have something to follow on the way out, it may have been foolhardy to attempt it on my own. Especially as it had already been established that at least one octopus was in residence in the area.

Turning away from the door I checked my air supply and instruments. They showed that it was time to leave and I moved across to the number five buoy cable and started the ascent. About twenty feet up I stopped and looking back realised how much my feelings toward this ship had changed since our first meeting.

Initially she had overawed me, for then she reminded me of a famous woman known to the world as a proud and well-groomed beauty, but who at the peak of her fame had completely disappeared under a veil of mystery from the world scene. Then twenty-five years later, with her looks gone and her hair tangled and matted she had suddenly been rediscovered. Maimed and caught unprepared, she was unable to even raise her head from the mud or flee from the curious eyes of this unexpected intruder and I was embarrassed for her.

But during subsequent dives this impression altered as I learned to see her in a new and different kind of beauty.

For where it once had been Carmen-like in its flashing fierceness, now her charm was of a calmer nature and where originally it had been her function and duty to destroy life, now like an oasis in this sea-bed desert her whole being supported it.

If anything, rather than being embarrassed, I was now even more proud of her.

25

One afternoon, just before the fishermen left, we were sprawled in the shade of a verandah in their village. Wishing to start the search for the *Houston*, I asked the headman if he, or any of his people, knew of other ships sunk in the vicinity of the *Perth*. With Sumantri acting as interpreter they listened intently as I told them of the *Houston* and of how this great ship had come to be in their waters.

Originally the pride of the American peace-time fleet, the *Houston* had also been a favourite with President Franklin Roosevelt and was often called the President's Yacht because of the many holidays he spent aboard her.

Shortly before Pearl Harbour the *Houston*, which was the flagship of the American Asiatic Fleet, left Shanghai for the Philippines, but when the Japanese landed she was forced to withdraw to Java. Initially as she steamed south to escape the enemy she was in the company of her sister ships *Boise* and *Marblehead*, but was left to run the gauntlet on her own after these two cruisers were put out of commission by Japanese aircraft.

Under almost continuous air attack during the lonely trip her commander, Captain Albert Rooks, eventually made contact with the Allied Forces in Java and the *Houston* joined the ABDA Fleet, a hastily thrown together group of American, British, Dutch and Australian ships, doomed to failure it seemed because of language and communication problems.

Following the battle of the Java Sea during which the ill-fated ABDA Fleet was reduced to two ships, the rest being either sunk or put out of commission, the

Houston together with *Perth* made a desperate dash to Sunda Strait again in an effort to escape. But along with the *Perth* in the early hours of 1 March 1942 and after a fierce engagement with the Japanese fleet supporting the troop landings in Banten Bay, the USS *Houston* was sunk off St Nicholas Point, West Java. Captain Rooks and some five hundred of the ship's company died with her.

At the conclusion of this brief outline of the American cruiser's history, the headman told me that when the battle of Sunda Strait started his people had fled up the mountainside behind the village and from their vantage point overlooking the bay had witnessed the entire action.

From what he said the allied cruisers never stood a chance. Surrounded and out-gunned by the enemy, they were hit with torpedo attacks from destroyers, pounded by cruisers and bombed by aircraft. In the illumination provided by the enemy searchlights, the Bantenese could see the planes diving again and again with the tracer bullets bouncing off the decks of the two ships as they were raked with shell and machine-gun fire.

In the morning following the battle the headman said that some of the survivors from our ships were actually swept by the currents into Banten Bay with the invading forces and although the survivors were unarmed, with many badly wounded, the Japanese had butchered them with their Samurai swords as they staggered exhausted on to the beach. He didn't know if the sailors were Australian or American, but later when the Japanese had moved inland his people came down from the mountain and buried the bodies in graves they dug in the sand.

Out to sea the masts of a large ship could be seen protruding from the water. The ship was there for a long time and none of the Bantenese was allowed to go near it. One day some more Japanese came. They were in what must have been fully equipped salvage vessels, for after working on the wreck for some months they finally finished cutting it up and took it away.

From this and other information received I evolved a theory on the fate of the *Houston*. I consider that it was she who was salvaged by the Japanese during their occupation of Java in 1942 – 45. I must emphasise that it is only a theory, based on the known fact and some supposition on my part.

It is generally accepted that the *Houston* sank closer inshore than the *Perth* and although the level of the bed of the Java Sea is patchy, with the recorded soundings showing current-scoured hollows of up to fifty fathoms in depth, it would seem the *Houston* sank in only twenty fathoms. Being a 10000 ton heavy cruiser, sinking upright in this depth would leave the tops of her masts well clear of the surface.

It is also known that the damage caused by *Perth* and *Houston* to the invasion fleet led the Japanese to think one of them must have been a battleship, as the Japanese wouldn't believe that two cruisers could put up such a fight. If the Japanese thought the *Houston* was a battleship, which represented a very valuable prize in non-ferrous metal, it is easy to understand their interest in what would be to them an easy salvage job.

Also it is not hard to believe that when the *Houston's* bell was recovered by the divers, one of the Japanese officers decided to keep it and in due course and by who knows what means the magnificently engraved bell ended up in Manila. That it should be a showpiece there in a private museum, where it was reported to have been sighted after the war, is also logical.

I wrote to Walter Allen, my friend in Houston, Texas, outlining my theory and he made further inquiries through the *Houston Post*. The information the *Post* uncovered was startling. Apparently when President

Johnson visited Corregidor in 1966, President Marcos of the Philippines presented him with the bell of the *Houston*. This was then loaded aboard the President's plane, flown directly to Washington and placed in the Presidential archives where it has been ever since.

President Johnson's press secretary, Mr Christian, advised the *Post* that the bell, which bears the inscription 'U.S.S. Houston, 1930', has an additional inscription of:

'This bell of the U.S.S. 'Houston', United States Pacific Fleet, sunk during the battle of the Java Sea during World War II, was recovered by the Republic of the Philippines. It was presented to Lyndon B. Johnson, President of the United States of America, by President Ferdinand Marcos of the Philippines at Batong Buhay, Corregidor 26th October, 1966.'

Mr Christian said that President Johnson was unaware of how the Philippine Republic had gained possession of the bell and as President Marcos made no explanation it seems he didn't know either. But I think that this last relic of the mighty *Houston*, the Galloping Ghost of the China Sea, was carried to Manila in a Japanese diving officer's baggage, marked 'spoils of war'.

The starboard signal lamp being transferred
from the dinghy to the *Aries*

26

During the thirty dives I made on the *Perth* we recovered some twenty-four different relics. These included shell cases from the four-inch gun turrets, navigational instruments and a signalling-light from the bridge, voice tubes and gyro repeaters from the wheelhouse and other miscellaneous pieces from different areas.

Some came easily and these I was mostly able to carry up with me. Some were more difficult to recover. The signalling light from the bridge probably caused us the most trouble. I had seen it on several occasions; it was about the size of a twelve-and-a-half gallon drum and looked as if it would be heavy and awkward to handle.

Lying half out of its mounts with one of its octagonal panes of glass broken, the light also had a large hole in its side indicating that it had been hit by shell fire. It took a whole dive to clear it completely from the ship and the next day when I dived again I took down an inch-thick manila rope that Sumantri had brought back with him from Djakarta. The rope was stiff and difficult to tie, but when it was secure I gave the four-pulls signal, indicating to the boys up in the dinghy that it was time to heave.

For the next five minutes we staged a tug-of-war with the light and as the men in the dinghy pulled I pushed, but it wouldn't budge. Panting with the exertion I gave the two-pull stand-by signal and backed off. I couldn't work it out as I felt sure the light was free of its gimbals, but something was holding it. Swimming down under the mounting I searched around carefully and after a minute or so found the trouble. There was an electric cable still feeding into the light. The cable was as thick as my thumb and as strong as a hawser and looking at it I knew we wouldn't be raising the light that dive, for it was definitely a hacksaw job.

Later with the bluntest hacksaw in Indonesia I finally succeeded in cutting the cable. This time, after the signal to pull was given, the light rose majestically from out of its gimbals and in fits and starts as the chaps pulled, it started its long journey to the surface. I was just about to turn away satisfied that the light was as good as recovered when it suddenly slipped lengthways out of the holding noose, catching at the last second on one of the signalman's shoulder rests.

Pushing off the ship I chased up after it and taking hold of the rope frantically gave the stand-by signal. But as the boys kept pulling I realised that the rope had so much weight on it the signal couldn't be felt and at every jerk the light threatened to slip clean out of the noose. Looking down I couldn't see the ship; it was already lost in the grey fog below and I had no option but to ride the rope up, for if I stayed with the rope there was a chance I could hold it onto the light, but if I left it the light was sure to be lost.

I wrapped my leg around the light and placing one arm through the noose held onto the shoulder rest with my free hand, thus keeping the rope from slipping off.

It was a slow, agonizing trip. Every now and again the pull would stop and the light and I welded together in our silent death-like embrace, would spin slowly round at the end of the rope. As the frequency of these pauses increased in number I couldn't help smiling at the thought of the boys in the dinghy, for with my weight to lift as well as the heavy light it must have been tough going. By the time we reached the surface I think everyone was exhausted, but if John and Sumantri hadn't jumped overboard and taken the strain we still could have lost it. All I could do after two of the leading seamen, Pati and Johnno had hauled me aboard was to lie gasping in the bilge, unable even to raise my hand to take off my mask. Scammell, who works on the principle that if you yell loud enough non-English-speaking people will understand you, was going great guns. But eventually he and Sumantri made the rope more secure and after a mammoth effort and a couple of near misses they wrestled the light up onto the deck of the *Aries*.

The four-inch shell cases while heavy enough, didn't present anywhere near the problem of the signal light. They were mostly recovered from 'S2', the starboard aft turret, about forty feet up from the sea-bed.

The first time I looked inside I could see a number of empty shell cases and several live rounds in a heap on the deck. Two of the live rounds were bent at right angles, again the evidence of a direct hit.

Thinking that Gordon Reid would like a shell case as he had been a four- inch gunner I moved in to pick one up, only to find that they were all fused together with calcified marine growth. I had my pick-hammer with me and sat down in the turret and started the delicate job of chipping the shells apart. I knew it was highly unlikely that one of the live rounds would explode, although it did cross my mind and after banging away for a while a spent shell broke free. Taking it in my arms I crawled out of the turret on my elbows, intending to place the shellcase in the rice sack tied outside.

The rice sack was a new idea we had evolved for the recovery of light weight objects and now I took it with me on every dive. It was attached to about ninety metres of special steel core sounding-line and at the conclusion of the dive it would be hauled back to the surface.

Clearing the entrance to the turret I scrambled for a footing, trying to stand up and at the same time reaching for the bag, but the unaccustomed weight

The heavy brass plough seat from the
Bridge range finder

threw me off balance and hugging the shellcase I plummeted down the canted gun-deck on to the sea-bed. Kneeling in the sand beside the huge bulk of the ship, I juggled the shellcase into a better position and then pushed off in an attempt to swim back up the forty feet. But I was like a fledgling that had fallen out of its nest and after a couple of pathetic attempts decided that it would be much easier to bring the sack down to the shell. This I did and after some trouble pushing the spiky shell into the bag, gave the signal to haul away

As I watched the bag starting its ascent, it occurred to me that there was something wrong with the angle of the rope — it was too perpendicular for the way the current was running. Looking up I could see why. The rope had fouled over a spar on the aft control and if the sack with the heavy shell hit the spar it would more than likely be torn off.

Shoving off from the sea bed I began a frantic race to the spar with the jerking sack. Just making it to the obstruction first, I straddled it and leaning down managed to heave the shell over. But as the bag scraped across it caught the quick-release buckle of my weight belt and this item, correctly doing its job, immediately released itself. My first knowledge that the belt had gone was when I sat up thankfully on the spar to watch the sack disappear upwards, only to see to my dismay, the weights going up with it. Once more I had to sprint after the bag and after catching up with it and retrieving the belt I sank wearily back on to the ship. By now the current had carried me back past the quarter- deck and rather grimly I started the long pull up-current to the number three buoy on the four-inch gun deck.

After I'd gone about half-way I stopped for a rest by bracing myself against a stanchion. Hanging there for a few seconds I realized I was cutting it fine for I was nearly out of air. Glancing up I couldn't help the sudden wave of fear that swept through me, for there like a group of larrikins waiting at a street corner, was the shark pack.

Lately when we'd met I'd noticed that the sharks were becoming more aggressive and I'd decided to give them as wide a berth as possible. But today it seemed I had no option, for the pack was between me and the shot-line and as I was nearly out of air there was no time to skirt round them or drop back down current to the number four buoy cable aft. Consequently I had no alternative but to go through the sharks and be quick about it at that.

Taking a firm grip on the stubby handle of the pick hammer and trying not to think about what would happen if they really got dinkum, I swam up on the deck and moved into the circling pack.

The sharks were about nine or ten feet long, somewhat smaller than the ones we encounter back in Australia, but lean and fast. By now they had become agitated and that didn't help matters. Almost immediately they started making their characteristic passing runs, like fighter planes strafing a bomber . . . coming in close but never quite making contact . . . and for a while they had me pinned down on the deck.

I was worried about my air and the fact that I wasn't getting any closer to the shot-line, but for the moment I couldn't move, for without the protection of the deck I could have been in trouble.

When the sharks came in too close I swiped at them with the pick hammer and hit one a glancing blow on the nose before he turned away. It was probably the best thing that could have happened for it seemed to discourage them temporarily and they kept their distance, which allowed me to make a dash over the open water separating me from the four-inch gun deck. But the sharks soon resumed their game and I

264

remember glancing longingly into the first of the four-inch turrets as I passed, for it offered a secure sanctuary, but by now my air gauge was showing a virtual nil reading and I had to keep going.

Finally I reached the shot-line and shakily stood up, pausing for a moment to wave my arm at them in what I hopefully imagined would be taken for an act of defiance. But it wasn't over yet, for the trip back to the surface was a nightmare as the sharks followed me up, making their sporadic torpedo-like passes from out of the grey fog.

About half-way they suddenly stopped as if by some pre-arranged agreement among themselves, but at the time I was unaware of the arrangement and the next eighty feet or so of ascent I think was worse, as I looked in all directions at once waiting for them to reappear.

There were odd days when I didn't see the sharks at all, but mostly we would play hide-and-seek at some time during my dives on the ship. Among my gear on the *Aries* was a heavy speargun fitted with a .303 power head and while this would have tickled them up, I was usually so burdened with ropes and other items that I couldn't carry the gun. Instead I tried to condition myself mentally to ignore the sharks and to some extent was successful, although their sudden appearance always gave me a fright.

It was the times they were on the surface before a dive that I disliked them most, for it would be difficult to imagine anything more sinister than the sight of their black dorsal fins cutting through the water as they lazily glided round the buoys. This was also perhaps the time of the greatest danger, that of entering the water and swimming down to the ship and I remember cursing them, as the long hard haul was bad enough on its own without worrying about the sharks. But although they came very close, they never actually attacked and I did learn to live with them after a fashion.

265

In contrast to my feelings against the sharks were my feelings in favour of the groper and in no time I had groper friends all over the ship. They seemed to stick to their own particular area, as I always saw the same ones in the same places. Huge creatures and insatiably curious, the gropers' sluggish movements give the impression that they are a bit dim-witted and it was obvious that my sudden appearance in their lives was the greatest event that had happened in years.

Dopey, the one I got to know best, lived on the bridge and as I worked away at recovering different items I could always rely on him to be looking over my shoulder. One day as I was carefully removing a voice tube mouthpiece, he became so attracted to the white cotton bands round the wrists of my gloves that, coming right in, he started to try to eat them. Without looking up from what I was doing I pulled the glove away and gave him a smart back hander on the nose. It was only after making contact that I realized what I'd done, for Dopey, all 300 pounds of him, could have bitten my hand off at the armpit. Looking quickly around to see how he'd taken it, I saw that he'd backed off, the great sad face registering his deep hurt at so unkind a cut. After a while he forgave me and once more came into peer over my shoulder, but I noticed that he didn't attempt to bite the glove again.

There were many other creatures who had made the *Perth* their home. The dozens of Green turtles, some weighing over 200 pounds, the hundreds of varieties of fish, the many different rays and something else, whose identity I never established, but which was so large that it completely blocked out the meagre light from above. It wasn't Dopey, as out of the corner of my eye I could see him alongside me. But as I was busy at the time I didn't look up and it was only later after it had gone that I started to wonder what had been poised above. It was probably just as well I never found out.

From inside the wheelhouse I recovered a beautiful copper voice tube mouthpiece, on the inside of which was an engraved brass plate reading 'No.44 Upper Bridge Starboard'. Also in the wheelhouse was a bronze gyro compass repeater and as it was extremely heavy, I cradled it in one arm and laboriously climbed up the front of the bridge to where I'd left the sounding line and the rice sack. Placing the repeater and mouthpiece in the bag I swam across the corner of the bridge to where shell-fire had partly exposed the wheelhouse below. Holding on to the deck I lay still and peered through the hole, but the visibility was under two feet and deciding that I wouldn't find anything that way started to push back out of the wreckage. As I did so something under my hand moved slightly and looking down I could see a round metal object about the size and shape of a hard-hat diver's helmet.

Dusting the silt away with my hand I uncovered two glass windows near the top and realized what I'd found; it was the ship's compass.

It was an exciting find and I carefully prised it out of the damaged corner. When the compass came free its weight surprised me and like the time with the four-inch shellcase I took off.

Sliding and crashing down the almost vertical deck I ended up in a heap on the port side. Appreciating that it was far too dangerous a manoeuvre for this depth, I berated myself for not being more careful, for not only had my mask been knocked off but the demand-valve supplying me with air from the cylinder had nearly been pulled from my mouth. Fortunately the mask was still stuck on the top of my head and quickly putting it back on I cleared it of water, for without the mask I was blind and would have had a difficult job finding my way back to the shot-line.

However I still had the compass and placing it carefully down on the deck I swam back up to where I'd tied the sounding-line. I nearly untied the sack containing the repeater, but as the line had a steel core I felt it would easily hold the extra weight. Once down on the port side again I securely lashed the compass above the bag and when completely satisfied that it was all right, I gave the signal to pull it up. Watching until the rice sack had disappeared into the fog I swam up to the number two buoy cable attached to the bridge and as fast as I could followed it back to the surface.

I knew the sounding line had broken and that we'd lost the compass as soon as I saw John's face. Holding on to the side of the dinghy against the tearing current, for a moment I was inconsolable. This was too much.

Vaguely I heard poor old Scammell trying to explain what had happened. 'I felt the line start to stretch,' he said, 'and I stopped the haul. Then as we were over half-way to the surface, I reckoned it should be okay and we started again, but at about sixty feet the rope snapped like a carrot. What did you have on it? Was it something valuable?'

Jerking my head up I glared at him over the side of the dinghy. 'Have we brought up anything yet that hasn't been valuable?' I snapped. 'It was only the bloody compass, do you call that valuable?'

I was being unfair and I knew it. John was as concerned about every aspect of the venture as I was and it wasn't his fault that the ropes were all rotten. But I was so put out at the loss that I could have wept and he was the only one handy that I could sound off at.

That afternoon we tied the inch manila rope to a fifty-six pound weight and dropped it over the bow of the dinghy, which was again being held to number two buoy. My theory was that the weight should land on the sea bed at approximately the same spot as the compass. If when I reached the bottom I couldn't see the compass, I intended making circular searches using the weight as a datum point.

Circular searching is the accepted procedure when operating in water of poor visibility. A rope is tied to the weight and the diver backs off until the weight is just visible. He then completes a 360 degree sweep and if the object for which he is looking is between him and the weight he naturally sees it. If it is not, the diver marks the rope by tying a piece of white rag to it and retreating again until this is only just visible he completes another sweep. If the visibility is zero, basically the same procedure is followed but it is all done by feel. As soon as I started down the rope I could feel the weight come off the bottom and by the time I reached it the force of the current had the weight streaming six feet off the sea bed. After a struggle I forced it down onto the sand and as my time at this depth was short, I quickly tied a piece of sounding line that I'd brought with me to the weight and began the search.

Crawling against the current reminded me of Scott of the Antarctic in a blizzard. Going with the current I was like a tumble weed in a desert gale. After one-and-a-half sweeps I was completely exhausted and realized that the circular searches were beyond me. In sheer desperation I paid myself out down the current to the full extent of the line, hoping to find the compass by chance, but there was nothing.

We were a quiet ship's company on the way back to Merak. I was having a bit of a sulk, John was busy preparing something special for tea in an effort to cheer me up and the boys had suddenly revived their lagging interest in chipping sponge and other growth off the signal light. After half an hour or so I stopped feeling sorry for myself and started to plan for another go at recovering the compass. The best I could think of was to take one end of the manila rope down with me and then after reaching the spot where I'd sent up the compass, I'd leave the ship and strike out down current following

269

The *Perth*'s binnacle showing shrapnel damage

the course the compass, took before the sounding line broke. If I didn't find anything I could give the haul-away signal and the boys would pull me up.

Next morning with this plan in mind I again dived down the number two buoy cable. Looped over my shoulder was my end of the heavy rope and so as not to foul it on the ship, when nearly there I pushed off the buoy cable and swam clean over her, landing on the sea bed at the port side of the bridge. Wasting no time I took my bearings and pushed off down the current. In seconds the *Perth* had disappeared and I felt very much on my own, but also within seconds I saw the rice sack and the compass. They were dead ahead and I was coming down on them as if directed by radar. From then on their recovery was just a matter of routine and after triple-tying the rope I gave the signal and again we were all pulled to the surface.

Back on the *Aries* we inspected the relics and found

that what we'd recovered was not the compass, but the compass housing or binnacle. Apparently the compass itself had been blown clean out of the housing, but its gimbal ring with the name 'Sperry' stamped on it was still inside along with the auxiliary batteries.

It didn't really matter, the binnacle was a beautiful piece and I carefully cleaned the sponge and coral from it. In my mind I could see the binnacle in its glass case at the Canberra War Memorial and it was with somewhat of a shock that I realized our job was nearly done and that we could start thinking about going home.

Back in Djakarta after the dive we inspect
the damage to the binnacle

27

There were still two important functions left to carry out. One was to photograph the *Perth* and the other was to hold a wreath-laying ceremony. While many such services had been held by passing British ships over the years, they had been many miles off her actual bearings and we considered that this was a wonderful opportunity to hold a service right over the ship.

I had already obtained the necessary permission from the Indonesian Navy and had arranged with Freddie Sherborne to come down from Djakarta with a wreath. At seven o'clock in the morning of the Sunday we had chosen for the ceremony, Freddie, Bobbie and young Kristen, arrived in Merak in the Embassy Landrover and after they had been piped aboard we cast off and moved up the Strait. Out at the diving area I had removed all the buoys from the ship bar number four, the one secured to the quarter-deck and after lining everyone up along the starboard side of the *Aries* we steamed slowly past the buoy, our object being to lay the wreath up current and let it float back as close to the buoy as possible.

With the crew at the salute, Bobbie and Kristen dropped the wreath over the side and it was then that a very strange thing happened. The current which had run a banker for the whole of the three weeks we had been diving suddenly stopped and the wreath as if drawn by a magnet slowly drifted towards the buoy and hung there, not three feet off it, for nearly twenty minutes. Any other day it would have been whipped away in seconds.

On the last two dives, the twenty-ninth and thirtieth, I photographed the ship. Working from the shot-line on

273

the quarter-deck I took flash shots of the Gorgonia coral on the bridge, the guns, the torpedo tubes, the quarter-deck itself and frightened hell out of poor old Dopey with a close up shot that I snapped of his head.

It was towards the end of the twenty-ninth dive that I got into trouble. I'd polished up some of the brasswork on the torpedo tubes and was just bringing them into focus with the camera, when something grabbed me by the back of the neck. It was as if I were nailed to a wall, for I couldn't move. Overcoming the desire to struggle, I cautiously felt around behind my head. At first there was nothing. Then I found the tangle of wire that had fouled tight round the Scuba regulator.

This wasn't the best place to be caught, for the Scuba regulator is only attached to the cylinder by a finger-tight fitting onto an 'O' ring seal and any sudden movement could dislodge it. If this happened I'd be without air. Checking the high-pressure gauge I estimated that there was only enough air for another five minutes. I'd have to act quickly and as stuggling was out of the question I decided to take the Scuba off and untangle the wire as I could see it.

This normally wouldn't have been so difficult but the current and all the extra gear I had on slowed me down. First I had to get rid of the plastic airways bag containing the flash bulbs that was floating above my head as the thin handles of the bag were twisted around the neck strap of the camera, which also had to be removed. It was a fiddly job, with everything having to be done either behind or above my head and it was aggravated by my mask and snorkel getting in the way and my rising consternation at the feeling I wasn't getting anywhere.

When I finally succeeded in removing the bag and camera I had nowhere to put them. Being suspended off the ship as I was and not wanting to lose the expensive camera and much more important, the film it

Suddenly the current stopped and the wreath drifted right up to the buoy which was still attached to the ship

contained, I wasted precious time desperately looking for somewhere safe to drop it. But as I couldn't see anywhere suitable in my limited range of vision, I let the bag go and hung the camera strap over my foot. Next came the weight belt. This I also draped over my foot and then I undid the Scuba harness. Slipping out of it I gently turned around and with the demand valve still in my mouth untangled the wire.

A glance at my watch and a quick check of the air pressure showed me about two minutes' time left. I'd made it . . .

That afternoon I dived to the *Perth* for the last time. First I finished taking the photographs and when this was done I made my way up to the bridge to hold a small service of my own. I'd discussed it with John the night before and we had already chosen the prayer. Originally we intended it for the boys of the *Perth* and *Houston* but I decided at the last minute to include the chaps on the Japanese trooper.

Crouching down out of the current behind the bridge screen, with the Gorgonia spray for an altar and my friend the groper, who had taken up his accustomed place beside me, standing as witness, I said the familiar words:

> Our Father, which art in Heaven
> Hallowed be Thy name
> Thy kingdom come
> Thy will be done . . .

★ ★ ★

At the conclusion of the diving we recovered the number four buoy cable and immediately sailed for Djakarta, arriving at Priok late that night.

About the first thing John and I did, after transferring our gear from the *Aries* to the *Bergamahl*, was to have a bath, or more correctly an Indonesian version of one. The Indonesian bathroom is about the size of a shower alcove and in one corner is a type of wash trough full of water and a dipper. The bather, standing in the middle pours water over himself with the dipper; once you become accustomed to it the system is most effective.

In the morning we supervised the transfer of the *Perth* relics from the *Aries* to the Yacht Club wharf, where they were picked up by a truck and taken to the Hydrographic Command with John and I following along in Sumantri's jeep.

The next step was to transport the relics home to Australia. There were two alternatives. One was shipping them back, but when we checked the departures from Priok the only vessel leaving in the foreseeable future was sailing to Hong Kong. She could have taken them, but if the relics went this way they would have to be transhipped to China.

'Not on your life', I said to Freddie. 'That's no good, hell we may never see them again'.

He agreed and we decided to have a go at asking Qantas to fly them home. The manager of Qantas, a golfing friend of Freddie's told us that the decision to fly the 600 pounds of relics to Australia on a no cost basis was beyond his authority, but he promised to send a cable to Canberra and see what he could do. This was a blow as we reckoned it would take the best part of a week to receive a reply and it meant that I would have to hang around Djakarta waiting. But although I had to wait John didn't and as he still had ten days or so up his sleeve before meeting his wife Nancy in Singapore, he decided to spend the time in Bali.

I'd have liked to have gone with him, but I couldn't leave Djakarta until the problem of the relics had been solved, so next day Sumantri and I put him on the train for Surabaya and laden down with his camera, faithful old Scammell left me. As Freddie had invited me to stay at his house for the remainder of my time in Djakarta, we transferred my gear from the *Bergamahl* and for the next few days while I waited for news from Qantas the Sherbornes gave me a great time.

With Bobbie and Kristen I went for a drive up into the mountains where we visited the tea plantations and bought water-colour paintings and other souvenirs from the wayside peddlers. I also helped them shop in the markets in Djakarta and bought a couple of colourful shirts at the Batik factory. One night we went to a party at the Indian Embassy and another evening they asked Sumantri and his attractive wife over for dinner.

After about five days Freddie rang from his office at the Embassy. He had bad news. The Qantas manager had called and my request to have the relics flown back to Australia had been turned down. He was as upset as I was and had pointed out to the Qantas chap that the relics were not mine, but they belonged to Australia and he thought it was a pretty poor show. Although the airways official was sympathetic there was nothing he could do.

There was now only one thing left. I decided to get help from Geoff Giles or Bert Kelly after I'd returned home and therefore arranged to have the relics crated and left in Freddie's care at the Embassy.

The night before I left Java, Jim Carr, the American Assistant Naval Attache, invited me over for dinner.

Another guest there was an Indonesian underwater salvage contractor, who was keen for me to dive on a ship that had been torpedoed in the Bali Strait. The ship was reported to have a million dollars worth of tin in her holds, but she was deep, about 300 feet. For a moment or two I considered having a go, but declined for I'd had enough and I wanted to get the relics home.

Actually I was more interested at the time in pinching one of Jim Carr's naval caps, as I was forming a collection of the three countries, Australian, American and Indonesian, that were involved in the Sunda Strait diving. I had already won caps off both Freddie and Sumantri and Jim was the object of my next attack. By the time the evening was over I thought he had forgotten about it, but just as I was leaving he slipped upstairs and came back with one of his US Navy caps. It completed the trio.

One morning Sumantri and I were browsing round a small antique shop in a back street in Djakarta when the proprietor, a wizened up little Indonesian, shyly asked me if I was the Australian who had been diving on the *Perth*.

When I told him I was he said he only had met one other Australian and added that he was the bravest man he ever knew.

It was during the war in 1943 at Bandung, in Japanese occupied Central West Java. The Australian, Lieutenant-Colonel Douglas Smith, had worked in the hotel that the Indonesians ran, disguised as an Armenian cook.

'Smithy', as he was called, taught them to play whist and during the six months he was with the Indonesians told them stories about his home town, Coolangatta, of the surf and beaches and of life in Australia. Every night despite their repeated warnings he would slip out of the hotel, never saying why or where he was going. They all knew it was just a matter of time before he was caught and eventually one night the Japanese were waiting as he tried to creep back in.

The Indonesians said that for some days 'Smithy' was tortured until finally, no doubt realizing that his position was hopeless, he confessed to having sent messages by radio to the Americans.

The Japanese then executed him by public hanging in the town square. Placing his hand on his skinny chest the Indonesian almost in tears at the memory of it

279

concluded sadly, 'At the time of the execution we were all quiet here in our hearts'.

★ ★ ★

Freddie just dropped me off at the airport. There was no point waiting, for the plane's departure could take hours. After clearing customs I sat down on one of the hard seats in the waiting area and almost immediately a scruffy-looking character came up trying to put over some sort of deal.

I was preoccupied and wasn't really listening, but after awhile I glanced up and said, 'Buzz off old chap, or I'll have you arrested. You may not know it but I have friends in high places'.

The Indonesian, who had no idea of what I was talking about persisted and I realised he wanted a cigarette. With a sigh I searched through my briefcase and handed him one out of my last packet of Rothmans.

As he ambled off one of my 'friends in high places' sat down next to me.

We had already said our goodbyes the day before but apparently they weren't enough, for hunching forward on the seat and staring at his hands he said, without even looking at me. 'Hullo Daddy, they tell me you don't live here anymore'.

The Japanese are an odd bunch. In the 1930s they were rated as cheap copyists of other people's brains and initiative, while during the war they earned for themselves the reputation of being dirty and brutal and something less than sub-human.

Consequently it was interesting to observe the crew on the Japan Air Lines flight from Djakarta to Singapore, as the hostesses with their delicate beauty and thoughtful attentive services were a far cry from the impressions left by the Knights of the Bushido.

One realized of course that the girls hadn't been

picked for the job because they resembled Phyllis Diller made up for her act, but nevertheless they were surprising and it was diffcult not to respond to their polite friendliness.

Harry Knight and Jack McDonough study photographs of *Perth* relics at West Beach Airport after I arrived back in Adelaide

28

The day after arriving home I was sitting at my desk in the office, staring morosely at the pile of work that had built up.

I'd just returned from *The Advertiser* building, the home of our morning paper, where I'd asked the chaps in the photographic section to develop the underwater film in my camera.

To their sympathetic dismay and my horror the exposed film showed a complete blank, not even a smudge. Somehow John and I had loaded the camera incorrectly. It was about the last straw and I was fed up but still had to face the job of bringing the relics back. Just then the phone rang. It was Perth, Western Australia calling. 'Peter Finn, Chief of Staff *Sunday Times*, speaking', the voice said. 'What's this about you having trouble flying the *Perth* relics back to Australia?' I told him the trouble. 'OK', he said, 'leave it with me. I'll ring you back in a couple of hours'.

By the time Peter Finn rang back he had the return of the relics all arranged, but he stipulated two conditions. The *Sunday Times* in conjunction with Malayan Singapore Airlines and Channel 9 in Perth would fly the relics home if a part of the ship was presented to the City of Perth and secondly I had to come over as their guest and be there when the relics arrived. 'Boy', I said, as the weight of the responsibility of it all slid off me, 'you've got a deal'.

There was a large crowd at the Adelaide airport the day Ona and I took off for Perth. I thought it was pretty decent of them all to come down and see us off, until Ona pointed out that we were on the same plane as the South Australian football team, which was also on its way to Perth.

I'd already flown over once since the return from Indonesia, when along with twenty or so of the *Perth* survivors, I'd met the MSA plane from Djakarta carrying the relics. They had travelled well and after we had inspected them the President of the *Perth* Association, Charlie Thompson, agreed to their being displayed in the foyer of the Rural and Industries Bank. Later I was told that during the five days the relics were on display over 10000 Western Australians came in to see them.

We decided on one of the four-inch shell cases as a gift to the city. As it needed to be properly mounted I said I'd take it home to Adelaide and when it was ready send it back. But they wouldn't hear of it. 'You can't just send it back', Arthur Bancroft, one of the survivors, said. 'The agreement was that you present it to the Lord Mayor yourself.'

When the shell had been cut in halves and suitably mounted I rang the Adelaide TAA Manager, Reg Rechner and thanked him for the proposed free trip. 'It's no trouble', he said 'perhaps your wife would like to go as well'. I assured him she would and it was settled.

The Lord Mayor of Perth, Mr Veryard, received the shell case at a reception in the Civic Centre and afterwards it was permanently fixed on the wall above his desk. On each side of it hang the two naval caps that I also gave to the City, one is Australian and the other American. The Indonesian cap I kept for myself as I considered that like the character who gave it to me, it was my own personal property.

The other half of the shell case that now hangs in the Perth Civic Centre I also had mounted and later in Canberra gave it to the American Ambassador to Australia, Mr Ed Clarke, with the request that it be sent on to the city of Houston in Texas, the thought being that as I couldn't find their ship, the people of Houston

The Lord Mayor of Perth, Mr Veryard,
receives the naval caps and shell case

The US Ambassador, Mr Ed Clarke, accepts the
other half of the shell case on behalf of the
City of Houston, Texas

Captain David Leach CBE RAN welcomes Ona and
me on the quarter-deck of the new *Perth* when the
voice tube from the original ship was presented

When the relics were on show at the Rural and Industries Bank in Perth, over 10 000 Western Australians
came to see them

may appreciate part of the *Perth*. In due course Mayor Louie Welch of Houston wrote thanking me for the shell and advised that it was now a permanent part of his office. Although it was not really planned that the two halves of the shell should find homes so many thousands of miles apart, one couldn't wish for a more appropriate ending.

Not all the relics made it to Canberra, for soon after the gift was made of the four-inch shell case to the city of Perth, requests for mementoes of the ship came thick and fast. The requests were all worthy and I had a difficult time deciding who should receive the limited number of items that were available.

A porthole rim went to the *Perth* Memorial Hall at the RAN shore-base in Fremantle and the Ex-Navalmen's Association at Elizabeth in South Australia has part of a navigational instrument from the bridge.

One of the other shell cases was cut in halves and after the two sections were mounted, one was given to Gordon Reid and the other to John Scammell. I offered the Captain of the new HMAS *Perth* a voice tube mouthpiece and after the Naval Board approved its acceptance, part of the old ship officially became part of the new one.

On the wall at Naval Memorial House Adelaide is an engraved brass plate from the engine room telegraph system and the different *Perth* Associations in each State all have their own special pieces.

During the transportation of the relics from one State to another the signalman's shoulder-rest from the starboard bridge broke off and as the light was Buzzer Bee's action station the night the ship was sunk, I sent the broken shoulder-rest over to him in Perth.

Here and there are some other pieces, like the brass bolt in the foyer of the Rural and Industries Bank, the copper container from the wheelhouse that Ray Parkin now has in his study and the voice tube mouthpiece on the wall in my office. Although all these relics are appreciated to the full, I think the one that is perhaps cherished the most is the lampholder from the binnacle.

Made of brass, it originally held the light that lit the compass at night. It was a wonder that the frail welds securing the lampholder to the binnacle held on as long as they did, but shortly after it arrived home the solder became brittle and it broke away. When I gave the lampholder to Mrs Waller I told her that it came from the bridge and that Captain Waller must have been standing close to it when he died. Now every year on Christmas Eve she places a lighted candle in it, the burning flame being a silent tribute to the memory of her husband, his ship and his men.

29

In Canberra on Remembrance Day, 11 November 1967, the Chief of Naval staff, Admiral Sir Alan McNicol, received the relics of the *Perth* on behalf of the Royal Australian Navy and the Australian War Memorial. There was quite a large audience packed into the Naval Gallery and as I listened to the speeches I glanced across at the painting of Hec Waller, remembering that other time when I'd first stood in front of it and although the occasion had been only a few months before, in some ways it seemed a lifetime. As my thoughts drifted back over the period I couldn't help realizing how lucky I'd been, for while it can be argued that what is frequently termed a 'lucky break' is not really luck at all but more often is the result of sheer persistence, I still did get the breaks.

That we worked hard and also that between us we had our certain abilities was incidental, for these things are the normal prerequisites, the basic requirements, without which no one should attempt such a project. But it is an accepted fact that in many fields of endeavour there is a very fine line between success and failure and this cannot always be determined by the degree of ability or effort. You still have to get the breaks.

There was no doubt that my breaks had come with the people I'd involved, the first being the day I said Jim Forbes was my friend, for this alone must have helped me more times than I ever knew.

Then there was General Kosasih, whose initial encouragement and advice showed me how to plan it all and Commodore Wardiman, who in spite of the considered opinions of his fellow officers and who at times had a few qualms of his own, continued to back me when nearly everyone else had baled out.

What would I have done without the support of old friends like John Scammell and Geoff Giles and that of the new ones such as Freddie Sherborne, Sumantri, the Bantenese fishermen and the crew of the *Aries*? As I sat musing over the long list my eyes drifted back again to the painting of Hec Waller and looking at it I knew he'd have understood, for he would have known the value of people and the value of getting the breaks.

I heard someone mention my name and with a start realized it was nearly time to make my speech. Looking into the sea of faces I picked out my wife and children and smiled at the sight of our four girls, sitting proudly bolt upright on their best behaviour.

Just in front of my family was General Kosasih, then Gordon Reid in his wheelchair next to Mrs Waller and around them *Perth* survivors from all over Australia. As I was about to stand up one more face caught my eye. It was Sumantri. He was attending the ceremony as the guest of the Australian Government who had readily agreed to invite him down and I thought how fitting it was that this excellent fellow should be there.

As our eyes met he flashed the grin I'd got to know so well and I smiled back. Then after taking a quick look behind me at the relics to reassure myself that I hadn't dreamed it all, I stood up to make the speech.

Mrs H Waller, widow of the Captain of the first HMAS *Perth*, during Remembrance Day ceremonies at the Australian War Memorial, Canberra.

Admiral Sir Allan McNicol, RAN, Chief of Naval Staff, stands behind her

Original HMAS *Perth* survivors at the Canberra ceremony

30

Ex-Chief Petty Officer Ray Parkin, RAN — the Chief Quarter-master of the original *Perth* — author, artist, historian — was the chap who willingly put aside his other work and produced the excellent pen drawing of the ship reproduced in this book. He also wrote the following acknowledgement and although it is complimentary to me I have included it in full. For a pat on the back from a man like Ray Parkin is one of those rare and valued compliments in life, that makes your own efforts seem doubly worth the while.

★ ★ ★

At just after midnight on 1 March 1942, with about one-third of our ship's company I lay in the water coated with oil fuel watching our ship sinking. Exposed and helpless in the glare of searchlights from surrounding Japanese warships, she had come to the end of as violent an hour's action as was ever fought at sea. Not many minutes before I had been on board, steering her through this last battle — a vessel complex, expensive and extremely efficient in speed and action. I had lived in her for two years and nine months, which was her whole life as an Australian warship. She had been hit by torpedoes and shell-fire had shattered her boats. The captain, just after he had given the order, 'Abandon ship — every man for himself', had been killed on the bridge by a salvo of shells. We watched the ship go down out of the searchlights' glare into the unknown blackness below, taking almost two-thirds of our shipmates with her.

Yet twenty-five years later a man left her alive.

This man was Dave Burchell. He was not a member of the ship's company but he brought back what we thought, on that night in 1942, had been blotted out for ever. This was a unique act carried out by a man of true sentiment: simply, directly, unselfishly and at his own expense. Some few have thought that such an act might have been a desecration. In fact, nothing could be further from the truth. Most Perth survivors now know that Dave Burchell's sentiment, humour and character, would have made him a most welcome shipmate in those hectic war years when men were held together by a single purpose. He has been made an honorary member of ex-Perth associations throughout Australia. Almost all the relics he raised are now in the National Memorial at Canberra: as a visible reminder of the ship, her dead and her deeds. The general public may have forgotten her, new generations may never have heard of her, but she has an undeniable place in Australian tradition.

Dave Burchell does not argue 'to be or not to be', he is and does. He lost a leg when young but that did not stop him joining the RAAF as an aircraftsman in wartime. He is now a diver, a no-nonsense expert to whom other divers are willing to listen. He is powerful and fit, but he is self-effacing. From his modest accounts you are apt to miss the full significance of what he has done. When the Japanese proposed to raise the Perth for scrap, there was a public outcry in Australia. To Dave Burchell it meant that she was in a diveable depth of water and it would not be long before people without sentiment or conscience would be able to reach her.

This story tells what happened when he decided to act. At first his prime objective was to bring back the ship's bell. In this he failed. I feel, however, that he has brought back something far more precious.

I remember how the ship, in her second-last battle,

made a vivid impression on men of another navy who saw her at work. During the action of the Java Sea, HMS Exeter was hit in the boiler room and stopped. She came under the concentrated fire of the Japanese fleet. Without hesitation Captain Waller at once took Perth in at high speed to lay a protective screen between her and the enemy. At the end of each leg in front of Exeter, Perth made 180 degree turns at high speed under full helm — black smoke pouring away from her two funnels and white smoke from the smokefloats on the quarter-deck filling the gap along the surface of the sea with a dense fog. (I can still feel the ship heeling away under my feet as I put the wheel over.) Thus she made an unforgettable picture for some men. Lieutenant Hamlin, of USS Houston, wrote later of what he saw as he looked out from Houston's number one eight-inch turret ' . . . there was Perth, a beautiful white bone in her teeth . . . three battle flags streaming . . . smoke pouring . . . firing all the time . . . rapid salvoes . . . shells falling all around her . . . it was one of the finest sights I have ever seen'.

Now Dave Burchell has brought back a different picture — one, because of the fatal suddenness of that night, we never expected to get. When men die at a distance from home in an unimagined place, with their bodies unrecovered and their graves unmarked, a terrible lack of finality gnaws with doubt and futile hope at the hearts of those left behind. Many will travel across the world just to see a wooden cross or a mound of earth to try to get that final acceptance. Now the bereaved of Perth have been given some vision of finality.

Altogether he made thirty dives, arduously piecing it all together. It is as if the ship, at last, is able to speak. He was the first man near her since the lucky ones had left her to save their lives and the rest had come with her to this faintly translucent Eden. Here, at last, was one who could take back news of those entombed when four of the eighty-seven torpedoes fired at her had hit. Now it was quiet and there was time to tell — and time to listen. She lay on her side like a mammoth resting. She looms like a towering block of buildings. In heavy weather she had often seemed tiny in a vast turbulent ocean; but in dry-dock she dwarfed the men who walked the wet barnacle-littered floor beneath her. And so she dwarfed this diver. He patiently explored, extending his endurance underwater and carefully reducing the time between dives so that he was able to make two a day. It was a calculated risk and he was never free of the possibility of an attack of the 'bends'.

There could not have been a better first visitor to the shrine of these dead men — never could they have been safer from desecration or vandalism. As well as fine feeling, Dave Burchell also brought uncommon skill.

The equipment had to be serviced, the compressor run, the bottles recharged and a hundred other things done that the non-expert has no idea of. Above all it took guts and perserverance to hang on and overcome the serious set-backs he unexpectedly met.

We now know that our shipmates' grave is not a sordid one. The relics were brought to the surface and photographed wet, just as they were. And they were unexpectedly beautiful, as if encrusted with gems. Coloured transparencies will attest the accuracy of this statement. Turquoise, topaz, emerald, pearl, onyx, opal and ruby were never more vivid than these sea-wet encrustations. They cloaked the profane relics with that kind of glory John Bunyan's Pilgrim might have expected in his heaven. The whole ship must look like this — 555 feet of her — and each funnel having as much area as a brig's main mast with all sail set. The whole is splashed with living colour; covered with the innocent, unprejudiced rainbow growth of animal and vegetable in harmony affirming indefeasible life-to-come. A mute sermon on the continuance of life, notwithstanding the most devastating havoc Man can wreak. The men who died so suddenly are now in a vast coffin decorated with a touching beauty which has the quality of impartial eternal justice: the significance of which, sadly, seems to escape Man as he seeks dominance and wins his successive pyrrhic victories.

Groper and other fish have established particular territories of their own now about the wreck. Where once Captain H. M. L. Waller, DSO, RAN, commanded and was killed, a large, good natured but sagacious groper now is the steadfast caretaker of the Compass Platform, the erstwhile nerve-centre of the ship in action. As I read of this it seemed to be an absolutely just and appropriate succession of command after our superb down-to-earth last Captain.

Nancy Waller, the Captain's widow who became a special sort of mother to all Perth survivors, gave it the nicest possible benediction when I told her about it. With blue eyes shining and a face lit from within, she said movingly, 'Oh, I am glad . . . Hec would be tickled pink to know that'.

Ray Parkin,
Ivanhoe, Victoria

31

Towards the end of 1968, a new involvement dawned for me when I was invited to stand for the Presidency of the North Adelaide Football Club.

Initially I wasn't too keen as my experience in football administration was limited and only covered a couple of minor jobs in the bush. Also North's previous president had been around forever and was sure to be a hard act to follow.

But the Senior Coach, Geoff Motley, a fearsome man known behind his back as Shark Jaw, rather felt I could do the job and as he wasn't the type with whom to argue I reluctantly agreed.

I think my trouble has always been that I never learn from previous experiences and unfortunately seem to be ready to plunge into situations for which I'm not adequately trained. Also that good old Australian adage of 'give it a go mate' may sound all very well, but it can get you into a lot of trouble.

However, some months later at the Annual General Meeting of the NAFC, I took over the reins of the club and with great naivety stumbled through the threshold into the hurly burly, rough and tumble of League Football administration.

I don't know what I expected at North Adelaide; probably I had a vision of myself floating around sorting out a few problems with Solomon-like wisdom and patting the players on the head. But I very soon discovered that to be pitch-forked into the Number One position of a league club, without preparation, was nearly suicidal and that first year was tough going indeed. Actually a working President's job is so complex that it could well be likened to being managing director of a large business and while the President isn't expected to physically do all the work, the ultimate responsibility is his and he is certainly expected to instigate and direct in the club's many and varied facets.

I found in my first bumbling year that it was presumed I was an authority on how to run bars and restaurants, how to out-think the Victorians during clearance wrangles, liaise with our landlord the local council, know where to get good deals on footballs, guernseys and boots and how to beat the nine other clubs to the best recruits and then if we did sign them, more often than not get them employment and accommodation.

On top of this was the advertising, letting of concessions, running bingo, staving off the bank manager, attending the half-dozen or so sub-committees, organizing players' contracts and so on and so on, ending up with constantly having to discipline the cheer-squad, who at that time always seemed to be in trouble. Also when things went wrong — which was often — I was invariably reminded by the old hands — whom were many — that my predecessor would never have let 'that' happen.

But such is life and I realized that I had been more than naive to have expected anything less and now having got into the thing it was up to me to try to get on top of it.

That first year we came a miserable fifth and the second year, when it looked as if we might know what we were doing, a disappointing fourth.

But the third year it all came together and with our new coach, Mike Patterson, at the helm and Barrie Robran taking all before him at centre, we were up, up and away and took out the 1971 premiership.

In 1972 we did it again and at the end of the season defeated Carlton, the Victorian Premiers and won the title 'Champions of Australia'.

In 1973 the third straight premiership just eluded us when North were beaten by Glenelg in a seven point desperate loss in the grand final.

They were great times and football has become a big part in both Ona's and my lives, as have the people that are also involved.

Chaps like John Blunden, who took over from me as president and many others, good workers, good blokes and it was a joy to work with them, as amongst the tears we also had a lot of laughs.

Then of course there are the players and what can you say about them.

Tough guys, weakies, iron men, characters. Some bursting with ability and no desire, others bursting with desire but no ability. Amateurs, pros, mercenaries. A few built like Tarzan with hearts like Jane and yet many built like Jane with hearts like Tarzan; the list is endless.

Then once in awhile if you are fortunate, you have a chance to associate with a chap like Barrie Robran.

In South Australia, in the opinion of the umpires, our Fairest and Most Brilliant Footballer each year is awarded the Magarey Medal. A player who wins this award becomes, in football circles, immortal — a legend. During his career Robran won three Magarey Medals and on top of this he captained and coached his club and also captained the State.

He had everything that goes to make a champion — the build, the skills, the commitments, even the modesty and over the years I got to know him like you would know your own son. For not only was I the president of the club for which he played, but he worked in my business with me for ten years and he was my friend.

Another friend to come my way from football was Neil Kerley, who I first met at a function at the Glenelg Football Club. We got on well right from the start and have been mates ever since.

Knuckles, the ominous nickname by which Neil is known, has played hundreds of league and State games, coached five different league clubs plus several State teams and is the most physically and mentally tough person I've ever met. Through Neil, who seems to be completely unfettered by the parochial restrictions of club interests, Ona and I have made many other friends in football circles.

Ken Eustice, who also won a Magarey Medal and played many games for the State and Wayne Jackson, that rare fellow who not only played for West Torrens League Club, but who at times was also the runner, the coach and the president.

Then there is John Cahill, another veteran of hundreds of league and State games and over the years coach of Port Adelaide, West Adelaide, and Collingwood Football Club in the Victorian Football League.

In addition to these characters are the other kind, generally colourful, frustrating fellows, who have a ton of ability and a total disregard for hidebound club rules and stuffy administrators.

There was the player we had to discipline at one time for his conduct off the field, an escapade which had so incensed the committee that it was decided to suspend him for two matches.

I was given the job to read him the Riot Act and as I was pretty cross with him was all set to give the lad a blast for his irresponsible attitude to the club, the guernsey, himself, life in general and anything else I could think of.

To set the right atmosphere it was arranged that he meet me in the club's boardroom at Prospect Oval and at the appointed time we sat down. I had hardly started to warm up when I noticed he was glancing at his watch.

'What's the matter?' I said, frowning at him. He gave me a sympathetic smile, as if he wanted me to know that he appreciated this was probably all necessary and that I was only doing my job. 'You won't take too long, will you?' he said, 'I want to be in town in about twenty minutes.'

Another player was finding it hard to get a job, so the club purchased three lawnmowers for him and set him up in the mowing business. They then circularised all the club members advising that it would help the player if the members used his services.

A couple of weeks later he was asked how the lawnmowers were going. 'Ah, I sold 'em', he said offhandedly. 'You sold them?' was the startled reply. 'Yeah,' he said, 'People kept ringing up and wanting me to cut their lawns.'

We were just completing transfer arrangements for a player from an interstate club and I was tidying up the end details over the 'phone. 'OK, that's it then,' said the interstate club's president. 'He's not very bright, but you've got yourselves a good player — if you can hold him.'

'Oh,' I said, experiencing a slight pang of alarm, 'why is that?'

The chap on the other end of the line laughed and replied, 'Well only last week I said in an effort to hold him, 'look son, we have arranged about ten different jobs for you during the last twelve months and none of them suit. Just what is it that you want to do? Name it and I'll do my best to fix it for you'.' Apparently the player thought for a moment and then his face lit up and he said, 'Well, yeah, there is something I wouldn't mind doing.' 'What's that?' exclaimed the exasperated official. 'Well, actually,' the lad replied. 'I've often thought I'd like to be a brain surgeon.'

Then there were the iron men, those tough guys whose resistance to pain and ability to carry injuries was incredible. Kerley and Robran are in this group, also Bugs Jaworskyj who had twenty stitches in his mouth at half-time and went back on and played the second half.

There were many tough guys at North Adelaide, but understandably injuries are not advertised and as they are kept under wraps as much as possible you didn't hear a lot about the opposition's problems, or their players ability to cope with them.

When I asked Neil Kerley who in his opinion qualified for the Iron Man class, he said after thinking for a moment, 'Freddie Bills was a tough bastard.' So with a recommendation like that from the original iron man, how could you leave Fred out?

★   ★   ★

At half-time during an interstate match in Tasmania, Knuckles fronted the doctor and sticking his chin about three inches from that startled gentleman's face, growled, 'There's something wrong with my jaw.' The doctor examined him and said, 'There's something wrong all right: it's broken. You'll have to come off.' 'Don't worry about it,' grunted Neil and going off into a corner on his own he sat down on a bench and with his hands helping to work his jaw chewed up eight packets of chewing gum. Then using this half masticated mess as a cushion for the break, he went back on and was voted as best man on the ground at the end of the game.

★   ★   ★

Over the years I've been fortunate to have been included in several interesting trips around Australia.

Once Geo Surveys chief mechanic, Alan Willmott and I drove a six-wheel drive Mac truck from Perth to Hall's Creek in the Kimberleys, the trip taking us through the historic towns of Meekathara, Marble Bar, Port Headland, Broome and Fitzroy Crossing.

301

The truck, which was fitted with over-sized smooth bomber tyres so that it could negotiate sand-hills, was needed for the carrying of helicopter fuel out to the Stansmore Ranges, south of Hall's Creek. On that trip Alan and I flew home in a light aircraft across the top end of Western Australia and the Northern Territory and on down to Adelaide via Alice Springs.

Another time with Darby von Sanden we did the reverse and flew up to the Alice then across to Hall's Creek, returning home via Broome, Mount Tom Price, Whittenoon Gorge and Kalgoorlie.

Also there have been flights with Ken Eustice, who flies his own plane and one in particular was when Ken took Neil Kerley, John Cahill and me on a trip around the north of the State.

Our first stop after leaving Parafield was 'Wertaloona' Station, west of Lake Frome and after spending three or four days with Bob and Dawn Wilson we headed off west over the Flinders Ranges to Ian Rankin's station, 'Mable Creek', twenty miles south of the Coober Pedy opal fields. It was here that Neil decided to play off the 'Marble Creek' tennis championship.

The scene was a far cry from Wimbledon, with the dress hardly classic Teddy Tingling. For the court surface was uneven cracked concrete, the balls we found after a search through the debris lining the backdrop and the racquets resembled tired snow shoes. Our dress, which was in keeping with the harsh surroundings was an assortment of odd footwear and our jocks.

Neil and I were to play Ken and Jack and as the three of them are fiercely competitive and hate to lose any form of contest, I could see that our opponents were all set to blast old Knuckles off the court and me along with him.

It was a blistering hot day with the temperature over the 110° mark and long before the game was over we'd all had enough. But as no one would give in the match dragged on, interrupted by loud and bitter arguments over the score and doubtful line calls. Then the injuries that the three of them had amassed over their long football careers, combined with the heat, started to take their toll.

Ken's 'Carnival Knee' went on him, Jack Cahill's ankles, sprained many times over the years, blew up, Neil's back got so bad that he could hardly straighten and due to the heat and sweat, my wooden leg was threatening to slip off. Towards the end, with the score at five all, I was serving.

It was deuce for the sixth consecutive time and as Neil went around behind the backdrop to retrieve the best of the bald balls, I fell down,uncaring, at the end of the court.

When he came back I told him I couldn't go on as I was having a heart attack. I should have known better. 'Get up,' he snarled. 'They don't know that, come on — two more strokes and we've won the match.' I looked towards the other end of the court where Eustice and Cahill were lying flat on their backs in the sparse shade of a tree. The whole scene reminded me of Banjo Paterson's marvellous poem, 'The Gee Bung Polo Club',when the players of both teams ended up dead or dying all over the field.

'OK,' I said struggling up. 'Give me the ball.'

The next serve aced poor old Jack, who couldn't move because of his ankles, this I followed with a weak effort that just cleared the net. Ken made a valiant effort and lunging off his good knee, returned the serve. But Neil, holding the small of his back with his left hand, sprang in and smashed it for a winner.

Turning on me, his back forgotten, he roared, 'Well done champ' and seizing me in a great sweaty bear hug he did a couple of spins, heaving me clean off the ground.

I just had time to see our opponents collapse back

under their tree when my leg, as if fed up with the whole deal, finally let go and complete with sandshoe, clattered on to the concrete court.

Two Aboriginal kids, attracted by the apparent ferocity of the match, had been timidly edging closer and closer in wide-eyed awe at the noisy antics of these strangers.

Their dismay grew at the sight of the two bodies under the tree, but when they saw the big fella attack his mate and fling him around like a dog worrying a rabbit until his leg came off — they had seen enough and fled shrieking.

★ ★ ★

At different times we have driven four-wheel drive vehicles up the Strzelecki Track to Innamincka and then across to 'Nappa Merrie' Station in South West Queensland. We always stop off with the Wilsons at 'Wertaloona' on the way and at 'Nappa Merrie' camp at a permanent water-hole on Cooper Creek, not far from the Burke and Wills 'Dig' tree.

These trips have not been without incident and once we burnt our camp to the ground at 'Gidgealpa' Station, when a gas refrigerator exploded while we were at the station homestead. Fortunately the vehicles survived but most of our gear, including the trailer with the booze and stores, went up in the spectacular blaze. On that trip Wayne Jackson and I travelled with Neil in his Range Rover, but on the second occasion, when our wives and Lyn and Malcolm Wuttke decided to come as well, we had a vehicle accommodation problem. But Ken Eustice,who was Australia's top Datsun dealer that year, fixed it with the Nissan Motor Company for us to take a Nissan 'Patrol' and test drive it for off-road conditions.

'Nappa Merrie' is an interesting station situated in

what is known as the Channel Country, where large areas receive the benefits of floods when the Cooper and Wilson Rivers come down.

It was originally settled by the Conrick family, who herded sheep in only ten years after Burke and Wills perished there in 1861. Apparently wild dogs and poor seasons proved too much for the sheep as now the station runs cattle, which are better suited to this type of country. The cattle, big Santa Gertrudis bullocks, are bred on 'Alroy' Station in the Territory and are walked down by drovers in months long overland drives. After three years at 'Nappa Merrie', which provides some of the best cattle fattening country in the world, the mature bullocks are then moved out on road trains to the Quilpie railhead and from there trucked to the stock markets in Brisbane. All this of course is not done without its problems, but in the expert hands of the 'Nappa Merrie' manager, John Rickertt and his wife Helen, the property is not only a picture to look at, but is highly efficient in terms of beef production.

John Rickertt, a stockman of the modern school, flies his own plane and where once it took six weeks and twelve men on horseback to muster cattle in the water-filled channels, now using the plane he achieves a twenty percent better result with half the number of men, in four or five days.

Mustering this country is made more difficult by the presence of rogue bullocks, virtually uncontrollable beasts, who either career off non-stop in the wrong direction or won't budge at all. Generally these fellows face a short life span, as not only are they a nuisance in themselves, but their anti-social behaviour soon rubs off onto the rest of the mob.

We came across a couple of these rogues the day John took me out mustering. Hiding under twisted Coolibah trees on the channel banks they wouldn't flinch, even when the plane with an ear-shattering roar clipped the

305

branches of the trees above them.

Aerial mustering is a dangerous business and demands intense concentration on the part of the pilot. John's system was to push the cattle out of the maze of heavily timbered and lignum covered channels towards his ringers, who were riding the firmer open ground at the sides. As the area we worked that day was two or three miles wide and about six miles long he had to continuously buzz the small mobs to keep them moving out, forcing them to plunge in and swim the larger channels. When he considered the cattle were within reach of the ringers he'd fly low over these chaps, advising through the loud speakers on the wings that there was a mob of say ten head, one hundred yards to their right. The head stockman, waving acknowledgement, would then despatch a rider to pick them up.

It was fascinating to me to witness the total picture from the air, that is, when we were in the air and not pulling G's as the plane dived in and out of the trees. John kept this up for seven-and-a-half hours the day I was with him and although I was exhausted, he didn't think anything of it.

On the way back to the homestead I called over the noise of the engine, 'What say we buzz camp?' John just grinned and heeled the plane over in the direction of the big water-hole. At the far end standing in the shallows we could see three naked figures. Doug Thomas was having a shave, Brian Linklater was washing his hair and Warren Brown was all soaped up.

At the sight of the plane coming in low along the water they jumped around waving and making rude gestures. I laughed, thinking how unwise they were to provoke this pilot, but even I wasn't prepared for the closeness of his passing run. When we were 100 yards away we were so low that I seemed to be looking up at them. For a second longer, they held their ground then the antics and the grins froze and like three hippos in a wallow, as one, they suddenly disappeared under the scant protection of the water.

Generally after a week spent camped on the bank of the 'Nappa Merrie' water-hole, we'd roll our swags and drive further north through 'Arrabury' and 'Cordillo Downs' stations, then on across the back country of South Western Queensland to Birdsville. Known internationally for its annual race meeting, Birdsville really comes to life during Race Week, when hundreds of light aircraft and motor vehicles bring in the converging crowds in their thousands.

Leaving Birdsville down the track which bears its name, the traveller has to be self-sufficient with regard to water, petrol, stores and spares when tackling the lonely trip to Marree, 540 kilometres away in South Australia.

Initially the Birdsville Track, before the advent of the road trains — those massive double-decker trucks and trailers that carry a 100 head of stock at a time — provided one of the few links for cattle stations in this area to the markets in Adelaide, 1200 kilometres to the south.

The cattle and the drovers, who herded the huge mobs down to the Marree railhead, were sustained by the brackish water in the string of scant water- holes and bores which dot the track.

The water-holes, fed by the occasional flooding of the Diamantina, Eleanor and Warburton rivers, in the north, are also replenished at times by Cooper Creek, the Clayton and the Frome further south.

Most of our outback is hard country and it takes a special breed to survive in it. It's hard on plant and stock and hard on people.

The Birdsville and Strzelecki tracks with their prolonged droughts and isolation are no exception and the stations that flank them, several now abandoned

307

with homesteads in ruins, can all testify to desperate times.

Neil Kerley 'helps' me into the water of
Cooper Creek

Ona and me at Burke and Wills 'Dig' tree
on 'Nappa Merrie' Station,
South West Queensland

32

In mid 1975 I had just returned from a trip to America and Europe where I'd studied a mixed bag which included trends in contract furniture, diving equipment and artificial limb manufacturing. Mostly it had been a pretty dreadful experience as like many first time travellers I'd tried to fit too much in to the time available.

Also in London I'd caught a massive dose of the 'flu and for the next month as I made my calls in the UK and Europe I lost over a stone in weight. For a normal bi-ped this wouldn't matter much, but for a uni-ped, using a suction type fitting on his artificial leg, it was disastrous.

Suction fittings are the modern method of leg attachment, completely doing away with straps and belts. But the attachment between the wearer and the leg relies entirely on a perfect fit and if the wearer suddenly loses weight the delicate fitting tolerance is upset, suction is lost and the leg falls off.

The first time this happened to me was in Stockholm. I was walking down the street when a chap tapped me on the shoulder and said, 'Excuse me, but is that yours?' I looked to where he was pointing and there lying on the footpath about ten feet back was my leg.

After that it fell off with increasing rapidity and reverted from being my once ever-reliable friend into a thing I could no longer trust. Without warning it would come off in taxis, restaurants, trains and once at a party at some people's place I hardly knew.

The big problem to a uni-ped is that if his leg falls off, he can't just whack it back on again hoping no-one has noticed. For generally when the suction lets go, it does so with a great blurting noise which is guaranteed to turn heads for a radius of twenty yards and if this is not embarrassing enough, the job of putting the leg back on is a personal affair, which normally is done in the privacy of his room.

Moving from one city to another became a nightmare. But by carrying my bags and crutches in one hand and bending over and holding my leg on with the other, I shuffled from one country to the next.

It was a humbling experience and not at all how I'd envisaged my visit to the great capitals of the world. For instead of strolling around, tall and handsome, taking in the sights, nodding and smiling at the girls, I was doubled over crab walking along and all too closely resembling Quasimodo at his pathetic worst.

However it wasn't all bad. I had a good time in America where I visited most of the main cities and down in Houston, Texas, where the four-inch shell case from the *Perth* had found a home, the city of Houston had made me an Honorary Citizen.

Also I'd squeezed in visits to nearly every castle and historic monument from the Tower of London to the Taj Mahal.

In Greece I made contact with the CO of the Greek Navy's Diving and Salvage teams, Commander Manoli Papagrikoratis.

Fortunately divers, like most minority groups, share a strong affinity with each other. It is a bond which seems to know no boundaries, either politically or internationally and once bona-fides are established, the understanding and respect to a fellow member of this tight Freemasonry is immediately given.

Such was the case with Manoli and I, for apart from being a diver he had also done para-scuba and was an experienced submariner. He was a real character, more than a bit of a devil and we hit it off straight away.

Through Manoli's help, then and during subsequent

trips to Greece, I've been fortunate to dive in most of the clear warm seas of the Aegean and Crete. I say fortunate, as the Greek Government is not always sympathetic to foreign divers, who over the years have pinched many historically valuable artifacts and sold them to overseas museums and collectors.

The Eastern Mediterranean provides top diving. Perhaps soft by our standards, as the water is warm and clear and there are no currents. Also, although the locals think they have sharks, they really don't know what a shark is. On top of this, as we were fortunate to do a couple of times, there is always the chance to dive on a BC wreck site.

But now in mid '75 I was back in Adelaide again and that particular trip was over. I wasn't sorry really for like most amateur travellers I'd come to the conclusion that wherever it may be, there's no place like home.

In the mail that had accumulated in my absence was a letter from Indonesia. It was from Sumantri and I smiled at the mental picture of him that it conjured up. It was the first letter I opened and relaxing back in anticipation of one of his usually interesting and amusing literary efforts, I was totally unprepared for the shock of his opening words.

'Dear Daddy' he said.

'The *Perth*'s bell is in Djakarta . . . '

I did a swift double take and read the line again. The words leapt out at me.

'The *Perth*'s bell is in Djakarta!!'

Desperately I scanned the page trying to take the whole report in at one go. Phrases caught my eye. 'Independent salvage company — Bell recovered — *Perth*'s — Japanese syndicate offering to buy it — all hush hush — nothing official — rumours — thought I should know — what was I going to do about it?'

I leaned back in the chair and made myself read the letter slowly in full.

Apparently an independent salvage company, run by an ex-Indonesian General, had been awarded contracts to salvage ships in the West Java area and in due course, inadvertently or without concern, they had worked on the *Perth* and recovered her bell.

The General, no doubt aware of the political implications involved, as he would have known that the Indonesian Government had promised the Australian Government to respect the wreck of the *Perth* as an official War Grave, had kept the damning evidence of the recovered bell under wraps until he decided what to do with it.

But rumours of the find had leaked out and at the time of Sumantri's letter, a wealthy group of Japanese were negotiating with the General to buy it. So far the General, who was now embarrassed by the whole affair, was sitting on the fence still contemplating in which direction he'd jump. Also, Sumantri added, that in the opinion of those in the know in Djakarta, if the situation became politically too hot, the bell would simply disappear.

I sat back lost in thought and stared unseeing out the window. 'What am I going to do about it', I thought. 'What can I do about it'. Letters and cables would be of no use. It was nearly eight years since I'd done the diving up there. I had no contacts. Everyone I knew except Sumantri would be gone. To go up to Indonesia myself was unthinkable. Hell, I'd only just come home. I hadn't even been in to the office. Even the thought of going to Djakarta made me feel ill — it wasn't known unaffectionately as the backside of Asia for nothing. No, that was out of the question — Ona would kill me. Wealthy Japs trying to buy our bell — I could just see them. What if this bloody General got cold feet and dumped it.

I thought of the *Perth* survivors and how, although I'd failed them in not bringing home their bell, they always

312

treated me as a special person. There was no doubt about it — it was still my job. I'd foreseen something like this happening ten years ago. Because of my previous effort in finding the ship — I was probably the only one who could really put the muscle on the General.

I thought of the War Memorial in Canberra and of my vision of the bell in its glass case. Following this came a clear mental picture of Captain Hector Waller, DSO, RAN and just as clear the memory of the promise I'd made him — to give it all my best shot.

I groaned in frustration. 'Jesus, Hec', I muttered resignedly, 'You're making it bloody tough'.

Ona came in with a cup of tea. 'What's the matter?' she said, 'you have been sitting there staring out of the window for twenty minutes. Aren't you glad to be home?'

'I'm going to Djakarta', I said.

'Oh good', she replied brightly. 'When — next year or the year after?'

I looked up at her and smiled sadly if such a thing is possible, realizing that it is always harder on the woman, as sometimes it is difficult for them to appreciate the old adage, 'A man has to do what a man has to do'. But I knew my girl. She would blow her top for a start, but after thinking about it for awhile, she would back me to the end, just as she had a dozen times before.

'No', I replied. 'Not next year or the year after — tomorrow'.

★ ★ ★

Sumantri was waiting at the airport when I arrived in Djakarta and as the passengers straggled across the tarmac from the 'plane, whilst I couldn't see him, I could certainly hear him.

'Hullo Daddy' came the cry from out of the faceless

313

The bronze gyro compass from the wheelhouse

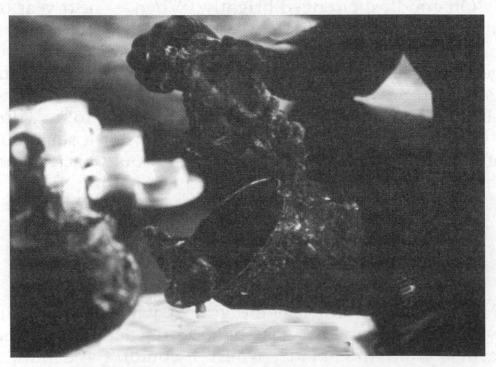

A voice tube mouthpiece from the bridge, before the sponge and marine growth was cleaned off

waiting crowd. 'That's my Daddy — the one with the wooden leg — Welcome home Daddy'.

Grinning ruefully, I silently shook my head and supposed it was good to hear that he hadn't changed.

We went straight to the hotel and up in my room Sumantri helped himself to a beer out of the 'fridge and filled me in on the latest developments in the saga of the bell. Things hadn't changed much — there was still only rumours — nothing official — the General hadn't made a move.

So deciding we might as well get stuck into it, I suggested to Sumantri that as it was still early evening we go and front the General straight away.

Eventually we found the place, it was in one of Djakarta's better suburbs, which didn't preclude it from requiring a couple of armed guards.

Sumantri and one of the guards, a mean-looking character who wasn't fussy where he pointed his automatic weapon, spoke briefly to each other in Indonesian. Then turning to me Sumantri said, 'Al Capone here says the General is not at home — he's gone out'.

I pondered this information for a second or two, there was probably no point in waiting — it could be hours before the General returned, I'd just have to make an appointment. 'Ah well', I said, 'tell him who we are and that we'll come back at 8 o'clock in the morning.'

It wasn't an ideal arrangement, as when mentally planning this first meeting with the General, I'd reckoned on using that well proven attacking element — surprise. For if the General was up to something, prior knowledge of my appearance would surely give him the opportunity of making any covering moves he'd feel were necessary. But as I had to be sure of seeing him, there didn't appear to be any alternative to making an appointment, so bidding Al Capone good evening and pleasant shooting, we left.

For a salvage contractor, the General's office was impressive. It was large and spartan, with creature comforts reduced to a brown linoleum covered floor, a single desk and a few uncomfortable looking chairs. Along the wall were stacked rusty and battered pieces of the salvage contractors trade.

Also as Sumantri ushered me in I noticed two hard-looking individuals, dressed in faded blue jeans, leaning against the wall. They were Europeans — young — perhaps in their mid twenties and I picked them to be divers.

The General looked up from the desk as Sumantri introduced us in English. I noted that he didn't waste time with the social graces, as he didn't stand up or offer to shake hands, but just nodded me into a chair. He was big and solid — I guessed in his fifties and looked exactly what he was — an ex-General now running a tough salvage operation — a busy man. He also looked as if he was used to giving orders and having them obeyed. There'd be no niceties here.

'What can I do for you?' he asked abruptly in a marked accent. I don't know what he was thinking, but my mind was racing and I needed a few seconds to replan. How best to handle it — the meeting wasn't going quite as I'd expected.

His discourteous attitude, which I guess was aimed at putting me off balance, nearly succeeded as my first thought was 'to hell with you'. I nearly snorted with amusement at the effect that sort of opening would make — no, keep calm — he's holding all the cards and he knows it. I covered these fleeting thoughts by the act of placing my briefcase on the floor, but calm or not, when looking back at the General, I couldn't resist the satisfaction of coldly eye-balling him for two or three seconds before replying. 'I understand that you have recovered the bell of the *Perth*', I said, deciding to plunge straight in.

'Yes' he grunted; at least he didn't waste words but his reply made my spirits leap.

'Then he did have it', I thought 'the rumours were right'.

I guessed he already knew who I was and of my interest in the bell, but this had to be established.

'Er — do you know who I am?' I asked, a bit embarrassed at having to put it that way.

'Yes', he replied 'you are the Australian diver who discovered the wreck of the *Perth* back in 1967.'

That was something anyway, at least I didn't have to go into lengthy explanations.

'Well', I said, 'I've come back up here to ask you to give me the bell, so that I can take it home to our War Memorial in Canberra'.

'Yes', he replied, just like that. 'You can have it'.

I should have been elated, but something was wrong, it was all going too easily and a glance out of the corner of my eye at Sumantri confirmed my doubts; he looked decidedly glum.

Asians generally, I've found, are no more honest or dishonest than any other race. That visiting Europeans are considered to be millionaires is understandable, as relative to the Indonesian economic situation they are and as such are thought of as fair game. This attitude is only directed at the faceless stranger, before they know him, for an Indonesian friend is just as honest and loyal as a friend anywhere. But they do tend to say what suits them at the time — it's to do with saving face. A promise made today, for one reason or another, is not always kept tomorrow and the uneasy feeling I had about this deal made me realize that we weren't home yet.

But in an effort to bind the transaction and to obligate him as much as possible, I stood up and

317

The bell

sticking out my hand said, with more confidence than I felt, 'Good — that's great. I'd like to thank you on behalf of the people of Australia'.

Under the circumstance the General had no option but to shake on it and continuing on as if it were all settled I asked, 'Now, would it be possible for me to see the bell?'

His reply startled me as I'd imagined the bell would be hidden far away in some vault or warehouse. 'Yes' he said, 'no trouble, it's there on the floor behind you'.

For a moment I appreciated how Jason must have felt when finally he found the Golden Fleece.

Almost unbelievingly, I turned and there it was — the *Perth's* bell.

Vision Come True
Before the bell finally came to rest in the Canberra War Museum it was briefly on show in a glass case in the foyer of the Adelaide Town Hall

319

Moving across I crouched down and placed my hand on the cold surface of this totally honourable piece. It was partly covered in calcified marine growth, but the inscriptions were plain and I traced over the etched letters with my fingers.

'HMAS *Perth* 1939' they read on one side and on the other 'HMS *Amphion* 1935'.

Lost in thought I stared at the bell for perhaps a minute, oblivious of the other people in the room, even Sumantri.

It had been a long road and although I knew it wasn't over yet, the sight of the bell hardened my resolve with an even fiercer intensity and I knew, come hell or highwater, there wasn't the slightest doubt as to its final berth.

'OK old son', I murmured half aloud, as if at last finding a long lost friend, 'its time you came home' and standing up I looked at the General hard — giving him the message. 'Right', I said, 'Where do we go from here?'

Sitting in the car outside the General's house it occurred to me how unusually quiet Sumantri had been. There must be something wrong, something of which I was not as yet aware. Perhaps his position in all this, that of being my declared ally, was proving to be more awkward for him than I realized.

I had to remember that we were dealing with the Top Brass in a Military State and it would be unfair after all he'd done if our association now compromised him.

In an effort to rouse him I elbowed Sumantri in the ribs. 'What do you think Admiral?' I asked, 'is it in the bag?'

He started the car without replying and we moved off down the road. His reply when it did come sounded the half-expected note of warning. 'Only 80% Daddy' he muttered, staring straight ahead, 'only 80%'.

We were on our way to the Australian Embassy, as

320

before leaving the office, I'd asked the General if he would like to personally present the bell to our Ambassador. My thought being that the kudos gained in making the presentation at such a high level, would more than compensate for what to him was the gift of just a few pounds of brass.

Also I'd started to formulate a plan. I reckoned that if the fact that the bell had been recovered was brought out into the open and people like the Australian Ambassador became involved, it would make it well nigh impossible for the General to renege. Consequently, I intended to inform and involve everyone and anyone.

At the Embassy I asked to see the Naval Attache and as Sumantri and I waited it reminded me of the first time I'd stood there and asked the same question eight years before.

I only hoped that whoever the present Naval Attache was, the fellow would be as helpful as Freddie Sherborne had been.

He came out of the lift and offered his hand. 'Clarke, Naval Attache', he said, 'how can I help you?'

I introduced myself and Sumantri and started to explain our business. 'Ah yes', he said, cutting me off. 'I thought I recognized the name. Perhaps you'd better come upstairs'.

Up in his office, I briefly ran through the events of the morning. 'Now I know it's short notice', I concluded, 'but could you ask the Ambassador to receive the General at say 10.00 am tomorrow and accept the bell?'

'Right,' he said, standing up. 'I won't be long'.

When Captain Clarke returned he looked worried.

'His Excellency feels that if we accept the bell, we will be condoning salvage operations on the ship,' he explained, 'and as this amounts to the desecration of a War Grave it could have serious political repercussions.'

'Hell,' I thought, taken aback, as I certainly hadn't

321

expected any problems from this direction.

'It's too late to cry desecration now and ask a lot of embarrassing questions,' I said. 'The deed's been done. Can't we just say that an independent salvage company was operating in the area and that the identity of the ship they were working on was unknown. When the bell came up they realized their mistake, they are sorry and they have offered it to us as a gesture?'

Knobby Clarke went off again to relay this suggestion to the Ambassador. When he returned this time he was smiling.

'Everything's OK,' he said. 'His Excellency has agreed and will receive the General in the morning.'

There was only one move left, that of obtaining permission from the Department of Marine, who technically owned the bell, for it to leave Indonesia. This, according to the General was a mere formality, so leaving the Embassy, Sumantri and I beat our way across the city to the Department of Marine.

About half-way there I gave him a nudge. 'What price now, old feller?'

'Still only 80%,' he said pessimistically. I didn't believe him — perhaps I should have.

At the Department of Marine the Minister received us and politely listened to the request.

When I'd finished he said everything seemed in order and that as far as he was concerned there was no reason why the bell couldn't be handed over.

Knowing how things can foul up with language and communication problems and also wanting to keep the whole affair moving I asked him to ring the General straight away and tell him that permission was granted. The Minister made some excuse to use a phone in an outer office and was gone a long time — too long. I became more and more uneasy. For awhile I tried to arouse Sumantri, who was in the middle of a rare downer, but finally gave up and we just sat there. After about half-an-hour the Minister returned and as he came in I stood up. 'Well, is everything OK,' I asked.

'Yes,' he replied. 'I think so, but before the General will hand over the bell he wants to know how much you are going to pay him for it.' For a moment I was genuinely puzzled. 'There must be some mistake,' I said, 'I have just left the General and he didn't mention anything about money.'

The Minister was suave. 'But he is a General,' he replied easily. 'He doesn't discuss such things.'

I looked at him in silence as it all started to come together — Sumantri's depression and his 80% — this smooth character no doubt in cahoots with the General — both of them playing me off against the Japs, who's involvement I'd forgotten — thinking they'd caught a real live one — with me and my naive Western way of shaking hands on a deal — just a boy on a man's job — a rank amateur let loose amongst the pros.

I felt the hackles start to rise — who did they think they were — how dare they!!

I leaned over his desk. 'He doesn't discuss such things,' I snarled with cold fury, 'well neither do I.'

'Pay for it!! Christ man — we have paid for it.' As I continued my voice rose. 'There are over three hundred of our chaps out there on that ship — they died helping to defend your country against the bloody Japs and now you want us to buy their bell back — how much a pound do you want for it?'

The Minister started back in his chair, surprised and embarrassed by this outburst, as no doubt he had been smugly anticipating some sort of educated horse-trading, with me of course ending up with the thin end of the deal.

'Mr Burchell,' he spluttered. 'I'm sure we can straighten this matter out.' 'I certainly hope so,' I grated, still boring in, 'because if you don't, you'll set Indo-Australian relations back twenty years.'

★ ★ ★

Walugo Sugito, the Colonel in Naval Intelligence who had been my initial contact eight years before, was now an Admiral and the Deputy Chief of Naval Staff. I had it down on my itinerary to call on him, more or less socially, but now I made a bee-line to his offices at Naval Headquarters to enlist his aid. Still feeling outraged, I guess I sounded off a bit to Walugo Sugito. I told him somewhat vehemently about the happenings over the past couple of days, ending up by saying, 'This General of yours is a crook'.

Fortunately he thought the remark was funny and snorted with amusement.

'David, David,' he admonished me, laughing. 'Your trouble is that you are too close to this thing. The moment someone doesn't respond as you would like, you condemn them. The General is a businessman, he has something he can sell. It would be the same if it was an Indonesian ship he had salvaged. You will get your bell — I'll guarantee it. But don't go round calling the General a crook.' He was of course quite correct — it was good advice and for a few seconds we sat there looking at each other; he was very astute, saying nothing, sensing that I needed a moment or two to get down off my horse.

It didn't take long and finally I sighed — relieved. 'OK, Wal,' I said. 'If you guarantee it, that's good enough for me.'

But I still slipped in a bit of insurance before ending it all. 'I'll inform our Ambassador that you have taken a personal interest and have guaranteed the bell's return,' I said innocently. 'He'll be very pleased.'

Sumantri was proud of me and my bit of insurance. Outside Naval Headquarters he said with a grin, 'At last Daddy — you learn the ways of the East.'

It was now obvious that my hope for a quick

324

handover of the bell was a lost cause, for I could see that it could take weeks for the red tape to clear.

This didn't really matter, I was confident that the job was done, but to make doubly sure I asked Sumantri to drive me around the traps again — the General — the Minister — our Embassy and finally Wal Sugito. It took two days to tell each of them what had been said and arranged by the others and after all the cross references were locked in tight and Sumantri had given me a 95% rating, I came home.

A month or so later I received a letter from Knobby Clarke advising that at a small ceremony at the Australian Embassy in Djakarta, the bell of the HMAS *Perth* was handed over — no charge.

The presentation had been made by the Director of Sea Communications on behalf of the Indonesian Navy. Clarke also advised that Lieutenant Colonel R. I. Sumantri had been in attendance.

We may have got our bell back without my trip to Indonesia — who knows? Naturally, I'd like to think I helped, but that isn't the point. How this eventuated doesn't really matter. The important thing is that it is back — where it ought to be.

We are a young country here in Australia, we need tradition and at times tradition requires the aid of both documented and visual evidence in order for it to build. As without these, the memory alone of an event, whatever it may be, can be a fleeting thing that sadly all too often fades with the life spans of the people who experienced it.

This is how I feel about the bell, as now the memory of the hard won tradition of the *Perth* will never fade. The bell will be in the Canberra War Memorial, visually reminding future generations of Australians of part of the cost of their heritage, for as long as we remain a nation.

The ship's bell showing HMS *Amphion* on one side and HMAS *Perth* — inscribed after she was recommissioned — on the other

33

Although many South Australian divers had searched for the *Loch Vennachar* for over a decade, it wasn't until 1976 that three members of the Society for Underwater Historical Research found the remains of this beautiful clipper.

Lost with all hands in 1905 during a voyage from London to Adelaide, the *Loch Vennachar* has always been one of South Australia's more intriguing shipwrecks. For although at the time there was much evidence of her loss, with identifiable cargo and smashed ship's boats being found, even after extensive land and sea searches there was no trace of the actual ship itself or of the twenty-seven members of her crew.

Some months after the *Vennachar* had been listed as missing, Trooper Thorpe and a Mr Charles May, whilst patrolling the desolate west coast of Kangaroo Island, discovered a large quantity of *Loch Vennachar* wreckage in West Bay. Also, half buried in the soft sand on the beach, they found the body of a lad whom, it was presumed, was one of the ship's four apprentices.

The Police Trooper reburied the boy in the sand-hills above high water and marked the grave with a simple cross that he made from one of the *Vennachar's* spars.

Incredibly, vandals recently burnt this original cross, but George Lanzar, the Flinders Chase Ranger, has since erected another.

Back in 1905 the news of the discovery of the West Bay wreckage, which included forty hogsheads of whisky, splintered decking, cordage and the stern of a lifeboat marked *Loch Vennachar* gave credence to the theory that the ship — off course and probably at night in a storm — had driven straight into the fearsome 200 feet high cliffs of Kangaroo Island's west coast.

However, no further evidence of the 250 foot long, 1 500 ton iron hulled ship, or of her crew was ever found.

Consequently the finding of the *Vennachar* in 1976 by the three Society for Underwater Historic Research members — Doug Seton, Brian Marfleet and Terry Smith — after seventy years of conjecture as to her fate, caused quite a stir in South Australian historical and diving circles.

At a hurriedly convened meeting the committee of the SUHR decided that the exciting discovery demanded a complete underwater archaeological survey. It was desirable that this be carried out as soon as possible, but it took a year to overcome the complexities, aggravated by the remoteness of the area and chancy weather conditions, that such a project presented.

Graham Seward, a man with wide experience in marine archaeology was appointed as Expedition Leader and along with an organizing committee was responsible for co-ordinating the whole venture. Finally over forty people, comprising divers, cooks, radio operators, etc. plus various vehicles, boats and other equipment necessary to carry out such an expedition, was transported to the West Bay base camp in February 1977.

My first job followed a phone call from Peter Christopher, the President of the SUHR. 'It is essential,' Peter said, 'that the government immediately proclaim the site an historic reserve in order to protect the *Vennachar* from possible vandalism. 'Also,' he went on, 'it would materially assist the project if the aid of the Police Under Water Recovery Squad and all its various equipment could be obtained.' He then pointed out that as I was the Society's Patron and as such was expected to have the necessary contacts to organize these things, how about I start organizing.

As it turned out, the job wasn't as difficult as it first sounded. I'd been at school with the then Premier, Don Dunstan and knew him well enough and fortunately the Assistant Police Commissioner, Lawrie Draper and I had previously both been on a committee, enquiring into the deaths of divers in the water-filled sink holes of the South-East.

After making appointments with Don Dunstan and Lawrie Draper I discussed the matter with them and they were both sympathetic to the Society's requests. The government proclaimed the site an historic reserve and promised financial assistance, also the Premier further gave the venture credibility by publicly announcing the proposed expedition through the media.

The South Australian Police Department, through Lawrie Draper, gave permission for the Under Water Recovery Squad, plus all their equipment, to accompany the expedition and subsequently the Police Squad was divided into two teams, with each team spending a week at the *Vennachar* site.

As the weather could make or break the project, much thought was given to this aspect . . .

February was chosen as historically it was the calmest month . . . So much for history.

In February 1977, out-of-season gale force winds lifted the huge Southern Ocean swells, smashing them onto the cliffs, and rollers that would have made the most ardent surfie hesitate, swept in through the heads of West Bay, finally ending up surging and crashing on the beach.

Consequently for the first week the project was grounded, as the sixteen foot inflatable Avons, the boats that were specifically chosen for the job because of their ability to handle rough surf, couldn't even leave the beach.

But during the second week the weather improved

329

and although the initial attempts by the more impatient divers resulted in their Avons rearing right over backwards in the heavy surf, finally boats started getting through and the diving commenced.

It was towards the end of this second week that I caught up with the expedition. Flying over to Kangaroo Island in a light aircraft, we landed at the Flinders Chase strip, a few miles from the West Bay camp. The next morning Sergeant Marty Harnath, who was in charge of the Police Under Water Squad, along with two senior constables, Big Al Cormack and Moose Marfleet, rustled me up some gear and we prepared to go out to the wreck site in one of the Police Department's Avons.

The first attempt to leave the beach was a disaster. A big wave, building up and just about to break, caught the boat head on, lifting the bow high in the air and even though we were ready for trouble, we were all flung head over turkey into the sea.

It didn't take long to right the boat and collect the loose gear, as we were fully kitted up even to wearing scuba and loose items had been purposely kept to a minimum.

Then, when we were all set, we tried again. This time we got through, admittedly we lost Big Al Cormack as the Avon shot into the air over one wave, but the rest of us refused to let go, as being dumped onto that sharp rising beach in full diving gear was something you tried very hard not to do twice.

Marty Harnath kept the long suffering Mercury outboard at full blast and after clearing the surf line we waited for Big Al to battle his way through the breakers and swim out to us. The Avon is an interesting craft. Made from tough rubber impregnated canvas, when inflated rather resembles a glorified tractor tyre tube. Its low profile makes it an ideal diving boat and under normal conditions it is excellent in the surf.

They can take quite a powerful outboard — the one

the police used was 40 hp — and the boat readily comes up on the plane.

Consequently it didn't take long to travel the mile or so out and around the North Head of West Bay to where the *Vennachar* waited under the formidable cliffs.

As a result of the maelstrom close inshore, created by the twenty foot ocean swells that were recklessly ending their long sweeps from the Antarctic against the base of the cliffs, it was necessary to anchor some 200 yards out to sea. The technique used when diving under these conditions, i.e. when a diver is unable to enter the water from the land and a boat can't anchor over the site, is for the diver to go over the side out in the safe area and then swim in underwater on the sea bed.

This is not without its danger, for a mishap such as the loss of a weight belt or any other accident that could force a diver to surface, would immediately place him in a perilous situation. As a swimmer on the surface in this type of sea would soon be cut to bits against the needle sharp rocks.

But these are the dangers and risks of first class diving and whilst they are not taken lightly, if a diver does go in at a spot like this, he must accept the risks as part of the dive.

Moose Marfleet was my diving partner and when we were ready he raised his eyebrows at me from across the Avon, I nodded and without a word we both went over the side backwards. Once under water I took a quick look around, as first-class diving or not, this was also first-class shark country and over the years I'd seen several big White Pointers along this coast.

Fortunately there didn't appear to be any and with Moose hot on my trail, I made for the ocean floor ninety feet down.

The water was exceptionally clear and even from the surface every detail on the bottom was revealed, with the thick kelp and a prehistoric creek bed, that wound its way through the mass of tumbled granite boulders, being stark in their clarity.

Moose and I quickly reached the sea floor and by holding on to any hand grips that we could find, braced ourselves against the surge of the ocean swells, whose influences are just as strong down at ninety feet as they are on the surface. Carefully we worked our way in, pre-planning every move from one hand-hold to the next. But even then at times we lost control and were swept along by the surge at breakneck speed, bouncing and slamming into the granite boulders. Then at the end of the surge, quickly trying to grab for a hand-hold so as not to be sucked back again, equally fast in the opposite direction. It was rough stuff and just as I was beginning to think it couldn't be much worse up on top, the first signs of the *Vennachar* started to appear. As we moved on into a point right under the cliffs we were surrounded by twisted iron plates, unrecognisable bits of heavy deck gear, wire hawsers, anchors and chains. Apart from the anchors there was hardly anything readily indentifiable as having been once part of the graceful *Vennachar*.

It was a sad scene, doubly so if you knew the *Vennachar's* history, as she had been unfairly tagged as a jinx ship after a series of misfortunes, the last one being when she was rammed and sunk whilst at anchor in Thameshaven in 1901. The accident was not of her making, but after she was refloated the superstitious old sailors of the day claimed the ship had died and that she had lost her soul. From the time I first studied her history I'd always felt that it was most unjust that the *Vennachar* had been branded a jinx and I admired the ship for the resolve she had shown during her thirty years of service. Now to find her like this, battered beyond recognition, to me the indignity of it seemed the most unkind cut of all.

I must say I lost most of my enthusiasm for the dive

when I saw how badly the ship had been knocked about, but Moose and I swam around peering and poking until our time was up and then, grabbing once more for the hand-holds, we started on the hazardous trip back to the Avon.

From the Society's point of view the expedition was a great success. Most of the objectives set were achieved and it was no mean feat to organize a show as big and complicated as this. They would have preferred better weather, but this is always the risk when diving on a natural wreck as opposed to say a war wreck. For if the weather in an area was predictable, the natural wreck probably wouldn't be there in the first place. The police were happy enough. The rigours of setting up a camp in such an isolated spot were really no problem to them and the arduous diving conditions presented the squad with useful practice runs.

Finally, although the society compiled an excellent report on the venture, which highlighted its successes and the lessons learnt, to me my dive on the ship was rather a sorry episode.

For whilst I'd seen several wrecks previously in as bad a state, I didn't have the same feeling for them and I'd have preferred to retain the mental picture I had of this much maligned ship, before the sea took its final unkind toll.

34

One morning in early February 1976, the phone rang, Jane answered it and called, 'It's Channel 7 Sydney for you Dad.' I took the phone and the chap on the other end of the line said, 'We're doing a documentary on the new *Perth* and during our research discovered your involvement with the old ship. How about coming over to Sydney? We feel you have something to contribute.'

'Oh,' I said cautiously, 'Are you doing it in conjunction with the navy?'

'Hell yes,' he replied. 'The navy knows all about it, they are co-operating fully.'

'Well in that case I'd only be too pleased,' I answered. 'What do you want me to do?'

'Just fly over' he said off-handedly, 'say about the 12th and we'll work it out from there. It will only take a couple of days.'

I checked my diary and the dates fitted in. 'OK,' I said, 'but how about I drive over and pick up the original *Perth*'s bell in Canberra. That should help the documentary.'

His reply held a strange note of excitement, but it didn't mean much to me at the time. 'It certainly would help,' he said, 'it certainly would.'

I well remember the day I left for Canberra — it was the morning after Derek Bollen's wedding. Marina, his new wife, has a Russian mother and the vodka had flowed. I still don't drink much but when I do it always seems to be the wrong stuff.

However Peter Butterworth and Don Davies helped me out to the car and Ona drove me home. The next morning I pulled up surprisingly well, but I haven't touched vodka since.

At about 6.00 am Ona and our four girls saw me off and pointing the car in an easterly direction, I headed for Canberra.

After arriving at the National Capital I looked up a few old navy friends — David Leach who had been the Captain of the new *Perth* back in 1967, when the gift was made of the voice tube mouthpiece and David Martin, whose father, a Commander, was killed during the original *Perth*'s final battle in 1942.

After a cup of coffee with Vice-Admiral Stevenson, Chief of Naval Staff, who wanted to see me and talk about the diving and final bell recovery, I then headed for the War Memorial to collect the bell.

A woman on the restoration staff of the museum workshop started in to give me a hard time. Fussily she told me how valuable the bell was and how careful I should be in looking after it and that it really shouldn't be leaving the security of the museum, I gave her a pained look, but before I could reply the Director of the War Memorial cut in, 'I think Mr Burchell is well aware of the bell's value,' he said reprovingly. 'Just put it in its box and get some help to carry it out to his car.'

In Sydney, as arranged, two burly young matelots arrived at the hotel room and took the bell to Garden Island, where the new *Perth* was waiting. I was to follow an hour later.

When I arrived, although they hadn't told me much about what to expect, I certainly wasn't prepared for the battery of lights and cameras that greeted me, or the startling shrill of the Bosun's whistle as he piped me aboard. On the quarter-deck, a bit flustered, I shook hands with the *Perth*'s skipper, Captain Hutson and some of his officers. 'What's going on, Captain,' I whispered. 'What are we meant to be doing?'

He looked decidedly nervous. 'Don't ask me,' he replied, mopping his brow. 'The producer fellow just said to try and act naturally, so far this is only the introduction to the documentary, apparently we're not on sound yet.' It all seemed pretty odd, but having had some previous experience with TV productions where the poor unprepared guests are just thrown in front of the cameras, I supposed they knew what they were doing.

At the producer's request we left the quarter-deck and trooped up to the bridge. There in all its gleaming glory, on an Ensign covered chart-table, stood the bell. I gave it a proprietary pat, just to let it know I was still around.

The producer was darting about issuing orders. 'Now, we're not on audio yet,' he said to me, 'we're still on the introduction — so if you and the Captain can stand each side of the bell — just be talking about it — that's right — looking down — good — everyone ready — lights — camera — action.' By now Captain Hutson wasn't the only one feeling nervous.

'Piss off,' I hissed at him.
'We're doing a documentary.'

We were in the middle of this charade when a chap virtually popped out of the scuppers and walking straight in front of the cameras said something like, 'You know why I'm here Captain — but Dave doesn't — Dave Burchell . . . THIS IS YOUR LIFE!'

I stared at him uncomprehending, startled; 'What did he say?' I thought, 'Who is he? — his face looks familiar — anyway what the hell does he think he's doing — walking in front of the Captain like that?'

'Piss off,' I hissed at him. 'We're doing a documentary.'

The producer, who apparently hadn't had much of a day, clapped his hands to his forehead. 'Cut!' he yelled.

Back in Peter Hutson's day cabin he and I had a much needed drink. I was still shaking my head, I just couldn't believe it. I suppose that show business people or international sports stars expect this kind of thing, but . . .

'Don't sit there shaking your head,' Peter Hutson said feelingly. 'It's happened all right. I don't mind telling you, even the thought of the bloody thing has been worrying me for weeks,' and I laughed at the memory of how nervous he'd looked when I'd first come aboard. Then I thought about the other people who must be involved.

'Did Admiral Stevenson know about it?' I was about to ask, but thought better of it. What a stupid question, of course he would. No-one would loan a multi-million dollar destroyer as a TV prop without the Boss's approval. The realization that the navy had been prepared to do this for me began to sink in and I started to shake my head again.

Momentarily lost in thought, the full appreciation of this unique honour swept over me. I knew, as well as anyone, that the navy is not given to idly handing out its bouquets.

You have to earn them and it came to me quite

337

clearly why the *Perth* had been loaned to the TV people. Those long years — the lonely dives — the equally lonely times in Indonesia — the verbal battles and confrontations — the bell. It was the navy's way of saying 'thank you — job well done'.

I felt very proud and yet with a strange mixture of emotions, in a way sad and suddenly the whole thing was almost too much to handle and I had to swallow hard.

I wished my mother was still alive, as she would have understood and I missed her not being there to share it with me.

In the car on the way to Channel 7's North Sydney studios, I tried unsuccessfully to find out who the other guests on the show would be.

I guessed Ona and the girls would be there. That was great and it meant I wouldn't miss Susan's and Cassie's birthdays after all. But as to the rest, I had no idea — I only hoped they wouldn't produce someone I couldn't remember. I mentioned this to the woman in charge. 'Just relax,' she said laughing. 'Enjoy the evening. We won't bring on anyone you won't know.'

In the main auditorium, Mike Willesee had finished telling the audience what was required of them. All was ready — even the bell was there — spot lit — centre stage — enjoying the limelight.

I came in and as requested sat down on a settee and from then on the night could only be described as a gigantic surprise party.

The first guest was Don McLeay, who told an unlikely version of how we'd fallen off the train, thirty-five years before. Then Tom Herraman — the tallest pygmy in the world — his story was how the other members of the State Diving Troupe had always envied me, as I didn't have to keep my legs together when diving off the tower.

After Tom, Reg Lindsay came yodelling through the

Ross Curnow, Bruce Berry and
Kym Bonython chat with Mike Willesee
on 'this Is Your Life'

curtain and insisted on paying the $1.40 he'd owed me
for about thirty years for his half share of the cost of a
record we'd made in our duo singing days.

Canon Alwyn Blaxell was next and he reminisced
about the church days at St Margarets in Tumby Bay.
After Alwyn the cameras panned round the audience
and as Mike Willesee introduced them, several old
friends stood up and gave a wave. Apparently because of
time limitations everyone present couldn't be on the
show. It didn't really matter, the main thing was that
they were there.

First the roving camera picked out Mac Lawrie, then
Don Brown and on to Bob Vollugi, my old form master
at school. After Bob was Snook Godliman, Ken
Langley, Barrie Robran and finally finished up on Peter
Hutson, who still looked nervous.

But back on stage they'd hardly started and a group
of three divers came on. Bruce Berry talked briefly
about the dive in the gold mine, Ross Curnow got
tangled up with the Englebret Caves at Mount Gambier

and Kym Bonython told how he'd nearly frozen to death waiting in his submarine after the Para-Scuba jump at Port Noarlunga.

Mike Willesee then asked about Bill Romeyn of the Royal Netherlands Harbours Works, wondering where he would be right now. The last I'd heard he was working an oil rig in the North Sea and I said that he was probably still there. But the next person through the curtain — all the way from Scotland — was Bill Romeyn.

Ona, the only guest I really expected, followed and I started in to jokingly remind her that a wife is not meant to keep these kind of secrets from her husband. But it was wasted, for I don't think she even heard me, as she looked a damn sight more nervous than Peter Hutson.

Then in a burst of colour and glamour came my girls, the four of them, all at once. Jane, Mandy, Susan and Cassie. Amid the confusion and the hugs they looked pretty good to me and I reckon they stole the show.

After things quietened down Ray Parkin appeared. He spoke of the *Perth* and of her final battle and of his

Mrs Waller

thoughts on the diving.

While he spoke, videos were shown on the TV screen of the ship in action and in the background there were the sounds of the guns and the men.

This set a more sombre scene for that top hand Freddie Sherborne who was next. We talked briefly of Djakarta before Mike Willesee broke it up by promising ample time to talk at the party afterwards.

Mrs Waller, that charming person, to whom the *Perth* had meant so much, came onto the stage after Freddie. She was very gracious and her presence on the show was most moving and appreciated by everyone.

By now I knew who the last guest would be. I was quite certain that it was Sumantri and when he came out with that ear to ear grin I just stood there with thoughts and memories tumbling. We clutched each other in bear hugs, then pushing me away to arms' length he glanced across at centre stage.

'The bell!' he said with great feeling and turning back, the grin gone and his eyes on mine, he made a remark that would have been lost to everyone else.

'One hundred per cent Daddy,' he whispered, 'One hundred per cent.'

'This Is Your Life' — The Cast

35

Among his many accomplishments, Chappy Charlesworth a good mate of mine, is also a very competent diver and good company, and when an opportunity to dive in the Truk Lagoon arose in 1978 I asked him to come with me. This he was pleased to do and after much preparation, we set off.

Unless you are a diver there would be few reasons to go to Truk as it has little to offer the modern jet-set tourist. Conditions are primitive and the dirt roads winding their way through the jungle are a pot-holed war-time legacy left by the Japanese. Being tropical it is very hot, but it still manages to average over an inch of rain a day and consequently everything is damp, with the exception of the booze situation, which is dry.

The flight to Truk which is roughly north of Papua New Guinea and east of the Philippines is a long one. going via Noumea in New Caledonia, Nauru on the Equator and Ponape in the East Carolines.

But to Chappy and me the problems of getting ourselves and our mountain of gear there was as nothing, for the place is considered a veritable Mecca by the underwater brigade and like pilgrims trekking to the Promised Land we were prepared to face any trial to get there. For at Truk the forty-mile diameter lagoon contains the greatest collection of modern sunken ships in the world, the water is clear and relatively shallow and because it is Trust Territory the wrecks are virtually untouched.

On the way to Truk we called at Ponape Island, a lonely volcanic peak in the North Pacific and all that is now visible of a long since submerged mountain range. Circling the island like a lace collar is a gently sloping coral shelf, extending out to perhaps a mile. At its perimeter where the depth is about forty feet and just before the shelf drops vertically away to the distant ocean floor thousands of feet below, are acres of spectacular table coral. Up to ten feet in diameter and supported on their delicate single stems, they are scattered over the myriad split levels of the shelf like so many huge flat-topped mushrooms.

Our accommodation on Ponape was interesting in that we shared a one-roomed native hut, built on top of a hill behind the settlement. The hut's base was made up by a network of logs lashed together with vines, it was open at the sides and had a palm frond thatched roof which although it leaked under the torrential rain was still relatively dry inside. This shelter not only provided a haven for us, but also for most of the things that flew, crept or crawled on the island as well and it was a brave man who jumped straight into his bed at night without first inspecting it for the presence of lizards, spiders or snakes.

Finally after a week of interesting travel we arrived at the volcanic island of Moen, one of the dozen or so islands, that when circled by the impressive outer ocean reef, formed Truk lagoon.

Known to many as the Gibraltar of the Pacific, Truk was occupied by the Japanese during World War II and it was here that they established the strategic Naval and Airforce Bases that were to prove such a problem to the Allies.

In 1944 when the American advance pushed up northward towards Japan, it was decided to bypass Truk, the plan being to land troops on Palau and Guam in the Marianas, as these islands were within closer striking distance of the Japanese mainland. However, as the enemy installations in Truk could not be left operable, the shore bases, airstrips and the ships at anchor in the lagoon, were destroyed by the

344

Americans in massive air attacks.

Operation 'Hailstone' as it was called, began shortly before dawn on 17 February 1944. The aircraft carriers *Bunker Hill, Enterprise, Yorktown, Essex* and *Intrepid*, under the command of Vice-Admiral R. A. Spruance and Rear Admiral M. A. Mitscher, were stationed about ninety miles north-east of Dublon Island, the main centre of operations for Japan in Truk. Seventy-two Hellcat fighters were launched against the Japanese forces inside the lagoon. This first wave of planes was given the task of destroying enemy aircraft and assuming complete air supremacy. The second wave of Dauntless Divebombers were to drop fragmentation bombs and incendiaries, the object being to knock out the airfields and render them unusable. These attacks were followed by a third wave comprising fighters, dive-bombers and torpedo bombers. Their mission was to destroy the fleet that was sheltering in the lagoon and at the end of the attacks, sixty ships, totalling over 200 000 tons were on the bottom.

Our first dive in the lagoon was on the wreck of the *Kiyosumi Maru* a transport of some 8 600 tons and over 450 feet long. She was lying on her port side in 110 feet of clear water. Swimming through the torpedo hole eighty feet down Chappy and I crossed through the engine room to the deck to find the whole ship covered in colourful hard and soft coral. These, combined with the garland-like marine growth flowing from her superstructure, gave the impression that she had been dressed for some festive occasion.

This of course was not the case, unless the scene is viewed as nature's answer to a Shinto burial shrine, for when the *Kiyosumi* went down she took seventy Japanese sailors with her and as we moved quietly about we saw several skeletons in the bridge area and in the cabins.

There were many reminders of the fateful day this

ship was sunk. A lonely water-logged tennis shoe, a pile of dinner plates, spilled onto the canted deck from a galley table, the tiled officers' baths in the ablution area behind the bridge. Then on the more lethal side were the silent coral-encrusted guns, the holds full of small arms ammunition and other war related material.

As the days went by we dived on many such ships. Massive armed aircraft ferries like the *Fujikawa Maru*, which is resting upright in 120 feet with the tops of her masts showing above the surface. In her holds we found partially stripped Zero fighters, machineguns, tyres, heaps of aircraft parts and a small outboard motor deep in one of the holds. On the *Yamagiri Maru* is a pile of eighteen inch shells that were destined for the battleships *Yamamoto* and *Musashi*, but thanks to the Americans these shells, the largest made during World War II, never arrived and now, guarded by a pack of restless grey reef sharks they never will.

In the bridge area of the 500 feet long oil tanker *Shinkoku Maru* we saw phonograph records, rifles, an operating table and even a typewriter still sitting upright on a desk.

As I looked at this last item I couldn't help thinking of the long since gone records clerk, who must have used it to tediously bang out his endless fleet refuelling reports, his thoughts possibly far away on his distant family and homeland.

The *Fujikawa* was a favourite dive, unfortunately she was so big and our time down so limited that even though we visited the ship on several occasions, we only just began to know her.

We sat in the soaking tubs in her two large bathrooms, swam in and out of the several bridge levels inspecting the instruments and gauges and explored her six holds.

Then when it was time to go we did our decompression stops by holding on to her masts for

346

stability, always looking down — thinking and wondering. During our two weeks in Truk we dived on twenty different ships, transports, tankers, destroyers, troopships and tugs. Some had strange sounding names, *Sankisan, Hoyo, Heian, Amagisan* and *Fugisan*, while others were more familiar, *Seiko, Susuki, Rio de Janeiro* and *San Francisco*.

During our 'up' time, filling in between dives, we would snorkel on some of the many aircraft that had crashed in shallow water just offshore from the old fighter and bomber strips. We sat at the controls of Betty bombers, Emily flying boats and Tony and Zero fighters. Again with imaginations running riot at the thought of the dramatic scenes that must have preceded the moment of their disappearance under the surface of this now placid lagoon.

Towards the end of our stay, Chappy and I dived 160 feet down to the sunken Japanese submarine the *I 169*. Just over 330 feet long and weighing 1 400 tons; she had submerged to avoid the US air strike in 1944 and after the raid was over, failed to surface.

Apparently the next day, a diver had been sent down to investigate. There were responses to his hammer signals from all the hatches except the conning tower, so it was assumed that very little water had entered the sub. A thirty ton crane was sent to try and hoist her bow to the surface, but the cable snapped under the weight and the sub sank again to the bottom. By then there were only feeble answers from the after torpedo compartment and efforts to signal to those inside to open the ballast tanks were unsuccessful. Shortly after, all signs of life from within the sub ceased and the rescue effort was abandoned. The *I 169* was declared lost with eighty-seven Japanese crewmen on board dying with her.

After all these years it was an eerie sensation to swim along the outside of her hull. At times I would stop, placing my hand on the steel plates, listening, almost expecting to feel and hear those long since gone hammer blows of the trapped crew inside. But of course there was nothing and it was with almost a feeling of relief that we left her, for somehow she seemed as evil in death as she must have been in life.

We left Truk for Guam, the first leg of our trip home on a clear afternoon a few days later. We said our goodbyes to new found friends, the US Navy diving team, our Trukese guides, the waitresses at the hotel and the few other divers that had gathered, like us, from all over the world. It had been a rare experience and Chappy and I both knew that whatever our diving futures held, it would never be quite like Truk with its sheer volume of ships, clarity of water and its nostalgic link with another race and another time.

Table coral at Ponape

36

Early in December 1978 the Navy rang and asked if I'd like to go for a trip in the new *Perth*.

Apparently several warships from the Australian Fleet were carrying out manoeuvres with the Royal Navy in the Indian Ocean and I was told that if I could get myself to Fremantle, the *Perth* would pick me up and I could cruise with the fleet back to Sydney.

'Great,' I said. 'What date should I be in Fremantle?' The chap from the navy told me and I checked my diary, purely as a matter of course as I felt I'd cancel almost anything rather than miss this trip. But there, right in the middle of the seven or eight days it was anticipated the *Perth* would take to get to Sydney, was an arrangement that was too late to cancel.

Ona and I had invited eighty people in for a Sunday morning Christmas party and there was just no way out of it — or was there — it was worth a try.

'Er — just a minute,' I said into the phone and turning to Ona and using one of those 'it's a bit of a nuisance, but I suppose I have to' tones — which incidentally never works and only makes women suspicious, as they always suspect an ulterior motive — I said, 'How about that dear. It's the navy on the phone from Canberra, they've invited me to do a trip on the *Perth*. It's a wonderful opportunity, but there's one small problem, if I do go it may mean that I could miss that Christmas party we've arranged. You see . . . '

'Forget it,' she snapped. 'If you think I'm going to run that show on my own, you've got another think coming. Half the people you have invited are business friends of yours, I don't even know them.' Then she slipped into top gear as only wives can. 'Who's going to clean the

349

pool and cut the lawns — what about the beer and the troughs for the ice that you are meant to pick up the day before — who will entertain all those strangers?' I thought of Greg Edmonds and John Thring who later became Jane and Cassie's husbands. They were going to give me a hand and act as barmen. 'What about Greg and John?' I said, 'they could . . . ' 'God,' Ona snorted, exasperated. 'You really are too much. You know very well that they know even less people coming than I do.' Resignedly I could see it was time to quit, 'Well — yes — I suppose you're right,' I ended lamely. Then turning back to the phone I asked, 'You did say the *Perth* was going straight to Sydney. She's not coming in to Adelaide?'

'No,' the chap replied. 'Straight through from Fremantle, she'll be in Sydney 0800 Tuesday.'

'I'm sorry,' I said sadly, 'but I can't make it. I've an appointment on the preceding Sunday that I just can't break.'

'Well, that's bad luck — would have been a good trip,' he said, then added, 'when did you say you had to be in Adelaide?'

I told him, 'Saturday at the latest.'

'Hmm,' he replied thoughtfully, 'I'll see what we can do.'

A couple of days later he rang back. 'Well, it's all arranged,' he started off, 'we contacted the Royal Navy and the Brits have agreed to transfer you at sea from the *Perth* to HMS *Mohawk*. *Mohawk* isn't scheduled to go to Sydney and as she's due in Adelaide on the Saturday morning it all worked in perfectly.'

'Hell,' I said, delighted, the whole thing sounding better than ever. 'That's marvellous, thanks very much.'

Ona wasn't impressed, her faith in the navy didn't match mine. Coldly emphasizing each word she said, 'If anything goes wrong and you don't make it back in time, I'll sink both you and the navy!'

On board *Perth* I had a great time. The captain gave me his day cabin along with the run of the ship. 'Do what you like,' he said after I'd asked him in what areas he didn't want me. 'If you get in the road someone will tell you.'

The navigator told me to use his elevated chair on the bridge, which meant that when things were happening I could be in the thick of the action and yet be out of the way.

Clad in anti-flack gear, I joined the gunners in their turrets during gunnery practice. Although these days gunners only man the turrets in case of power failure, as the guns are automatically loaded, trained and fired from a control station deep within the ship.

We did a RAS — refuel at sea — from HMAS *Supply*, with the two ships ploughing alongside each other at twenty knots, the heavy oil hoses having been dragged across by a light line that was shot over the gap between the ships. Thousands of tons of controlled steel and horsepower against the sea, with the *Perth's* navigator, concentrating, committed to keeping his ship on station, as a drift of a few feet in any direction would mean snapped lines and hoses.

During the week along with the complicated night manoeuvres by radar, we fired guns and mortars, ran missiles out onto their launching pads and rendez-voused with land-based aircraft. There was something happening all the time.

Out in the Great Australian Bight, 300 miles south of the coast, the weather was deteriorating and by the time Thursday came — the day of my transfer to *Mohawk* — it was blowing a gale with the waves thirty feet high.

At breakfast the navigator looked at me and raising his eyebrows queried, 'I believe you are leaving us today?'

'Yes,' I replied, 'this afternoon I think.'

'Hmm,' he said. 'That should be interesting. I must try not to miss it.'

When the time came, *Mohawk*, dead in the water 200 yards off our port bow, lowered a cutter and as it approached, the small boat disappeared completely from sight in the troughs of the huge seas.

On board *Perth* the Executive Officer and six stout lads had me ready and waiting, hanging over the side of the ship.

One end of a rope was looped under my arms and the other, after passing through a pulley fixed to an outswung davit, was held by the six stout lads. The idea being that as the Royal Navy cutter came alongside they were to lower me into it.

But the sea had different ideas.

One second the cutter was six feet below me and the next, in a great sickening drop at about the speed of an express lift, it was thirty-six feet below.

Seeing the cutter momentarily within reach the *Perth*'s EXO called 'drop' and the sailors let go of the rope, but even though I plummeted down like a condemned man through the trapdoor, I still couldn't catch up to the Brits.

'Stop,' yelled the EXO and six pairs of hands closed on the rope. Then, as he saw the cutter rearing up on the next wave with me hanging defenceless in its path, the EXO called 'pull'. Up I went, the Royal Navy in hot pursuit, clutching at my fast disappearing legs above them. I had to laugh. 'If they grab the wrong leg,' I thought, 'they'll be in for one hell of a shock.'

This yo-yo like exercise continued for some time and once a I rose majestically up to the *Perth*'s deck level, after the EXO's repeated calls of 'stop', 'drop', 'pull', I heard one of the sailors complain, 'Jesus Commander — I wish you'd make up your mind'.

Although they didn't beat me by much, it was the

Brits who threw in the towel first. Their Bosun, unimpressed by the sight of his beautifully varnished railings being smashed to bits by the steel side of *Perth*, finally cast off and headed his battered craft back to *Mohawk*.

After I'd been swung back inboard, the EXO, undeterred by this initial setback was preparing for round two in what was becoming a saga.

'Rig for Jackstay transfer,' he called and immediately there was a bustle of activity as sailors hurried to their respective stations.

A day or two previously we'd done a Jackstay transfer and at the time as I'd witnessed the line shot from one ship to the other and looked upon the unhappy countenance of the poor wretch who was to be transferred, it occurred to me that there must be an easier way.

But that had been in relatively calm conditions, with the waves merely friendly ten foot ripples and the slow speed of the ships just maintaining steerage way. Even then, to the heartless delight of the watching ships' companies, the poor fellow being transferred had been dipped in the sea.

Several chaps whom I'd got to know came up and ominously shook hands. 'You're going to get wet,' they said. Shortly afterwards I saw the same fellows complete with cameras, at various vantage points round the ship and although my faith in our navy is unbounded, even I was starting to get alarmed.

It wasn't the prospect of being dunked that I minded, that might even be a bit of fun. But I knew in this weather, *Perth* and *Mohawk*, would have to travel at speed to keep on station — and there I had a problem. For if I hit the water at speed the first thing to leave the scene would be my leg.

As I waited around in my life-jacket for the Jackstay to be rigged, possible newspaper headlines flashed

353

through my mind — 'Civilian Loses Leg In Bight From *Perth*', I thought with a nervous snigger, or perhaps worse 'Civvie Lost In Bight — Only Leg Recovered'. However as it turned out it didn't come to that for to the disappointment of the crew the EXO decided it was too rough to attempt the transfer and cancelled it. I didn't know whether to be pleased or sorry as whilst I hadn't exactly been looking forward to a confrontation with the angry sea, now as I'd be going straight on to Sydney, it meant that I'd miss our Christmas party at home and in due course would have to face a confrontation with an angry wife.

As the ship's engines increased in tempo and we started on the long non-stop run to Sydney, I wondered what the hell I was going to tell Ona. I knew, no matter what I said, she wouldn't believe me and would probably demand to know why I hadn't just swum ashore and thumbed a ride from Eucla.

In the middle of these depressing thoughts a Leading Seaman appeared. 'The Captain would like to see you on the Bridge,' he said. 'Right,' I muttered 'He probably wants his day cabin back.' 'No,' he replied with a grin 'I think you are in for a Helo transfer.'

'A Helo transfer,' I thought, startled, I'd been round long enough to know that meant helicopters. But *Perth* didn't have a heli-pad, how were they going to pick me up?

With a new sense of foreboding I made my way up to the bridge.

'Well,' said the Captain briskly. 'There's no doubt about the Royal Navy. They said they would pick you up, so far they haven't succeeded, but now they have signalled that they are going to have a try with a helicopter. The Brits are not allowed to carry civilians in choppers, unless it's an emergency, it tends to get a bit messy if there's an accident, you know, all that paper work. However the RN has declared you an emergency,

354

so if you'd get yourself down aft to the quarter-deck the Chief here will look after you.' 'Well,' I said hopefully, 'if it's against regulations, I don't want to . . .' But it was a forlorn hope. 'Have a good flight,' he cut in. Obviously the matter was closed.

With me clambering after him, the Chief carried my crutches and bag down the several flights of steps and we finally reached the quarter-deck. By now it was getting quite dark and his voice came to me out of the gloom.

'I must say you've got guts,' he said admiringly. 'But as I was saying to the boys, you would have been better off going on the Jackstay.' Then as he helped me into a life-jacket he asked, 'Have you done a Helo before?' I didn't like to admit that I hadn't even been in a helicopter before, let alone been plucked off the deck of a heaving destroyer in a gale at night. 'Well no, not a Helo,' I said trying to sound casually professional. 'I've jumped down out of 'em plenty of times, but I've never jumped up into one.'

We both thought that was pretty funny, but while his laugh was hearty, I noticed mine held a slightly shrill note which fortunately was lost in the howling wind.

'I'll give you a tip then,' the Chief said confidentially, moving in close, 'when they drop that noose down from the chopper, once it's under your arms they're off like a shot and you'll go with 'em. You see they don't like hanging around in the air turbulence that's created by the ship. Also when you're up there don't raise your arm to wave goodbye, or you'll slip straight out and be back down again.'

'Oh God,' I groaned under my breath, 'how did I get into this?' Also I still had a wooden leg problem, as while suction sockets are not designed for being doused in the sea during Jackstay transfers, neither are they designed for the wearer to hang in space from helicopter cables.

Already I'd nearly lost the leg a couple of times with the jerking stops and starts during the cutter exercise.

'Ah well,' I thought, trying to be philosophical and forced to accept the fact that the leg could well give up 200 feet in the air. 'If it goes — it goes.'

It required the support of two hefty seamen to keep me upright out on the open quarter-deck, as without their help, the heaving deck would have pitched me straight over the side.

Above us in the darkening sky, lights flashing, was the RN helicopter, its rotary blades thrashing out their characteristic bat-like beating sound and for the first time I was really aware of the danger of the situation, not only for me, but to the other people involved.

Up until now, although I'd realized that whatever was coming would probably be a bit hairy, I hadn't known what to expect and had just gone along, doing as I was told.

But here on the quarter-deck the position became clearer. The *Perth* was now travelling at speed and even though the Captain kept her steady on course, the turbulence, as the wind boiled over her superstructure, made it a hazardous business for the RN pilot. One error or slip in judgement on his part and he could well be down on top of us.

But they were good — very good, all of them. Not only the Captain and his men on the Bridge and the two sailors holding me, bracing themselves against the sharp quick movement of the ship, but the Chief watching and ready and the pilot, expertly positioning his buffeted helicopter above. To me it was good dangerous stuff — exciting — the sort of thing that brings the best out in people — I was glad to be part of it. Then, like a reverse version of the Indian rope trick, the noose appeared. It was heavy — weighted and bound in leather, but even then it streamed in the wind.

Making a grab for it, the Chief staggered back across

the deck and slipping the noose over my head, secured it under my arms.

I just had time to give him a wink then, with crutches in one hand and bag in the other, I soared aloft like Mary Poppins into the now black sky.

What I must have looked like, as the winch hauled me up parallel with the open loading bay into the glare of the chopper's spotlight, one can only imagine. My pants had slipped down round my hips and my polo-necked jumper had been pulled up by the noose to somewhere under my armpits. As I hung there, rigidly at attention in the fierce downdraft of the rotors, with arms pressed firmly to my sides and hands grasping my rather odd bits of luggage, I wasn't your normal everyday kind of visitor.

But the Flight-Sergeant, who greeted me, displayed all the calm of a well trained door-man at the Hilton. 'I'll take those Sir,' he called, reaching for my crutches and bag. After they'd swung me inboard the pilot turned in his seat, 'Welcome aboard Sir,' he yelled. 'I'm afraid it was rather a rough old transfer for you. Sorry about that,' and as he turned back to his controls, to concentrate on chasing the far distant lights of *Mohawk*, I noted he looked about sixteen.

It was unfortunate that *Mohawk* pitched violently just as I reached the Wardroom, for instead of pausing for a moment outside to adjust my dress and smooth down my sparse hair, I shot straight into the middle of a dozen officers dressed for dinner in white mess jackets. They eyed me off curiously. I was their first Australian and my appearance — unkempt — hair on end — the crutch of my pants down round my knees — seemed to measure up to their expected impression of a Colonial.

The pause before anyone spoke was only momentary then a Commander, hand outstretched in greeting, moved across and in one of those unflappable Oxford accents drawled, 'I say old boy, would you care for a drink?'

Grinning, I returned his grip, they had no idea how pleased I was to be there, as my attendance at our Christmas party was now assured. 'A drink?' I echoed happily, 'what a bloody good idea.'

37

Recently I had a call from a friend, Langdon Badger, who flies his own twin-engined Aerostar. He was planning a trip to Misima Island, east of Papau New Guinea in the Louisiade Archipelago and asked if I'd like to go with him.

We had spoken on several occasions over the years about Misima and the Louisiades, as whilst I'd only been there once, Langdon and his family were frequent visitors.

His plan this time, was to leave Parafield and fly North-North-East across Australia, refuelling at Cloncurry in Queensland, stop over at Weipa, the bauxite mining town at the tip of Cape York and clear Australian Customs at Horne Island.

After crossing Torres Strait, clear the Papua New Guinea Customs at Pt Moresby and head due east some 600 kilometres to Misima.

I was pleased to accept, for while in itself it sounded an interesting trip, I had always wanted to return to the Louisiades, as I remembered them as one of the most beautiful tropical island areas I'd seen.

My first visit to the area was as 'Diving Supervisor' to the Rhodes Fairbridge Expedition, when the Louisiade Archipelago, the second largest reef complex in the world, was scientifically described for the first time, in 1968. My involvement started when Colin Freeman, the librarian at the University of Papua New Guinea, arrived in Adelaide to organize the diving gear for the expedition.

I'd taught Colin to dive a year or two previously, before he'd gone to Pt Moresby and while he was competent enough, it came out during conversation that he hadn't had much further experience, especially with regard to diving in the tropics.

After about an hour I could see that they had problems and I asked who was going to be in charge of the operation. Quite out of the blue Colin said, 'I wish you could come. It would cost you a few bob to get to Samarai, but the rest of the trip would be free'. I laughed, it wasn't much of a business proposition, but then it seemed none of my diving ventures ever were.

For a moment or two I thought it over — New Guinea — Louisiades — I'd never dived there — it appeared that this mob needed someone to look after them — I guessed I could get away.

'OK' I said, 'when do you want me to be in Samarai?'

A month or so later I flew out of Brisbane to Moresby and then by light aircraft over the Owen Stanleys to Gurney strip on Milne Bay, the historic place where we gave the Japs their first setback in World War II. From Milne Bay to Samarai, a small island in the China Strait on the Eastern tip of Papua New Guinea, I travelled by boat. After a day or two there, organizing equipment and waiting for other members of the party to arrive, we headed off.

The expedition, backed by the University of Papua New Guinea and Columbia University, New York, was also assisted by a mixed bag of scientists from the UK and Australia. In all there were twenty of them — marine geologists, oceanographers, botanists, herpe-tologists, geo-chemists and one chap whose special interests included the lighter and more humorous side of science — sedimentology, tectonics and regional geology. I made the mistake once of asking him what all that meant and he immediately launched into an harangue that was so technical I couldn't understand a word he said.

The Papuans, who crewed the two chartered trading vessels that were used, must surely have wondered at the peculiar occupations of these strange white men, for in no time the decks were littered with specimens of rocks, plants, lumps of coral, fish in bottles and sea snakes that the herpetologist, kept all alive and slithering in a forty-four gallon drum. The herpetologist, Dr Harold Heatwole, an American from the University of New England, was most single-minded in his purpose, for if he saw a snake, whether on land or sea, he caught it. Once, out between different groups of islands, we passed an eight foot long, thick as your arm, evil looking yellow sea snake. Harold casually picked up his catching pole and without a word to anyone just stepped over the side. The fact that he had been meaning to learn to swim, but hadn't as yet got around to it and that apart from being fully clothed he also had on his heavy jungle boots, didn't really occur to him.

Unfortunately for me I saw him go and as I was the 'Diving Supervisor' and more or less responsible for everything aquatic, I had no option but to go straight in after him.

Somehow Harold caught the snake, but instead of the catching noose holding the brute just behind the head in the accepted manner, it slipped halfway down the snake's body, which allowed it to double back on him at the other end of the pole. Harold, who was drowning at the time, then gave the pole to me as he said he had to use both his hands to hold onto my shoulders. I can still see those curved yellow fangs striking with enraged fury at my desperately curled back fingers, while from behind me, in his strong American accent, I could hear Harold yelling 'Jeez man — ain't he the most beautiful thing you ever did see?'

Later he put this snake in the drum with his other specimens and by the end of the trip it was half-full, or so he told us as no one, especially the Papuans, would lift the lid to find out.

Rhodes Fairbridge, the leader of the expedition,

Professor of Geology at Columbia University, educated to the 'nth degree and world authority in his field, is in some ways not entirely practical. For like many of his kind he becomes so engrossed with what might be over the next horizon, that he doesn't trouble himself with tiresome day to day problems.

But in Rhodes' case he's fortunate, as his wife Delores is there to clean up after him and as he crashes through the jungles of the world, Delores follows behind, expertly cracking the whip over the lackies, organizing and sorting out the problems.

Between them they are a great team. However it was generally agreed upon by the members of the Louisiade Expedition that Delores was not the person with whom to fall out of favour.

As it turned out, after an incident that occurred early in the trip, I had no problems in this direction.

One morning Rhodes asked me if he could try out a wet suit. He said he didn't want to learn to dive, but only wished to go for a swim. This was just as well as we were anchored in about thirty feet of water, several hundred yards off shore, with the only means of getting back on board being a temperamental rope ladder. In all, not ideal conditions for a novice Scuba lesson, as in the open sea I prefer to start pupils off in shallow water where they can stand up if necessary. I find this gives the pupil and the instructor more confidence.

I got old Rhodes kitted up in a full wet suit, complete with boots, gloves and hood.

He wouldn't entertain wearing a weight belt or mask and when he jumped in, encased in all that rubber, he floated on his back like a plank. I watched him pretty closely, as while I felt he couldn't possibly come to any harm, he was after all Delores' husband. There was a slight current and Rhodes drifting with it was soon about twenty yards out from the boat, halfway to the edge of the reef, where it dropped away hundreds of feet into the depths.

I had just decided he'd gone far enough and was about to call him back when to my horror I saw the dark torpedo like shapes of several sharks appear from over the edge of the drop off and glide towards him. 'Hey — Rhodes' I called, 'come back'. There was no response, he lay there flat on his back, eyes closed like a great black seal and I realized because of the rubber hood covering his ears he couldn't hear me. 'Bloody Hell' I groaned, the already doubtful honour of being 'Diving Supervisor' to these boffins completely losing its appeal.

There was only one thing to do and while I couldn't believe I was actually doing it, I dived in and started swimming across the twenty yards to the oblivious Rhodes to warn him.

When you stop to think about it, there are really very few ways you can casually tell swimmers that there are sharks in the water with them. But as I didn't have time to stop and think, although I tried to break it to him as gently as I could, I suppose it was a bit traumatic. He received a big enough fright when I suddenly appeared beside him, but when I peeked back his wet suit hood and whispered in his ear, 'Now don't panic — but there are sharks underneath you', I guess his reaction was understandable.

I think it would be fair to say that there's nothing wrong with Rhodes' reflexes, for without a split second's hesitation he performed a most extraordinary athletic feat. Rising out of the water like a Polaris Missile he spun around and heading for the boat in a sort of stumbling run, clawed his way straight up the rope ladder.

I was so impressed by his efforts that for a moment I forgot that I'd been left behind with the you know whats.

I've always subscribed to the theory that sharks, being predominantly fish eaters, are attracted to splashing or sudden movement. This theory is supported by the fact that many sharks are reflex eaters, as having to catch their prey in their mouths tends to make them bite first and think afterwards.

Fortunately, being the bearer of this invaluable knowledge I then rather sneered at Rhodes' ignominious retreat and slowly commenced a controlled move towards the boat, studiously avoiding any sudden movements.

I kept this up for about five yards, but a mental picture of fifty man-eaters tearing in with mouths agape got the better of me and as my nerve broke, theories forgotten, I struck out and with arms flailing, I too made for the ladder. Although the incident probably took a year off Rhodes' life span and at least ten off mine, it did put me in big with Delores. From then on, as she was firmly convinced I'd saved her husband's life, nothing was too good for the 'Diving Supervisor'. I was always first to be fed and never wanted for a top-up when we had a few drinks during the happy hour each night.

But I wasn't entirely off the hook, as Delores wouldn't let Rhodes go in the water unless I was in there with him.

This wasn't much of a restriction on me, as somehow he'd lost most of his enthusiasm for swimming in the Louisiades.

On the notice board on the foredeck was a list showing each member's name and special interest. At the top read — Burchell, Dave — Diving Supervisor. 'Hell' I thought, quite impressed. 'They must be pleased to have me on board, putting my name at the head of the list over these other guys with all their titles and degrees'.

It wasn't until a couple of days later, as I was having

another surreptitious peek at my name right up there on top, that I realised the list had been made out in alphabetical order.

One of my jobs was to help describe the incidence and variety of species of fish life in selected areas. Previously this work was done with nets and lines and understandably, the end results were not very conclusive. But in the Louisiades we planned to use liquid nicotine poison dispersed underwater by divers. This stuff, after about ten minutes, knocks off everything in the area and it was reckoned that a 100 percent result should be obtained. The method may sound a bit ruthless and extravagant in loss of fish life, but the area treated each time, a grid approximately thirty feet by thirty feet, was so minute in relation to the thousands of miles of coral reefs, that in the interests of science it was an acceptable procedure. After the poison takes effect the stunned fish are collected from the sea and taken up top for identification.

At the end of the expedition, although results at that time were not complete, it was expected that something between five percent and ten percent of the fish recovered were previously undescribed. A surprising result in this day and age.

As well as the Misima area we worked the Conflict and De Boyne Groups of islands, then sailed down the Calvados Chain passing Jomard Entrance and its wrecked ships with the vast coral sea stretching away to the south.

Looking at these ships, left to rust away since ploughing into the treacherous reefs, I really felt for their crews. For the Jomard Entrance, a passage from the Coral Sea into the Louisiade Archipelago, must be one of the loneliest places in the world.

Now, fifteen years later, flying over the same area in Langdon Badger's Aerostar, I could see the place hadn't changed. The Conflicts and De Boynes looked just as attractive and Jomard looked just as lonely. To the west the dark outline of Misima was starting to take shape and further south the Calvados Chain of islands dotted their way to the horizon.

Mountainous, rugged, shrouded in cloud, Misima, the second largest island in the Louisiades, along with its copra and fishing, has produced over 300 000 ounces of gold since the turn of the century.

The tough adventurous Australians who first worked the mines came over from Sudest, the largest island in the group, after the gold there petered out in the late 1800's.

The courage, skill and tenacity of these men, who without the aid of modern equipment built miles of roads and railways through the jungle and mountains, is still in evidence. For Misima, remote by even today's standards, a hundred years ago with sailing ships the only form of transport, must have been likened to the end of the earth.

Our host, Alby Munt, who was born on Nivani Island in the De Boynes, is an institution in the Louisiades. He and his wife Ruth own several copra and cocoa plantations on Misima, a gold mine or two, an inter-island shipping company and a general store that would rival Harrods for its versatility of merchandise.

The Munts, great friends of Genny and Langdon Badger, set us up in one of their plantation houses a few miles up the coast. They also loaned us a four-wheel-drive vehicle and the five of us, Genny, Langdon, their son Langdon jnr, a friend Bob Lindsay and me used the vehicle daily and drove hundreds of miles over the pot-holed roads, to the island's scenic spots. These included panoramic views from the top of two hundred feet cliffs, rarely visited rocky beaches and a cave full of ancient skulls that we reached after a tough climb up narrow mountain tracks through the jungle.

We chartered one of Alby's trading vessels and for a

few days cruised down the Calvados Chain, stopping at islands, fishing and diving on the reefs and collecting shells. During this trip, out from Nivani Island, we dived on a Japanese Zero that didn't make it home during the Battle of the Coral Sea.

The pilot of the plane was killed when it crashed and Alby, who was just a child at the time, remembers the Japanese commandeering the wire mattress from his bed which was then used to lie the poor fellow on when they cremated him.

The Zero, after all these years, is still in good shape and we tried to salvage the port wing cannon for Langdon, who is an aircraft buff, but short of pulling the whole wing up, the cannon wouldn't budge, so not wanting to unduly damage the 'plane, we left it.

Back at the plantation house the locals soon saw us as a steady source of pocket-money and most nights they'd turn up to do a bit of bartering with the Dim Dims — we were told that Dim Dim is Papuan for European, but we couldn't help wondering how the term originated — pineapples, vegetables, shells and even a sulphur-crested cockatoo were brought to the door by these shy traders, who often as not, had walked miles from their distant villages.

But finally the holiday was over and we left the Louisiades, stopping off at Pt Moresby for a night then, after the customs check at Horne Island, flew on to Normanton in North Western Queensland. This historic old town now pretty much a relic from a past era, with its quaint mid Victorian railway station and great empty shell of the original Burns Philp building, lies twenty miles inland from Karumba, the headquarters of the prawn fishing fleets on the Gulf of Carpentaria.

From Normanton we moved on down to Windorah in the heart of the Channel Country in South-Western Queensland and then across to 'Nappa Merrie' on the SA border.

After a couple of days spent with John and Helen Rickertt we loaded the Aerostar for the last time and taking off from 'Nappa Merrie' commenced the final leg to complete the 8000 kilometres round trip back to Adelaide.

38

I first met Commander Jake Linton, RAN, at a Mine Clearance Divers Officers function at HMAS *Penguin*, a shore station in Sydney, after I'd been invited to be the guest speaker at this, the MCDO's inaugural dinner. Most of the people present were Clearance Divers (CD's) and Explosive Ordinance Disposal (EOD's) experts and when we sat down at the beautifully laid-out long table, with everyone in full mess dress and decorations, I noticed that the chap next to me was in British Army uniform.

Slightly puzzled at why an army man would be at a navy dinner, I whispered to the Naval Commander on my other side, 'Who's this bloke on my left, the Army Colonel?' He glanced across and then sitting back said, 'Christ, don't you know who that is? He's McKenzie-Orr, Mr EOD himself. He was awarded the George Cross for bomb disposal work in Northern Ireland. The IRA put a price on his head.'

When the commander saw that I was suitably impressed by the company I was in, he relaxed and sticking out his hand, introduced himself. 'Jake Linton,' he said.

Since then each year that there is a dinner, I've been invited and Jake and I have become good friends. He's a tough old boy and made the rank of commander from the lower deck, which is an achievement in itself.

One day in mid 1980 he rang from Sydney and asked, 'What are you doing in September?' 'September,' I queried. 'Hell I don't know, that's months away. Why, what's on?'

'Well,' Jake said, 'I'll be up in the Solomons doing a job with Clearance Diving Team 1 in HMAS *Labuan*. If you can get yourself to Honiara on Guadalcanal, we'll come and pick you up. I'll show you some real diving, not that soft stuff you've been used to.'

'OK,' I said, 'cut the comedy, just tell me the date you want me there.'

But Jake wasn't ready yet to get down to exact dates. He'd just phoned, he said, to find out if I could make it before he went to all the trouble to obtain his admiral's approval to take me along as a passenger. He'd ring back with the details later.

After Jake had hung up I thought about Guadalcanal, that desperate place with the horrific memories of World War II, where thousands of American marines had died in the struggle to wrest the island, with its strategic airstrip, from the Japanese. Ona and I had visited Guadalcanal and had seen the battle-fields — Red Beach, Henderson Field and Bloody Ridge and I'd also studied the naval battles of the adjacent Savo Sound. There, during a hit and run action, in one night we lost four heavy cruisers, HMAS *Canberra* and the United States ships, *Astoria*, *Vincennes* and *Quincey*.

Although I hadn't asked Jake what he intended doing in Guadalcanal, I knew it would not include diving on these ships, as they lay thousands of feet down on the bed of what is now called Iron Bottom Sound and were well beyond compressed air diving limits.

He rang back a few weeks later and gave me the dates. I was to be in Honiara on 20 September, also he expected to be at sea for about three weeks.

'Right,' I said. 'I'll be there. By the way, what are we meant to be doing?'

Jake laughed. 'We're going to blow up the Solomon Islands,' he said. 'Didn't I tell you, we'll sort of shift 'em sideways.' Then he went on to explain that as a goodwill gesture, from time to time the RAN cleared harbours and blew channels in reefs for our near neighbours. The exercises were also regarded as excellent practical experience for our clearance diving teams. On this occasion it was the Solomon Islands turn and HMAS *Labuan* complete with CDTI and 150 drums of high explosive, was nearly ready to set off.

⋆ ⋆ ⋆

In September, as I climbed out of the battered taxi on the wharf at Honiara, I was met by a smart looking US Navy Chief Petty Officer.

'Chief's happy,' he said in a strong American accent, giving me a smart salute. 'Well,' I thought, 'I'm certainly glad to hear that.' But as I found out later, what he actually said by way of introduction was 'Chief Slappy'. For that was his name Chief Petty Officer Harmon Slappy EOD, USN and who else but an American could have a name like that?

Slappy, who was temporarily attached to the RAN was a member of CDT1. This shuffling of military personnel is a common occurrence between the Americans, the Brits and ourselves, with the consequent exchange of ideas and procedures being invaluable, as the exchange is made not only at all levels of rank, but also in all departments. The other members of CDT1, apart from Jake Linton who was the CO, were CPO Tony Ey CD, and three Able Seamen CD's, Peter Hughes, Paul Winney and Graham Husband.

I'd first met Tony Ey while diving at Truk, when he was there on loan to an American EOD team who were working on bomb disposal jobs in Truk Lagoon.

To me chaps like Jake Linton and Tony Ey form the backbone of our armed services.

Tough and efficient, they are experts in their field of bomb and mine disposal and although they are not given to talk much, they handle their always dangerous and sometimes deadly work with cool professionalism.

On 22 September at 1 pm *Labuan* cast off from

Honiara on Guadacanal. First we sailed north-east across Iron Bottom Sound to the Florida Islands.

The next day at some wild and primitive thatch hutted village, whose name was unpronouncable, Jake and the headman studied the problem we were there to try and solve.

The village, which was situated right on the beach, was fronted by a beautiful lagoon. But this was bound in tight by a partly exposed ocean reef some 150 yards offshore and the reef was the problem. For to reach the open sea to go fishing, visit relatives or take their copra out to the ships, the villagers were forced by the presence of the reef to paddle miles to get around it.

'Would it be possible,' the headman asked timidly, 'to make a big bang, like the Americans did during the war and blow a hole in the reef for our canoes?' 'Sure,' Jake said confidently, 'no trouble. Anything the Yanks can do, we can do better. Where do you want it?'

Late the next afternoon, from the bow of the assault craft from which we were operating, Tony Ey lit the fuse and called 'Fire in the Hole!' the time honoured cry of the explosive expert.

Five minutes later, when we were well clear of the area, twenty-eight strategically placed 120 pound drums of high explosive went off in one almighty blast. Rock, coral and water shot straight up hundreds of feet in a spectacular eruption.

Early the next morning, after the tides had cleared the debris, we carried out an underwater inspection. There it was. A channel forty yards long, thirty feet wide and six feet deep, straight as an arrow out into the open sea, where no channel had been before.

The locals were ecstatic. The channel presented a whole new lifestyle to them and the exciting future prospects of this, along with the noise, the activity, the great feast they were preparing with the hundreds of stunned fish and the picture show that the navy had promised for that night, turned the day into a gala occasion.

After this first blow on Florida we blew channels and cleared harbours on Malaita, Ulawa and San Christobal Islands, which are all part of the Solomon Islands Group and finally finished up back on the south-west end of Guadalcanal. During the three weeks it took to complete the project there were one or two unscheduled incidents that bear reporting. For instance the work boats used for surveying different areas and for laying the charges, were two twelve foot aluminium assault craft, powered by 75 hp outboard motors and one afternoon off the island of San Christobal one overturned in a squall.

I'd been working with Tony Ey's group in the first assault craft and after we'd finished laying our charges we were sitting around waiting for Jake, who was ferrying more high explosive in from *Labuan* which was anchored about a mile up the coast. Time went by and still the second assault craft didn't arrive so deciding something must have gone wrong we went to look for them.

At first there was no sign of the boat in the choppy water, but further on we saw a very strange sight — the figure of a man carrying what appeared to be a cross, standing upright on the sea.

This apparition had a traumatic effect on a young Roman Catholic AB in the bow. 'Holy Mother of Mary,' he gasped, crossing himself. 'It's the Second Coming.'

But I must hasten to add this was not correct. For as we got closer we could see it was only Jake, balancing on the flat bottom of the overturned assault craft, strumming on an oar like Elvis Presley.

We rescued Jake, Lieutenant Care Wickam and two AB's from the water, righted their boat and then towed it back to the ship. But nine drums of high explosive and a heap of assorted gear, including four cameras, had been deposited 100 fathoms down to the bed of the sea.

One day Jake let me organize a blow. It was on Malaita and after the job was over it was officially entered in the records as 'Burchell's By-Pass'. It wasn't really my blow, he just let me think it was, but under his and Tony's watchful eyes, I did the survey, planning where to place the charges deep inside underwater caves and ledges in order to obtain the best results. Then when they were satisfied, with the aid of Slappy and the three Able Seamen Clearance Divers, we wrestled twenty-six drums of primed high explosive into their various positions.

The process of setting off explosives is interesting. It involves a chain reaction from an initial time fuse, that burns at forty seconds per foot, to a detonator which is attached to a detonating cord, that burns at 22 000 feet per second.

This detonating cord is run out and connected up to the individual drums of high explosive after they have been placed in position.

In the Solomons the high explosive that the navy was using was a DuPont product, brand named Tovex 650, chosen for its power and spreading effect instead of TNT, which has a higher shattering factor.

The initial slow burning time fuse is used to give the operators time to 'shift their butts', as Slappy would say.

After my blow was all set, with the calculated five minutes or so of getaway fuse wrapped around the float, I leaned over the side of the assault craft and trying not to think of the twenty-six primed 120 pound charges of Tovex 650 underneath us, I pulled the water-proofed hand activator.

Immediately the fuse started sparking and sputtering and resisting a strong temptation to throw the thing away as far as possible, I forced myself to place it carefully on the float.

'Fire in the Hole,' I yelled, a bit too loudly. Tony Ey just smiled, he probably remembered his first time and easing the throttle of the outboard open he took us in a leisurely sweep away from the danger area.

All eyes were by now on the sweep hands of wrist watches, as it is a matter of great kudos that the charges blow at the time the fuse-setter calculates.

A good man never misses, a poor effort could be out by four or five seconds, mine went off ten seconds late. But as Jake said, 'If they don't go off at all — it's a disaster'.

We had one of these, when for some reason the system broke down and the charges didn't blow. It was an eerie feeling, cruising back into the charged area in the assault craft, not knowing what had gone wrong, hoping it wasn't some sort of delayed action fault that might rectify itself at any moment.

Then it was over the side to make an inspection and I can still see those sinister blue painted drums, appearing one after the other, as we swam along the white detonating cord that linked them together. We found the cause of the malfunction, it was a faulty detonator and when this was replaced and the whole system rechecked, the time fuse was again lit by the hand activator. Cautiously we moved off about a quarter of a mile and waited.

This time, right on the button, the surface of the sea shook and a second or so later the familiar KARRUMP as the sound of the exploding charges came to us. Then the surface erupted in a gigantic column of water and rock, which rose majestically hundreds of feet into the air.

It was exciting work, hard, exhausting and not without its danger, but the sight of a successful blow shooting skywards and knowing the benefits it represented to these remote people, made it all very worthwhile.

KARRUMP . . . Up goes 'Burchell's By Pass'
at Malaita — Solomon Islands

At the beginning of the project, when we'd arrive at a village it was to find that about half of the population had taken to the hills, as many of them could still remember the war and wanted no part of bombs and explosives.

But as time passed the word spread from island to island that no one had been killed.

Also stories of the feasts everyone was having with the stunned fish and the nightly picture shows that were put on from the deck of *Labuan* tended to stop this mass migration. This caused Jake a real problem, for if anything the pendulum swung the other way and where initially the villagers had been timid and cautious, now they were becoming over-confident.

Jockeying for position, either hidden in the fringes of the jungle or out on the water in their canoes, they would jam around the blast area vying for vantage points so as to be first to get at the fish.

Consequently before each blow it was necessary to clear the area of people, or I should say attempt to, for as fast as the excited islanders were pushed back on the one side, others would crowd in from another. On top of this, although pre-publicized safety briefings were held to inform the locals of the danger, there was always the chance that some of them, bored by the prospect of all that talk, would just skip the safety lecture and go fishing in their canoes instead. If this happened, using Murphy's Law, it meant that these chaps would come paddling back into the primed and charged area, four minutes after the five minute delay fuse had been lit.

This would have proved to be most embarrassing for Jake and the members of CDT1, as they were very aware of the fact that the navy had sent them to blown up the Solomons — not its inhabitants. However this didn't happen and the only casualty we had during the three weeks was the Chief of Ubuna Village on San

Christobal, who required six stitches in his hand after a Moray eel bit him.

The enraged Moray, which had been blown up onto the exposed reef, sank its teeth into the Chief's hand when he gleefully made a grab for it to add to his collection for the feast. Later I watched the nervous young RAN medic stuff in the first stitch, but had to turn away shuddering, as obviously the lad had learned his trade by practising on wheat bags.

I had to admire the medic's courage, for it took a brave man to keep at it and stitch up that wild-eyed Chief, who was only a couple of generations removed from being a head hunter and who also up till then had never felt the pain of a roughly applied sewing needle. The next morning I saw the Chief on the beach, his hand swathed in bandages.

'How's the hand Chief,' I asked.

He looked at me, glowering from out of his muddy brown eyes. 'Moray — OK,' he grunted and then simulating a stitching movement with his uninjured hand, he shook his head emphatically and added, 'That — no bloody good.'

I nodded gravely, full of sympathy, at the same time deciding that if I cut myself badly enough to need stitching on this trip, I would definitely demand a general anaesthetic.

It became the diver's job to keep the rest of the ship's company supplied with fresh fish and mostly we did this by competing with the villagers over the smorgasbord that appeared after each blow. But on the off days, when no charges were fired, we went fishing with 1 lb bombs of plastic explosive. Cruising out to a likely spot in one of the assault craft, snorkel divers then picked the target which was generally a small school of fish and after calling the boat over, the swimmers would climb back on board and the PE set on a five second fuse, was tossed over the side.

BANG!! and the crew in the assault craft would rise six inches as the charge went off underneath them. After that it was straight back over the side to beat the sharks to the catch. To give the diet a bit more variety most nights we went diving for lobsters. Night diving is always an eerie business, especially if you don't happen to have a torch which was the situation in my case. But by holding grimly on to Tony Ey's weight belt, even though I knew it was irritating him, I got by.

Except when he'd shrug me off and dive deep into some underwater cave, leaving me in total blackness holding on to a coral outcrop, puffing on my scuba and hoping that one day he might return.

Slappy was the undisputed lobster catching champ, although we reckoned the reason for his success was that he had the best torch. I think it used to be a Boeing 707 landing light and lit up the underwater scene like day. But nevertheless he was darn good at it and one night in his best effort, he bagged a dozen beauties.

A strange, wild place, the Solomons, full of anomalies. For while the areas at which we called were generally primitive and rarely visited by the outside world, on occasions we'd stumble across some remote mission and not only be surprised by its substantial churches and schools, but also to learn that missionaries and the buildings had been there for a hundred years. Another time, tucked away out of sight up a river estuary, we found a busy timber mill, turning out its sawn and treated timber with all the proficiency of one of its counterparts in a city suburb.

In addition and typical of tropical volcanic island chains, these contradictions continue geographically. Wide and deadly malarial swamps, fed by the freakish storms and torrential rains of the monsoons, being offset by beautiful lagoons, rugged mountains and vast primeval forests.

Finally, back in Guadalcanal, our team split up.

Slappy and the A.B.'s of CDT1 set off with the crew of *Labuan* for the long trip back across the Coral Sea to Brisbane, Jake and Tony Ey went on up to the New Georgia Islands in the Western District of the Solomons, to survey a future project there and I flew home to Adelaide.

As the jet aircraft passed over the city, on the approach to West Beach Airport, I was reminded of the marvels of modern transport. For it was hard to believe that just a few hours previously, I'd been in the steaming jungles of the remote Solomons and I couldn't help thinking of all those chaps during the war, who would have given plenty to have made the same trip in such a short time, forty years ago.

39

Dressed in camouflaged battle-dress, with the renowned Green Beret set squarely on his head, the Royal Marine sergeant made his way purposefully across the foyer of the Harbour View Hotel in Kowloon.

At my wave he deviated towards me and for a moment it appeared I was about to be run down, but with a double stamp of his heavy boots, he came to a halt with a quivering salute three feet away. 'Captain Peart's compliments- Sah!!' he barked. 'If you will come with me please, we have a Land Rover outside to take you to 'Tamar'!!'

'Righto,' I replied mildly, 'let's go,' not even attempting to compete with the elan of the Royal Marines.

As the sergeant jockeyed the Land Rover through the traffic in the brightly lit tunnel under the harbour, I thought how fortunate it had been that I'd casually mentioned to Tony Bennett, my bank manager back in Adelaide, that Ona and I were going to Hong Kong. Tony, a retired Naval Commander and wise in the ways of the navy, promptly decided I needed help and in spite of my startled protest, immediately placed a call to David Leach in Canberra. David Leach, who later became a Vice-Admiral and Chief of Naval Staff, but who at that time in 1981 was a Rear Admiral and Chief of Naval Personnel, came on the line.

'Dave Burchell's going to Hong Kong and I'm ringing to ask if you can do anything for him up there,' Tony said into the phone — I squirmed with embarrassment as I felt sure David Leach would have one or two more important items than this on his plate. 'Sure, he's here in my office,' Tony continued, 'I'll put him on.' I took the phone and started making apologies to David Leach but he swept them aside. 'No trouble at all,' he said. 'I'm glad you rang. When are you arriving in Hong Kong and where are you staying?' I told him and he went on. 'Right, I've got all that. I'll send a signal to HMAS *Tamar*, the Royal Navy base in Hong Kong. We don't have a base there, but the Brits will be pleased to look after you.'

I don't know what David Leach said in his signal, or whether the Royal Navy were in fact pleased, but look after us they certainly did.

Captain Waugh, the CO of HMS *Tamar*, the RN Headquarters Establishment on Hong Kong Island, invited Ona and me over for lunch and afterwards arranged for me to accompany his troops on a couple of sorties. The first was a ride in one of the RN Hovercraft, which operate from a base on Stonecutters Island and the other was to go with the Royal Marines in their Sea Riders, the fast power boats that are used to apprehend Chinese smugglers.

The hovercraft jaunt, when we'd skimmed at fifty knots along the Chinese coast, had been quite an experience. I'd never been in one before and their unique ability to glide at speed over solid obstructions, such as sandspits and partly exposed rocks, was most impressive. Huge affairs, carrying a crew of five, they are equipped with wireless and radar and fit the popular conception of futuristic flying saucers. Roaring around each night with searchlights blazing, while policing the bays and backwaters, they would doubtless further frighten the devil out of the already terrified Chinese, who illegally are trying to leave Red China and enter Hong Kong.

However today was the trip out with the Royal Marines and after passing through the imposing entrance gates, the sergeant brought the Land Rover to a halt outside their section of the British Naval Base.

Captain Bill Peart, the CO of the Royal Marines contingent, escorted me into his office and over a cup of coffee he eyed off the grey suit I was wearing with distinct disapproval. 'You can't go out in a Sea Rider dressed like that,' he said and moving across to his locker he took out a pale blue nylon jump suit. 'Here,' he continued with a grin, 'you'd better put this on. All the tourists out on the harbour will think you're James Bond.' I discarded the grey suit and zipped up the much smarter blue one and after I'd pulled one of Sumantri's old baseball type sea caps down on my head, with its full Colonel's gold braid across the peak, modestly I had to admit that I did look like James Bond.

Down at the wharf, two Sea Riders and their crews were waiting. They were open fibreglass boats powered by outboard motors with the two-man crew riding one behind the other astride a central console. The chap in front operated the controls, which were basic enough and comprised a T-bar type hand throttle and a steering wheel.

I was introduced to the corporal in charge of my boat and after climbing aboard I straddled the console and settled onto the passenger seat.

Glancing down I noticed for the first time the heavy webbing foot straps, bolted to the deck. They looked ominous in that they gave notice this was no pleasure craft and there was every chance of a rough ride ahead in the lumpy waters of the harbour, as the wakes of a thousand ferries, tugs, junks and sampans fought with the wind and tide rips. It was certainly no place for the novice and I hoped my driver was an experienced hand.

From the top of the wharf, the corporal saw me sitting in the passenger's seat. 'No, not there sir,' he called. 'You're to take the controls.'

I looked up at him in alarm. 'I'm to take the controls,' I echoed, 'There must be some mistake.' 'Oh no, sir,' he called back, 'Captain Peart said you were to be in

383

charge of the boat sir.'

I felt like a man who had unsuspectingly accepted an invitation to watch a demolition derby, only to find that he was the feature item in the main event.

'Like hell I will,' I thought in dismay. 'I've got to get out of this.'

The corporal came down the steps onto the landing and I indicated for him to come over with a jerk of my head. 'Now look son,' I said in a low understanding voice. 'This is your boat, I don't want to just come along and take it over. I know how proud you lads are of your individual commands,' giving him the old wink I added, 'You can steer. I won't say anything.'

He started back, shocked that I'd even suggested such a thing. 'They were Captain Peart's orders sir,' he said reproachfully. 'Now if you would move forward into the driver's seat, I'll show you how to start the motor.'

Tentatively I eased the Sea Rider across the smooth surface of *Tamar's* enclosed boathaven toward the chopped up water of the main harbour outside.

Behind me the big outboard motor burbled at idling speed and the corporal clutched lightly at the spare tyre around my waist. 'Just give her about a third throttle when we clear the basin entrance,' he said in my ear. 'It looks pretty rough today and there's a fair bit of traffic out there.'

'A fair bit of traffic,' I thought, feeling a bit sour on the whole deal. 'What the hell is he talking about, it looks like an LA freeway — Ah well — here we go,' and taking one hand off the wheel I gently pushed the T-bar throttle forward.

Immediately the Sea Rider's bow lifted and she came up on the plane. 'That's enough for the moment,' I told myself, 'we don't want any heroics,' and leaving my hand on the throttle I carefully steered out into the harbour.

It was unfortunate that the four foot high wake of a

passing ferry hit us before I had any chance to get set. I saw it coming and started to lean forward to compensate my balance in an effort to ride it, but the solid wall of water slammed into us so hard that just as I moved my weight forward the bow came up sharply and my hand, which was still on the throttle, shot the lever straight through into full bore.

Several things happened at once. With a roar, that would have done credit to an enraged Bengal tiger, the outboard hit full revs — the Sea Rider, assisted by the initial bow lift from the wake of the ferry, reared straight up on its tail and as we started our leap into the sky, I felt an excruciating stab of pain round my midriff as the corporal's fingers, closing instantaneously, sank deep into my spare tyre.

On the way down I let go of the throttle and grabbed for the wheel, as I felt I'd need both hands to brace myself when we hit. This left the outboard on full power and after a bone-jarring crash the Sea Rider took off and at forty knots we shot straight out into the maze of the shipping that was ploughing up the Hong Kong freeway.

In the split second that I had to assess the situation, I could see we had three alternatives. The first was to be run down and cut in half by a fast moving freighter, the second was to take a chance and try to go under the jet-powered hydrofoil, that was on its way with 300 gamblers to the dens in Macau and the third was to take a Chinese sampan straight up the middle. The sampan won. Heaving the wheel to port, I just missed the sharp bows of the freighter, a heave to starboard and we sliced along only inches from the side of the hydrofoil, then with nowhere else to go, we speared straight at the sampan, which was about twenty yards away dead ahead. I knew it was a forlorn hope, as we were about to cover the distance in a flash, but with one last effort I gave the wheel full lock.

Normally it wouldn't have been anywhere near enough, but a freak cross chop caught our stern and flicked us ninety degrees sideways, thus saving the day, but as the Sea Rider broached a wall of water descended on the unfortunate sampan. In the instant it took before we were up and off again, I looked down at the Chinese family who had been happily cooking a meal in the half cabin which was their home.

All was chaos. The fire was out, pots and pans were scattered and to further add to my embarrassment an elderly man, who must have been doused by the full impact of the deluge, was lying flat on his back with his legs in the air.

For the next few minutes, although there were fewer ships to dodge, it was still too rough to let go the wheel and ease off the throttle, so we careered onward virtually out of control.

This was misinterpreted by my passenger, who thought I was having a great time and turning to the direction of his mates in the accompanying Sea Rider, he called 'Yah-hoo — come on you chaps — we've got ourselves a cowboy.'

How the cowboy in his James Bond jump suit made it across the harbour I'll never know, but finally somewhere behind Stonecutter's Island we roared into calmer waters and with a shaking hand I reached over thankfully and eased the T-bar lever back. 'Bloody hell,' gasped the corporal, sitting back and releasing his grip. 'That was some ride sir. You must do a lot of power boating back in Australia.'

For a moment or two I didn't reply as I couldn't trust my voice, but when I reckoned I could handle a short sentence I said nonchalantly, 'Yeah, I guess I do. You see we've got these surf boats down there,' — I was thankful that I'd recently seen a documentary about surf boats on TV and that it was still fresh in my mind — 'and sometimes me and a few of my mates take a couple out and . . . '

Before we left Stonecutters to return to *Tamar* the corporal called me aside.

'Look sir,' he said apologetically. 'I'll go out with you in a Sea Rider anytime, but would you mind slowing it down a bit on the way back? You see Captain Peart takes a dim view of us opening the boats up and he's sure to be watching when we come in.'

I gave him a fellow conspirator's punch on the shoulder. 'No worries boy,' I said. 'I know what the brass is like, they don't always appreciate you having a bit of fun.' Then, so as not to let him down, I set the throttle at one third while we were still in the calm water behind Stonecutters and religiously left the lever alone until we were back at the wharf at *Tamar*.

Later, over a drink in *Tamar's* wardroom, Bill Peart remarked off-handedly. 'The boys tell me you gave them quite a ride today.'

'Ah well,' I replied, 'we do a bit of that sort of thing back home you know.'

'Is that a fact?' he said in feigned surprise, 'why, when I saw you take off, it looked to me as if you had no idea what you were doing.'

'Abe Lincoln was right,' I thought sadly as the James Bond image crashed, 'you can't fool all of the people.' I realized that it was about time to change the subject, but before I did I gave him a wink, just to let him know that I knew that he knew and then asked, 'Tell me about these Chinese smugglers who give you so much trouble.'

'You mean the AA's?' he said, then added with disgust, 'Ugh, they're dreadful people.'

'The AA's,' I repeated, 'who are they?'

'The Aiders and Abetters,' he replied. 'The smugglers — we call them AA's for short. They are the ones we like to catch. There's not much joy in ambushing the poor old Chinese refugees. You see we are obliged to hand the illegal immigrants to the Red Guards back on the mainland. Christ knows what happens to them. Especially after all they've gone through to get this far. It's hard to imagine how bad it must be back there, to make them take the risks involved in trying to escape. Then when they are caught — to be sent back — it would be pretty grim.'

'Yeah,' I said thoughtfully, 'it sure would be.' It was obvious he didn't like the job. 'Do you catch many?' I asked.

'We arrest about twenty refugees a night, one way or another,' Bill Peart replied, 'but the AA's are a different story. They're slippery bastards, their boats are faster than ours and they are up to every trick in the book.'

I'd heard something of the problems the Royal Marines faced in their thankless task of halting the flow of illegal immigration into Hong Kong. Apparently the smugglers, or AA's, make a highly lucrative living by nightly running the British blockade ferrying Chinese refugees. This luckless human freight has no friends, as they are illegally leaving China and just as illegally trying to enter Hong Kong. When they reach the point of no return, by now desperate with nowhere else to go, they are forced to make deals with the ruthless AA's.

During these negotiations, if the refugees find they haven't sufficient cash to satisfy the smugglers, and these characters greedily assess each situation, their daughters are taken and sold into prostitution.

Bill Peart told me that a few nights previously he had been chasing an AA's boat and just as he thought he had them in his grasp, the smugglers sufficiently slowed the fast approaching Royal Marines down so that they could escape, by throwing their cargo of illegal immigrants overboard one at a time, knowing full well that the Brits would stop and pick them up. Bill said that two of the women they pulled out of the water that night were dead, but tied to the back of one of them in a pathetic bundle was a baby, it was still alive and later was given into the gentle hands of the nuns at a Catholic orphanage.

The whole thing is a nasty, depressing business and although the British realize that it is impossible to stop the immigration entirely, if the policing ceased the trickle of refugees would immediately become a flood, the result being utter chaos. For the island of Hong Kong and the adjacent British area of Kowloon across the harbour, are relatively minute when compared to China and being already overcrowded they continuously experience the many and varied problems that overcrowding spawns.

Consequently if the trickle became a flood they would be engulfed. Of course these are only some of the problems and few Democratic countries, if any, would wish to take on the responsibilities, plus the cold unsympathetic neighbours, of this lonely outpost and relic of Queen Victoria's empire.

40

Early in 1981 — The International Year of the Disabled — I was asked to speak at a seminar being held at Northfield Hospital. Initially I was at a loss to know just what to say as I felt that the people involved, dedicated medical professionals, should know all about the problems of the disabled. However, while searching for a theme, the thought came to me that few of these people, if any, where physically handicapped themselves and because of this, they could at times have difficulty in identifying with the deeper psychological problems of the disabled.

For over the years experience in visiting many new amputees in hospital had shown me that nearly all of them had responded positively to any advice I'd offered, accepting it and hopefully benefiting from it, without question. The reason being — I was physically qualified.

Bearing in mind that the medical profession is a touchy crowd, not given to accepting advice from laymen, I warily used this theme for the basis of the talk. Reminding them of the point that when a disabled person is having a psychological downer even though the professionals may be deeply involved in a case and can overcome most of the problems, because of their very wholeness of body, they are not physically qualified to understand all the problems. By this I meant that if a quadraplegic is having trouble coping, either mentally or physically, then the best person to help them is another quadraplegic. A quadraplegic who has 'successfully' come to terms with quadraplegia, some-one who has been there and knows the terrors and who, because of this, really understands.

The same principle applies to all forms of incapacity

— from amputees to asthmatics, from the deaf to diabetics — if the person handicapped is having trouble, the best effective help can come from someone similarly handicapped. For despite the old adage to the contrary — the blind can lead the blind.

The disabled are the ones who have to live with their disabilities — not just at the clinic on Wednesdays and Fridays but for every minute of every day for the rest of their lives.

This breeds a freemasonry amongst the handicapped, a common bond of understanding, for they know first-hand of the pain, the constant indignities and embarrassments and the endless frustrations. Theirs too is the heart thumping near panic that comes to all, especially in the beginning, when alone in the middle of the night they have to face the fact, that unlike a broken arm that will soon mend, their limbs, or loss of sight, or total deafness, or any one of a dozen chronic diseases, will never mend.

In the hope that it is of help, I have compiled a few thoughts for the disabled and those close to them. The list, of course, is not complete and never could be, as the facets of the subject itself are limitless. But these are some of the main problems that are not always understood.

Convalescence is that difficult time of rehabilitation when anxious parents and friends take the place of skilled hospital staff. When the orderly confident routine of the institution is replaced by the well meaning, but clumsy and unskilled efforts of the family at home.

It is also the time of the most adjustment by all concerned. Lifestyles are disrupted and because of this, tempers can become frayed and bitter words and recriminations are said. This in itself needn't be a bad thing if kept in bounds within the family and recognized in retrospect as having served its purpose by letting off a bit of steam. But convalescence is a difficult time and needs great patience and understanding.

If Aunt Mary continues to burst into tears every time she calls to see 'that poor dear crippled girl' as she so stupidly refers to the patient, then tell her not to come back until she can control herself. For the last thing your girl needs, just as she's coming to grips with her problem, is Aunt Mary bursting into tears at the sight of her.

Then there is hearty Uncle Harry. An authority on all medical problems as he had flat feet and was rejected by the Militia during the war.

'We can lick this thing boy,' he roars, clapping your ailing son painfully on the back. 'Us Thompsons don't let little things like leukemia stop us.'

Then, having made his obvious monthly 'duty' call, he leaves making the loud statement that he's off to play a round of golf.

Uncle Harry being so insensitive that it doesn't register with him that your son loved the game and was a promising junior golfer before the leukemia crept in.

It generally takes a couple of days to get over one of Uncle Harry's visits.

The handicapped have to suffer many embarrassments and while sheer exposure to them over the years helps form some sort of protective shell, in the early days it can be tough going.

When I first lost my leg I'd just turned sixteen and I remember burning with embarrassment over practically everything that happened to me — from the bed pans in hospital, to being pushed around and stared at in a wheelchair. Since then, when I'm on my crutches, I wouldn't mind a dollar for every time some kid has called out, 'Hey Mister, where's your other leg?'

I was more than fortunate to have my mother to help me. She was a South African of Scottish stock, but left her family and friends when she married my father. They met when he was on his way home from France at the end of the First War and she came to live at Rendelsham, a small town out from Millicent in South Australia and although my father died from his war injuries when I was two, Mum chose to remain in Australia. It must have been very difficult for her to decide as she was only in her early twenties, was very homesick and desperately wanted to return to her beloved Capetown.

But in spite of all this she decided to stay, for although she could have gone home, I think she saw that as the weak way out. For she realized that this was her husband's country, here was where her sons were born and that Australia was where their destinies lay.

Many's the time just the memory of her strength has made me lift my game, as I didn't ever want to let her down.

Although I was too young and inexperienced to realize it then, this accident that laid me low, wouldn't have done her much good either. It was only when I was older and became a parent myself, that I could better appreciate the heartache she must have gone through.

However, she never let it show, but instead devoted herself to steering me through the maze of setbacks, repeated visits to hospital, frustrations and moods of depression that plague the newly handicapped.

Another influence that helped me come to terms with the early embarrassments, was joining the RAAF.

Almost before I'd become used to seeing an artificial leg myself, I was thrown into a war-time service life that completely lacked any semblance of privacy.

Hundreds of us slept, bathed and dressed in open discomfort and the sight of me hopping on one leg from the hand basins to the showers, drew many a startled stare from my comrades-in-arms.

One chap in particular gave me an especially visual hard time. He always seemed to be next to me at the ablutions in the morning and his intent interest in watching me put my leg on, made me squirm with embarrassment.

After a week or so he introduced himself, at the same time apologizing for his rather crass interest.

'My brother has just lost his leg,' he explained. 'He's in the AIF and my mother was pretty upset about it. But I wrote to her and told her how well you cope with things. I got through to her on the phone last night and she said that hearing about you has greatly eased her mind. I want to thank you.'

We shook hands and I remember feeling quite touched, as it was the first time anyone had complimented me or used my efforts as an example. But that chap didn't know, nor did I realize then either just what he did for me. For many's the time since I've used the experience to lean on when being stared at. We all know there are people who are morbidly curious, but most just like to see you getting on with the job and I tell myself that perhaps the person staring also had a brother in the AIF, or more typically these days, a son who has come off his motor bike.

Care should be taken by those wanting to help the handicapped, in not pushing other incapacitated peoples' achievements too much. It becomes very boring and even worse, frustrating, to be continually told about Freddie Bloggs and how he can do this or that. Incapacitated people generally can't wait to get on with the challenges in front of them and it doesn't help to over-feed them on good old Freddie's exploits before they are ready.

Also be careful not to unnecessarily qualify praise for work well done by the handicapped.

So often when the incapacitated person, say a leg amputee has painted a landscape in watercolours, he is told that the work is excellent — for a fellow without legs. Or a girl, say a polio victim, working at her electric sewing machine and who has just completed a pretty new dress for her niece, is told, 'that's lovely dear — for someone with polio.'

This happens much more frequently than people realize.

If the chap without legs suddenly got up and ran a four minute mile on his prostheses, then it would be a hell of an effort — for a fellow without legs.

Or similarly, if the girl climbed Ayers Rock, in record time in her leg irons, it would be a tremendous performance — for a polio victim.

But don't unnecessarily qualify the handicappeds' efforts, when qualification doesn't apply.

Often in times of trouble, friends find it hard to make contact with those affected, as they don't know what to say. Really they don't have to say anything much, certainly not the platitudes and clichés.

If the person troubled wants to talk, let them, if they don't just assure them that you are available if they need anything, give them a few days and then make contact again. At the start the mere fact you were concerned enough to call, will be of comfort.

Don't be slow in offering assistance to the disabled. Contrary to popular belief the handicapped get sick and tired of constantly having to show their independence — mostly they are just trying to survive.

Hold open the door for them, carry the parcel, help them up the steps. For that door or parcel or steps are only one of a dozen frustrations they have had to battle with so far that day.

It doesn't have to be a big deal, but your casual help over just one of these hurdles will always be appreciated.

Parents, wives or husbands of the physically handicapped have always had a heavy cross to bear. They know all about the problems of convalescence and readjustment and in the case of parents of the congenitally handicapped, there is added heartbreak.

For through no fault of their own, but in all good faith and their trust in their God, these parents have brought a handicapped child into the world. The responsibility or blame for this — no matter what the doctors, or the clergy, or their friends may say — they will always feel is theirs.

The greatest joys and deepest sorrows come to us through our children. It is the parent who knows the fierce pride when a child has performed beyond its capabilities. It is also the parent who feels the bitter hurt of an unkind cut, more deeply than the child itself who received it. Imagine then, how much worse it is for the mothers and fathers of the physically or mentally handicapped, when their children are thoughtlessly snubbed or ridiculed. Think twice before you scrub little Mary off the birthday party list because her wheelchair's a nuisance and don't omit young Charlie just because last year he got over excited — of course he's not quite all there you know — and threw his jelly across the room onto your new wallpaper.

For some reason, usually normally average kids can be very cruel and often make the handicapped the target of their gibes. I will never forget being involved myself in the baiting of a dear little girl at Tynte Street Primary. She was a victim of polio, with her legs in irons and because of this, being slow and awkward, hadn't made it in time to the toilet and she'd had an 'accident' on her way across the school yard.

When I came on the scene she was surrounded by a dozen jeering kids, whose heartless circle I promptly joined. At the height of this shameful turnout a young teacher, not much more than a boy himself, pushed through the yelling mob and bending down, picked up the sobbing girl, mess and all. Without a word, or any show of distaste or regard for his clothing, he carried the child firmly in his arms over to the staff amenities block, where some women teachers cleaned her up. This simple or perhaps not so simple, Samaritan-like gesture had a profound effect on me. For although I must have been only about seven at the time, I remember it still as one of the most truly Christian acts I've ever seen.

The parents of physically and mentally handicapped children are also all too familiar with those lonely, frightening times, in the middle of the night. The whispered talks about this child — loved no less for its disability than the others — perhaps even more. Explain to the others why the disabled one on occasions receives more attention, why it needs more.

It is surprising the depth of a child's understanding when these things are explained and discussed. Share the load, it will make it lighter for everyone, especially for the one handicapped, as they'll be better understood by the others, if you are completely open about the problems.

Husbands or wives of the physically handicapped have their own peculiar problems. Often the result of an accident, this incapacitation, whatever it may be, which has suddenly wrecked their lives, cruelly brings home the real meaning of those words . . . 'For better or for worse, in sickness and in health'. Words, to which on that happy day they somewhat lightly agreed, never thinking at the time that they would be called to account so soon.

For the man it is the worry about his job. Can he still hold it? He and his wife both worked so hard, denied themselves so much and now this. Is he still able to provide for his family? For the woman who has lost her sight, or become a paraplegic, it is the thought, 'how can I cope with this thing, what about the running of the house, the meals, the washing, the children?'

This is the group, the husbands or wives, who can gain most from talking with someone similarly disabled.

To save unnecessary anguish this should be done quickly. A doctor will know who to contact and the person newly incapacitated will always get a tremendous lift from the old hand, who knows what it's all about and has overcome most of the problems.

Being an amputee and consequently a bit of a chameleon — as sometimes I wear a wooden leg and look fairly normal, while other times, I leave the leg at home and walk on crutches — I'm very aware of the change in attitude of strangers. For when I use the leg I get no consideration or assistance at all from strangers, but if I'm on my crutches and the loss is obvious, it is a completely different story. People smile and open doors, they step out of the way on crowded streets and the traffic stops while I cross the road.

I remember one time when old Knuckles and I arrived in Singapore whilst on our way home from a trip to Athens. As we came down the steps from the plane, we were met with a tropical downpour. Immediately two young Chinese hostesses ran up with umbrellas and escorted me across the tarmac to the terminal building, while Neil, who was struggling along behind carrying all our baggage, was left loudly complaining out in the rain. All this is a normal reaction to the sight of the obviously handicapped and whilst it can't be used as an excuse to feel a girl's leg on the bus to find out if it is artificial or not before giving up your seat, it does help make the point that things are not always what they seem. That fit looking chap who makes no effort to help push the stalled car or lift the piano, may in fact have a dicky heart or multiple sclerosis. So don't judge too quickly on appearances, show some tolerance and remember, handicapped people are not keen on being handicapped. They'd much rather be able to lift the piano.

One day, Cassie, our youngest daughter, said to me, 'Dad, what's the first thing you'd do if you had two legs?' I laughed as the question was rather academic and at the time made some light reply that sufficiently eased her mind. But now she is older and can understand life more, I can tell her what I'd really like to do, probably what we would all like to do, we members of this incapacitation club.

Early in the morning as the sun is rising I'd go down to the beach — and in bare feet, just at the place where the waves wash in over the hard wet sand — I'd take off. Then, released forever from leg irons and wheelchairs, and sound in wind, limb, heart and mind, I'd run — strong and free — and run and run and run . . .

THE END

We do hope that you have enjoyed reading
this large print book.

Did you know that all of our titles
are available for purchase?

We publish a wide range of high quality
large print books including:
**Romances, Mysteries, Classics,
General Fiction,
Non Fiction and Westerns.**

Special interest titles available in
large print are:
**The Little Oxford Dictionary
Music Book
Song Book
Hymn Book
Service Book**

Also available from us courtesy of Oxford
University Press:
**Young Readers' Dictionary
(large print edition)
Young Readers' Thesaurus
(large print edition)**

For further information or a free
brochure, please contact us at:
**Ulverscroft Large Print Books Ltd.,
The Green, Bradgate Road, Anstey,
Leicester, LE7 7FU, England.
Tel:** (00 44) 0116 236 4325
Fax: (00 44) 0116 234 0205

THE SAVAGE SKY

Emma Drummond

1941: Rob Stallard, the unworldly son of a farmer, leaves war-torn London for a Florida airbase along with a group of RAF pilot cadets. He quickly develops a great passion and talent for flying, but is not so happy when he encounters US cadet James Theodore Benson III, son of a senator. Rob is instantly averse to a man who appears to regard flying as merely another string to his sporting bow. For his part, Jim sees Rob as a'cowpoke from Hicksville'. Personal dislike rapidly extends to professional rivalry, and a near-fatal flying incident creates bitter enmity between them that will last more than a decade.

THE UGLY SISTER

Winston Graham

The Napoleonic Wars have ended as Emma Spry tells her fascinating story . . . One side of her face marred at birth, Emma grows up without affection, her elegant mother on the stage, her father killed in a duel before she was born. Her beautiful sister, Tamsin, is four years the elder, and her mother's ambitions lie in Tamsin's future, and in her own success. A shadow over their childhood is the ominous butler, Slade. Then there is predatory Bram Fox, with his dazzling smile; Charles Lane, a young engineer; and Canon Robartes, relishing rebellion in the young Emma, her wit, her vulnerability, encouraging her natural gift for song.

NOW AND THEN

Joseph Heller

Here is the writer Joseph Heller's Coney Island childhood, down the block from the world's most famous amusement park. It was the height of the Depression, it was a fatherless family, yet little Joey Heller had a terrific time — on the boardwalk, in the ocean, even in school. Then, a series of jobs, from delivering telegrams to working in a Navy yard — until Pearl Harbor, the Air Force, Italy. And after the war, college, teaching, Madison Avenue, marriage, and — always — writing. And finally the spectacular success of CATCH-22, launching one of the great literary careers.

NIGHT PASSAGE

Robert B. Parker

When a busted marriage kicks his drinking problem into overdrive and the Los Angeles Police Department unceremoniously dumps him, Jesse Stone's future looks bleak. So he's shocked when a small Massachusetts town called Paradise recruits him as a police chief. Jesse doesn't have to look for trouble in Paradise: it comes to him. For what is on the surface a quiet New England community quickly proves to be a crucible of political and moral corruption replete with triple homicide, tight Boston mob ties, flamboyantly errant spouses, maddened militiamen, and a psychopath-about-town who has fixed his sights on the new lawman.

A RUNNING TIDE

Ann Swinfen

Tirza, a successful and respected war photographer, tries to escape her past by retreating to a remote Scottish island. But even thousands of miles and four decades cannot erase the memories of a childhood summer in Maine: a community profoundly altered by war, a family thrown into conflict, and the British airman, who changed all their lives. Tirza has spent a lifetime trying to banish that fateful summer from her mind, but it is not ready to let her go; only by revisiting Maine can she solve the mysteries of that past and complete her journey of self-discovery.